Shooting the War

The Memoir and Photographs

Shooting the War

Otto Giese
and Capt. James E. Wise, Jr., USN (Ret.)

· · · · · · · · · · · · · · · · · · · ·

of a U-Boat Officer in World War II

LEO COOPER
London

First published in Great Britain in 1994 by
LEO COOPER
an imprint of Pen & Sword Books Ltd.,
47 Church Street,
Barnsley, South Yorkshire. S70 2AS

ISBN 0 85052 421 0

A CIP catalogue record for this book is available from the British Library

SHOOTING THE WAR originally published in 1994 by the Naval
Institute Press, Annapolis, Maryland, USA

Copyright © 1994
by the United States Naval Institute

Printed in the United States of America on acid-free paper ∞

Frontispiece: Otto Giese, fourth officer on the SS *Columbus,* at North
German Lloyd's New York docks before the start of a Caribbean cruise in
autumn, 1939.

To the gallant men of the U-405 *who were lost in battle in the North Atlantic on 1 November 1943*

Contents

· · · · · · · · · · · · · · · · · ·

List of Equivalent Commissioned-Officer Ranks (World War II)

. . . .

GERMAN NAVY	ROYAL NAVY	U.S. NAVY
Grossadmiral	Admiral of the Fleet	Admiral of the Fleet
Generaladmiral	No equivalent	No equivalent
Admiral	Admiral	Admiral
Vizeadmiral	Vice admiral	Vice admiral
Konteradmiral	Rear admiral	Rear admiral
Kommodore	Commodore (captain in a post usually held by a rear admiral)	Commodore (a Kapitän zur See holding a flag officer's position)
Kapitän zur See	Captain	Captain
Fregattenkapitän	Captain (junior)	Commander
Korvettenkapitän	Commander	Lieutenant commander
Kapitänleutnant	Lieutenant commander	Lieutenant
Oberleutnant zur See	Lieutenant (senior)	Lieutenant (junior grade)
Leutnant zur See	Lieutenant (junior)	Ensign
Oberfähnrich zur See	Sublieutenant	Senior midshipman
Fähnrich zur See	Midshipman/cadet	Midshipman

Foreword

· ·

This is the story of one man's journey through six years of strife during World War II. Born in Bremen, Germany, of military lineage, Otto Giese went to sea as a nineteen-year-old cadet on board the merchant marine training ship *Schulschiff Deutschland* in 1933. Subsequently he served aboard numerous merchant vessels, ocean liners, and cargo ships. After attending the nautical academy in Bremen and receiving additional naval instruction, he was assigned as a junior officer on board the North German Lloyd liner SS *Columbus*. When war broke out in September of 1939, Giese survived numerous adventures before joining the German navy's U-boat arm, the "gray wolves" of the sea. Battles in the Norwegian Sea and Barents Sea against heavily defended convoys aboard the *U-405* were followed by long and lonely raids on the *U-181* in the South Atlantic and the Indian Ocean.

What follows is the war diary of Captain (Kapitän) Giese. It is unique in its scope and detail. His accounts of the *Columbus*'s scuttling, little-known German blockade-runner operations, and the arduous life of U-boat men in remote parts of the world are vividly portrayed. In addition to firsthand accounts of his experiences, Captain Giese captured his adventures with an extraordinary collection of photographs, many of which are included in this book. He bought his first Leica camera while on board the *Schulschiff Deutschland*, then proceeded to record his wartime experiences with great skill and a keen sense of historical perspective.

The military tradition of the Giese family has continued. Captain Giese's youngest son attended the U.S. Air Force Academy and, like many other fine young Americans, fought for his country in Desert Storm.

After two years as a cadet aboard the three-masted, full-rigger training ship *Schulschiff Deutschland*, Giese became an O.A. (officer's aspirant) and served as an assistant to the officers training cadets.

It was my good fortune to meet Captain Giese through a former crewmember of the destroyer USS *Borie* (DD 215), which fought the *U-405* in an extraordinary North Atlantic night battle in November of 1943. Our three-year joint adventure preparing this wartime journal has been a most gratifying personal experience. Though I served twenty some years in the U.S. Navy, I soon found that I had much to learn from a seasoned warrior, skilled seaman, and gifted artist, whether it be with a pen, a brush, or a camera. Captain Giese is all of these things and more. He is a highly cultured, articulate gentleman steeped in the traditions of the old navy. What a pleasure these last three years have been.

CAPTAIN JAMES E. WISE, JR. (RET.)

Shooting the War

Prologue

On 18 October 1945 I entered Changi jail in Malaya as an "SP" (surrendered person). I had been captured by the British colonial army after lingering for months on a rubber plantation following the surrender of Germany and the relinquishing of our U-boat, the *U-181*, to the Japanese. Thus ended a six-year seafaring journey. I had sailed on most of the oceans and seas of the world aboard German oceanliners, merchant ships, blockade-runners, and U-boats. I had spent years away from my family in Bremen and my future, along with the future of those who waited at home, appeared uncertain. How vividly I remembered the dreams and ambitions of a German youth who yearned to see the world!

It was in the spring of 1933 that an old friend of my family, a sea captain and owner of some of the fastest colliers that sailed between Hamburg and England, asked me about my plans after school. I answered that I would like to see the world. "Young man," he said, "I suggest that you see the world as I have, by becoming a sailor on one of the large square-riggers." During frequent visits to my house he would describe life at sea in such a way that my imagination filled with thoughts of sea ventures in exotic corners of the world. Far-off places like China, the arctic, South America, Africa, the Indian Ocean, and America suddenly seemed within my reach. I was so impressed with his tales and the seafaring books he left for me to read that I didn't wait to finish school but set about becoming a seaman. Later that year, I passed a health exam and reported to the owners of the Deutscher Schulschiff Verein (German Training Ship Company) in Bremen. They assigned me to one of their cadet training ships, the *Schulschiff Deutschland*, a square-rigger.

This seemed to be a natural course to take at the time, for throughout my boyhood and teen years I had been drawn to the sea. I roamed the North Sea, the Baltic, the Sunds, rivers, brooks, and marshes in all sorts of vessels.

My family was apprehensive about my going to sea at such a young age. The sea had already taken its toll on our family. My mother's only brother had vanished in 1912 when the fast mailboat *Seestern* was lost in the Pacific. Serving the imperial German government in the colonial islands of the South Seas, she had set sail from Brisbane for the Huon Gulf via Samarai. The *Seestern* never arrived at her destination. It was surmised that she either blew up—she was carrying a large amount of dynamite—or ran aground on a reef and capsized in the heavy seas and rollers that prevail off Australia.

The three-masted *Schulschiff Deutschland* was white with beautiful lines. At first, life on board was so hard that some cadets, at night in their hammocks, secretly shed a tear. We got kicked with seaboots or beaten with ropes when we broke the honor code. Often we stood in the rigging for hours on end, in the tropics barefoot (when there was no time to put on canvas shoes) and up north in heavy seaboots, unsecured on the foot wires, leaning against the yardarms trying to fasten the wildly flapping canvas sails. Our hands were blistered and often bleeding. Hurricanes bore down on the ship, which was steadied by the barest of sails and with oil bags hanging in heads and gulleys.

After fifty months before the mast, which included tours aboard various steamers, I went to the German Nautical Academy in Bremen, Germany, to sit for my mate's license, which I received in 1938. That year I went through basic training with the navy at Wilhelmshaven, in north Germany.

Finally I was commissioned a junior officer on Germany's third largest ocean liner, the SS *Columbus* of North German Lloyd in Bremen. When I reported aboard the 32,000-ton *Columbus*, one of the queens of the German merchant marine, I knew that all the hardships endured up to this point had been worth it. My dreams of sailing to the far corners of the world were about to come true. I had found the life I was looking for, a life on the open sea.

. . . .

PART ONE

The Scuttling of the SS *Columbus*, 1939

One

West Indies Cruise

. . . .

The SS *Columbus* was a beautiful sight as she plowed through the bright blue waters of the Caribbean in the summer of 1939. She sported a black hull with a white belt slightly above the waterline, a shiny white superstructure, and sand-yellow smokestacks, the trademark of one of the most famous German shipping companies, the North German Lloyd. Completed in 1922 at the Schichau yard in Danzig, in 1929 she was refitted with modern steam turbines and remodeled with 1,750 cabins to house luxury-, first-, second-, and tourist-class tourists. The *Columbus* measured 775 feet in length, had an 83-foot beam, listed a gross tonnage of 32,581, and boasted a maximum speed of 23 knots. She had been chartered for a number of years by Cooks Travel Agency in New York and cruised into West Indian waters about every two weeks with occasional trips around South America and Africa.

My duties aboard the *Columbus* were varied and quite numerous. Primarily I acted as assistant to the chief officer, Mr. Ruppert. I had to report to his cabin every day at 0600. While he ate breakfast we discussed the proceedings of the day. Afterwards I went to the enlisted mess quarters where seamen were assembled at 0800 sharp to inform the boatswain of special requests by the chief officer and to supervise the distribution of work assignments. Also, I was to welcome the harbor pilots at the lower outer door, conduct them to the bridge, and then take them downstairs again. In case of accidents on board involving passengers, I had to fill out insurance questionnaires and file reports. If a passenger died, I had to attend the embalming of the body and its placement in a freezer compartment.

One of my more exciting tasks was making the "gold run" each time we docked in New York. After we tied up at our pier and my job was done on the bridge, I would grab a pistol out of a drawer in the chartroom and hasten along the passages down to our steel chamber, where gold bars had been stacked. Nearby, only a single gangway had been lowered to the pier, where an armored truck and police cars had been drawn up. Police officers with ready guns had cordoned off the entire area. I checked the pieces of gold as they were hustled down by guards and placed in the truck with its motor running. All this was done with incredible speed and precision. There was not much talking. Two special guards, plainclothesmen, stood at my side and watched every movement around us. Once the gold had been transferred to the truck, I put my papers in my pocket and rushed down the gangway to be locked up in the truck with the two detectives. Off we went at top speed, sirens howling. It seemed as if the truck, flinging us from one side to the other, had no brakes. Finally it slowed down, I heard various gates rumbling open, and then the vehicle stopped with a jolt. We were in the basement of a great bank on Wall Street. Again, numerous guards surrounded us and the gold was hurriedly checked out. After collecting my receipt, I was conducted upstairs to the main exit of the mammoth building and suddenly found myself alone in the busy and crowded streets of the city. I returned to the ship and handed over the receipt to the chief purser. Gold transfers were only carried out on our Germany-to-New York voyage. I assumed these activities to be commercial banking transactions. I never did learn their true nature.

I was also the crew's sport's officer, tasked to arrange events such as soccer matches, boxing events, and handball games. Our raceboat crew competed against foreign crews docked at various ports of call. Following the job as chief officer assistant, I was assigned as watch officer together with Second Officer Jan Kampen and Third Officer Heino Lampe.

That same summer on one of my trips I had met my American sweetheart, Pat, who resided in East Orange, New Jersey. Spellbound by her, I decided to become an American citizen and join the U.S. Coast Guard. These hopes were dashed by what was to come in the months ahead.

In August 1939, we berthed in New York Harbor and began training for the 13th Annual International Lifeboat Race to be held on Labor Day. This was to be our third attempt to win the cup, against strong Norwegian and American competition. While relaxing in my cabin I would listen to the latest news broadcasts from Germany that spoke of a world about to be thrust into turmoil. Chaotic flashes of unrest and insecurity crossed the distant horizon. But in New York all seemed to be normal and quiet.

One day the booking agency of North German Lloyd reported that the *Columbus* was fully booked with 850 passengers. It was time for immediate departure. The gongs sounded, signaling visitors to go ashore; happy crowds continued to fill the promenade decks, embracing each other, singing, and dancing. We had to urge them politely down the gangways. Ribbons of colored leis thrown by passengers to friends on the pier drifted merrily in the wind. Our ship's band played the German farewell song, *"Muss I Denn, Muss I Denn zum Städtele Hinaus?"* (Must I now leave the small city?). Some wept, overwhelmed with sentiment, while others sang jubilantly. Our lines were dropped into the water and heaved on board, the ship's sirens on the foremast and on the second smokestack roared three short blasts, and Captain John Miller, our customary dock pilot, had the officer at the telegraph put the pointer on half astern.

With the help of several tugs we slowly backed away from the pier into the Hudson and pointed our bow downriver. It was my job to

Whenever there is time in a Caribbean port, I take our race crew out to prepare for the international boat races conducted each Labor Day in the Hudson River. Here we are enjoying a short rest on the beach (I'm standing fourth from the left). The *Columbus* can be seen in the background.

Track of the SS *Columbus*

conduct the dock pilot to a small gate at the side of the hull not far above the waterline, where he descended the pilot-ladder onto a waiting tug. While walking back to the bridge, up the broad and thickly carpeted staircase in the first-class section, I was fascinated by the mahogany rails carved so delicately and the beautiful goblins and pictures framed in exquisite white and gold.

After passing the fire station I had a short and hearty chat with the alert men of the fire brigade, went on the dark, now-deserted boat deck, and entered the bridge where I saw the ship's commandant, Captain Willibald Dähne, Chief Officer Ruppert, and Second Mate Kampen huddled together. "Anything else, sir?" I asked. "No, thank you, that's all," said the captain. With that I went down to my cabin.

Captain Dähne was greatly loved by the American passengers. He was exactly what they wanted in a captain, modish in appearance, amiable, always ready to smile, a perfect politician and diplomat equal to any situation that arose. He was slim but athletic, especially good in boxing. As far as his officers were concerned he set a superb example. He liked to see his officers mingle with the passengers. Many parents with daughters were happy to have a young officer accompany them to dances. Captain Dähne was one of the younger captains in command of high-seas liners such as the *Bremen, Europa, Columbus,* and *General von Steuben.* Politically he seemed neutral. I often typed memos of his speeches for him; he was just a great diplomat. He didn't communicate his feelings about the rapid approach of war with the ship's junior officers. He probably discussed these matters with Chief Officer Ruppert, the chief engineer, and Chief Purser Tielbar. He acted calm and polite with the passengers in order to ease their apprehensions.

Several of the officers and most of the crew (with the exception of various foreigners, such as those found in the Chinese-manned laundry room) were from the area around Bremerhaven. The noncommissioned crew often spoke amongst themselves in *Plattdeutsch,* spoken in Germany's northwest coastal area or in the flatlands of nether Saxony. These men were born to become seamen and they were a proud, reliable, weatherbeaten gang that included some unique characters.

We had hardly reached the open sea when the whistles of the vessel sounded the signal man overboard, and while rushing to the bridge I felt the *Columbus* swinging into a circle. "What happened?" I whispered to one of my fellow officers. "One of the passengers jumped over the side from the starboard promenade deck," he answered. "God only knows why. He was having dinner at a table in the first-class section and was dressed in a white tuxedo jacket and pants. A few shocked passengers in deck chairs saw him vaulting over the rail."

"Giese, quick, get your race crew into a lifeboat. We'll lower you together with the motorboats!" called Chief Officer Ruppert. The ship had not yet stopped in the water as our boat hit the rolling sea and we cast off. It was dark now. The decks were crowded with spectators. Strong searchlights illuminated the scene.

For two hours we combed the entire area until we realized that the poor man had probably wanted to die. Strange, I thought afterwards on board, why would someone so disturbed go on a pleasure cruise?

Late that night I had to enter the man's cabin together with the ship's doctor and chief steward and make a thorough search of his belongings. We found no clues as to why he might have jumped to his death. We took an inventory of his effects, then packed and sealed his suitcases so that all would be ready for subsequent legal proceedings by our lawyers and the court in New York.

A cruise liner is like a small world, full of life and not devoid of its sadness. But our cruise passengers didn't want to face the hard side of reality. With their tickets they had "bought their fun," and our good *Columbus* and her crew tried hard to fulfill their expectations.

Following this tragic incident we continued south and passed Cape Hatteras during a driving rainstorm. Soon idle sunshine warmed the passengers and once again the decks were full of activity.

At the height of our summer cruise in the Caribbean many young couples used hatch no. 3 for sleeping instead of their hot and stuffy cabins. This hatch was directly under the bridge. Here they had the bright stars over their heads and the slightly rolling vessel lulled them in a soft, fresh breeze. Here there were kisses and whispered promises of love. They were never quite alone in their romantic reverie. From time to time two round, dark binocular eyes appeared on the railing of the bridge, scanning the lovers. Each couple had been secretly numbered clockwise by the young officers on the bridge. When the watch changed at midnight the young officers reported on the progress of each couple. One night an officer dropped an apple and it fell on a couple. Desperately embarrassed, he tried to murmur an apology. The couple continued their lovemaking undisturbed.

The crew followed the events in Europe by listening to Deutschlandsender broadcasts from overseas. We were sure the passengers were aware of the situation in our homeland, but they remained calm and undisturbed. They would hardly discuss such topics, being on vacation and headed for the Caribbean. All was well!

On 22 August the *Columbus* dropped anchor off St. Thomas. There was no trouble with the British authorities; they were kind and polite as ever. Our lifeboats rendered fast and steady service between ship and shore. It had been my duty as one of the junior officers to supervise the boats and see to it that no passenger had an accident, especially when they returned from ashore and boarded the boats in high spirits.

The following day we arrived during the early morning hours at the port of St. Pierre in Martinique, where the French police prevented our crewmembers from coming ashore. Our ship's photographer, however, slipped ashore with the passengers and threw himself into taking pictures. He was arrested and his camera equipment confiscated. During a subsequent trial presided over by a German-speaking inspector who had once been a German prisoner-of-war, the photographer was accused of being a spy and trying to photograph military objects under the pretence of taking pictures of passengers. And indeed, the film showed that a military object had been photographed, an old fort that was used as a background for a group of passengers. The photographer was ordered off the island and directed to pay the trial charges. We quickly resolved the situation and were soon back on board and off to our next port of call, Barbados.

After a brief stay in Bridgetown we weighed anchor and headed for Grenada. Captain Dähne decided to bypass that British colony because of the worsening political situation and the sighting of two submarines riding at anchor in one of the bays. We directed our course westward and steamed at high speed towards Curacao, leaving our next scheduled port, La Guaira, astern.

When we arrived at Curacao on 26 August the air was humming with disturbing news. The German overseas broadcasts reported that many atrocities were being committed by Poles against Germans on the frontier. Fearing a deteriorating European situation, Captain Dähne decided to return to New York and land his passengers in order to free his ship should a crisis arise. We took on fresh provisions and sailed that afternoon. Again the turbines hummed, speeding the large vessel northward. The older passengers were slightly shocked and nervous. The younger ones, resenting the fact that their trip had been cut short, continued their festivities undiminished. In a way, though, even they were happy to be going home, back to safety, since it had dawned on most that war was unavoidable. The crew became quite excited; we thought we would make it back home in time to do our duty for the fatherland.

On 27 August, around 1200, I took over the bridge watch for an officer who had fallen sick. Heat rose from the glimmering decks. There was not the slightest disturbance in the air, everything seemed timeless, sea and horizon blending into one hazy panorama. I was drowsing when suddenly Captain Dähne appeared on the bridge with Chief Officer Ruppert, who said to the quartermaster, "Hard starboard, please, course 190 degrees!" "Aye, aye, sir! Hard starboard course 190 degrees," answered the quartermaster. The time was exactly 1235 Eastern Standard. The captain had the famous QWA 9 telegram in his hand. QWA telegrams were coded messages transmitted to all German merchant ships apprising them of actions to be taken in the event of war. QWA 9 ordered all German merchantmen to arrive in a German port within the next four days; if this were not possible we were to take refuge in any Spanish, Italian, Japanese, Russian, or Dutch port. American ports were to be entered only as a last resort. Naturally, we were bound as officers to discretion and could not communicate the contents of this secret cable to the passengers. Rumors continued to circulate in the ship and one found ready listeners. Someone had distinctly seen in our wake a partially submerged German submarine passing orders to us. I was told later that this tale was related in American newspapers.

We reached Curacao on the twenty-eighth and drifted off the entrance to Willemstad, which was guarded by a small Dutch cruiser, until the governor gave us permission to enter port. It was quite natural that our passengers became angry at not being allowed to go ashore that night. The lights of the port city were alluring and they had not set foot on land since Barbados. The next day we remained at the oil pier and bunkered as much fuel as the Dutch could spare. There was restlessness in the air. The rumblings in Europe could be heard louder and louder. No settlement could be reached between Poland and Germany over the Danzig question. Hitler sent an ultimatum to Poland and warned the world to abstain from a repeat of World War I.

I agreed with our pending move against Poland. My feelings towards that country were influenced by events after World War I. German lands had been ceded to Poland, lands which, according to our school history books, had been conquered once by the German Order of Knighthood and colonized by German farmers. I also had sentimental attachments to Poland, having fallen in love in Danzig while a cadet in the sailing ship *Schulschiff Deutschland* in the early 1930s. With its high walls and towers Danzig was the epitome of a German fortified town of the Order of the Knights. It was beautifully preserved. I could well appreciate Poland's desire to keep Danzig since it was her only port on the Baltic Sea. On the other hand, I felt that Hitler's offer (with some diplomatic alterations) could have eased the present tensions. I also hoped that our nonaggression pact with Russia might have some influence on Poland's decisions. As it turned out, events at the German-Polish border boiled over so fast that both powers clashed without a declaration of war.

When England and France, allied with Poland, entered the war against Germany, I was determined to help my country. I made this decision without any hatred against Germany's enemies. It was a natural reaction born of patriotism, pride, honor, and the conviction that my family and friends expected me to be one of the many thousands of young Germans hastening to join the colors. Furthermore, I was convinced that this war would be of short duration considering Germany's military might and its able leaders. Neither England, France, nor Poland was prepared to withstand massive attacks by our armies and air force. Our objective was clear to me—to connect East Prussia with Germany again. The question of the "Polish corridor" would be settled at a later time, depending on the outcome of the war.

The *Columbus* was not the only German vessel in Curacao. There were several other ships, including merchantmen, awaiting orders from Germany. We got under way once again on 30 August and sped northward. New York couldn't be reached in time for us to land our passengers and return to Germany. At 1230 the big liner veered around again. We had received another QWA telegram ordering us to land the passengers in Havana. They grew more anxious and some nervously joked that their trip would end in a German concentration camp. Others wondered which island would appear next. Their questions were soon answered when the skyscrapers of Havana appeared below dark clouds on the horizon. Within a short time we dropped anchor in the murky waters of the spacious bay.

Over the radio we heard Hitler's dramatic speech in the Reichstag reporting that the Poles had neglected to accept his offer of a peaceful settlement of the Danzig and corridor questions presented two days earlier. They had not sent an emissary to Berlin to discuss the issues. On 31 August, the Poles had occupied the German border town of Gleiwitz and seized the radio station. Hitler went on to state that with this latest action, Germany and Poland were at war as of 1 September 1939.[1]

While these events were occurring in Europe we hastily loaded the American passengers in our lifeboats and landed them ashore. The departure was hearty and warm since many friendships had been made during the trip.

Havana was still asleep. The awakening sun had not yet touched the veil of haze lingering over the houses of the city when the links of our heavy anchor chain clicked silently into the chain locker. Slowly and carefully the large hull of the *Columbus* moved towards the open sea. I wondered if the guards in the entrance fort, Castillo del Morro, had noticed us. Safety watches were established and all blinds and portholes were closed. For days the lifeboats had been under preparation for war, and already the crew, its daily rations reduced, had been put under the "war auxiliary law" (*Kriegshilfsgesetz*).

Two ———————————————————————————

War Clouds Gather

· ·

Before the sun rose the following day we had painted black rings around the tops of our smokestacks, although any enemy ship could have easily detected our vessel as the *Columbus*. Behind us lay Havana in the morning haze, ahead of us, the open sea. We set our course for Germany.

During the morning hours of 2 September, Captain Dähne wrote in the log, "By preparations, which had been made, it is assured that the vessel can be scuttled within the shortest time!"[2] This demonstrates the change of mood in our one-time luxury liner. Either we would manage to reach Germany or a friendly European port, or we would open up the sea valves and send our proud vessel to the bottom of the ocean. At 1200 Captain Dähne noted in the journal, "On account of the danger of war with England it was decided to change our route and call at a port of distress, Veracruz, Mexico." Veracruz had a large German colony at the time that might prove useful to the ship. We turned westward towards the setting sun.

Meanwhile across the Atlantic Prime Minister Chamberlain instructed the British attaché in Germany to communicate to the Reichsregierung (the German government) that it was to give guarantees of instant withdrawal of all German troops from Poland. If it failed to do so, England would fulfill her obligations towards Poland with all the consequences that would bring. If an unsatisfactory answer was received, the attaché was to ask for his passport and return to England immediately. France had already called for general mobilization of its forces. Hitler's answer to England was unsatisfactory. On 3 September 1939 England and France declared war on Germany.

On that fateful day, the *Columbus* entered the Gulf of Mexico making full speed for Veracruz. The evening passed without a sight-

The *Columbus* at anchor in the roadstead at Veracruz, Mexico. She is waiting for orders from Germany to brave the British blockade and return to the fatherland.

ing of the British. The situation was tense: We knew that the British Admiralty would do everything possible to capture our ship since she would make an excellent troop carrier. Towards 0800 Central Standard time we could see the glare of Veracruz ahead and at 1154 our anchors thundered into the dark waters at the city's roadstead. No light could be seen from our vessel as we rolled gently in a long swell. The first stage of the war was now set for us—waiting patiently in a neutral port.

The Mexican authorities were quite friendly. However, for the next fourteen days there was no shore leave for the crew. Three other German vessels were also in port awaiting further orders, the North German Lloyd (NDL) freighter *Hameln,* the Hamburg America Line (HAL) freighter *Arauca,* and the *Orinoco.* Then two Norwegian freighters entered Veracruz. I contacted one of their officers to arrange a football game between the crews of our ships, a pretense to get better acquainted with the facilities for stowing away in one of the ships. Along with two fellow officers I asked the permission of our captain to make a trial escape by stowing away in the Norwegian vessels. He granted our request, and soon I was hidden in a lifeboat on one Norwegian ship while my friends tried their luck on the other. The time of departure was set and I waited for the signals to have the lines cast away. Suddenly one of my co-conspirators, the second mate, appeared at the lifeboat with a worried look on his face and said, "Boy, get out, we're running to England!"

Eager to join my country's cause, I was deeply disappointed by this change in events. I had to find a way to cross the Atlantic, preferably landing in Spain. Subsequently I planned to offer my help as a seaman on a Mexican fishing boat, hoping to gain the captain's confidence. Within a short time I would bring more "helpers" on board, including Fritz Welcke, the fourth mate, Doctor Lenz, our ship's physician, an engineer, our champion boxer Steward Rayhofer, and five reliable sailors. On a given day, we would overcome the Mexican crew and sail to an island close to the *Columbus* where we had secretly stored provisions, nautical equipment, drums of gasoline, and so forth. We intended to leave the Mexican crew on the island and set sail, saving the gasoline for a later time.

I discussed my plan with Captain Dähne and got his permission to proceed. Our plan was dashed, however, when we shifted our anchorage and I learned that the owner of the fishing boat suspected my intentions. Luckily, the proprietor of the boat did not legally pursue the matter; otherwise I might have ended up in a Mexican jail without any help from the German consulate.

While in Veracruz many of our young crewmen had some sort of girlfriend or at least a favorite señorita. Personally, I loved to visit the dance hall Lucha Maria situated some miles out of town. What a pleasure it was to sit on the flowered patio with its beautiful Mexican tiles! I could see the blue sky like a tremendous dome over me, could hear the palms move and feel the cool night breeze.

For reasons of safety, Captain Dähne decided to shift our anchorage from Veracruz to an offshore point eighteen miles to the south. Soon the dangerous and hazardous *nortes* (northern gales) would set in. If we had stayed at anchorage off Veracruz heavy swells might have broken our anchor chains or slipped our anchors, causing us to drift onto a reef. On 7 October, reports circulated in Mexico City that the *Columbus* had sent out a boat with two mechanics to effect repairs on a German submarine cruising in Mexican waters. These sensational reports were denied by the marine department of Mexico's Ministry of Communications, which said that our vessel was under constant surveillance by a Ministry of War coast guard cutter. It was further reported in the local papers that the *Columbus* had started loading considerable quantities of provisions that had been sent by rowboat from a nearby village, Antonio Lizardo. This was true:

Stores had been taken aboard for use by the 600-man crew in case a *norte* should cut off our supply. In any case, these reports gave rise to rumors and suspicions that we were preparing for departure.

In early November, the German embassy in Mexico City received orders by secret code instructing the captains of the *Columbus, Arauca,* and *Orinoco* to make ready for an immediate departure and blockade run to Germany. In a special meeting all officers were briefed and received information about individual assignments. The entire matter was handled with strict secrecy. However, it wasn't long before rumors of our departure spread on board and ashore. Even newspapers in New York seemed to know more about our situation and our departure than we did. Of course, we couldn't hide our initial preparations, especially since some of our international stewards were sources of information for American and British consulates. The British, who had been observing our activity for some time, were now on the alert. The Admiralty had not forgotten about the breakthrough of the NDL liner *Bremen* from New York to Murmansk.[3]

On 1 December the old tanker *Cuauthemoc* tied up on our port side and started to pump oil into our bunkers. This task continued for a day and a night. Then she left and appeared a second time to complete our refueling. The *Columbus* took on 25,000 barrels of fuel, enough to keep her at sea for forty days. By this time all non-German crewmembers were put ashore. Everyone on board knew that our departure had finally arrived.

Most of the crew was relieved to know that the interminable waiting would soon end. Some, however, were deeply concerned. We would either have to scuttle our vessel, drown, be picked up and taken by the British, or arrive in Germany to join the fighting front, the latter a possibility that some did not like. The crew crowded the local bars and restaurants as if to find courage and strength in liquor. Beer and *Habanero* (Cuban rum) were brought on board and drunkards swayed through the passages. The parties seemed endless. There were speeches full of passion and spirit, of bravery and courage, but also of insubordination, discord, and hatred.

For elderly and married crewmembers it would perhaps have been safer to stay with the vessel in a calm place, far away from home and family, from war, terror and death. The strain of West Indian cruises was considerable—the work, heat, sweat, and endless hours of toil endured by the crew, many of whom were obsessed with making money to secure their future back home. Now all their sacrifices had proven to be in vain. They were deeply disappointed and felt betrayed. They began to hate Hitler and rejected the idea that they had to fight for him.

Some crewmen conspired to sabotage our departure. The ship's command, not unaware of who was involved, watched them closely until one day someone broke down and communicated the entire plan. The conspirators had managed to acquire pistols and intended to kill the captain and chief officer, set fire to the ship, and throw sand into the turbines.

I admired Captain Dähne's calm reaction after he heard all this; he simply called the entire crew to a general assembly and spoke in clear, direct terms. He appealed to the men's honesty, comradeship, discipline, and courage. Only cooperation and order would spell success in the dangerous days ahead. The enemy was alert, we had to be more alert and outsmart him. He ended his speech with "Long live our fatherland, Germany!"

He ordered that the isolation hospital be made ready to imprison the conspirators and asked that all officers use a sharper tone with the crew. We were greatly assisted by a so-called *Selbstschutz* (self-protection) group voluntarily formed by World War I veterans. They gradually reported a remarkable improvement in behavior and discipline among the crew.

In the meantime, our Chinese washermen had been conveyed to the care of the Chinese consul in Tampico and our Italians to their consul in Mexico City. We allowed our crew their last shore leave on 7 December.

The following day the ship's boatswain distributed brushes and paint to all hands. All that had been shiny and bright now became gray and monotonous. Superstructures, ventilators, smokestacks, masts, loopholes, boats, deckhouses were covered by fast-moving paintbrushes. The heavy ice blinds of the bull's-eye portholes were closed, and other windows and openings were fitted with covers so that not the least gleam of light could escape. The large salon, library, smoking quarters, bars, and many state cabins were cleared of belongings and converted into sleeping quarters, dormitories, hospitals, guard rooms, and other stations. All lower decks that contained crew's quarters were evacuated. All lights were extinguished with the exception of a few dim blue lamps that shone day and night.

A certain tension hung in the air as the crew waited to depart. Day in and day out alarm bells and gongs hammered through the vessel,

The crew of the *Columbus* keeps busy painting smokestacks, ventilators, and the entire superstructure gray.

The Columbus in her "new dress," at anchor outside Antonio Lizardo, Mexico. We are sure that the enemy will still easily recognize Germany's third largest ocean liner.

calling the crew to boat maneuvers. Boats were lowered into the water and rowed and sailed. With the motorboats, towing maneuvers were conducted until everything passed near perfection. Additional ropes had been coiled up on the boat decks and rope ladders lay ready for instant use. Boats had been permanently swung out to port and starboard. All stores were carefully inventoried. Rum, cognac, and even champagne, dried fruit, milk and preserves were added to the usual boat provisions of hardtack and water.

Since the early days of our preparations for departure we had detected unidentified warships far out at sea. On 9 December an article appeared in a Mexican newspaper with the headline, "Mysterious Warship Seen off Veracruz." After much guessing and checking on silhouettes we were sure that they were U.S. destroyers. They disappeared on the twelfth, much to our relief.

Finally on 13 December we heard, "Man all stations! Heave anchors!" and slowly the anchor chain clicked around the capstan. Next the captain ordered, "Standby engines! Slow ahead." It was a sensational feeling when the dark hull slid through the water again. For the present, however, we were only to sail as far as the Veracruz roadstead; there we would receive Mexican authorities who would count the crew and clear our papers. While we waited, a *norte* started to blow again and we feared that the authorities would not dare come out. A small boat from the German consulate approached during the night, but it couldn't come alongside because of the heavy seas. As we expected, the Mexican authorities failed to show.

In the early morning hours of the fourteenth, we heaved anchor again and tried to press nearer the breakwaters of the entrance. The small boat from the consulate approached us, battling the choppy seas. We managed to hold our vessel against the wind and current until the boat lay alongside the small gate where I stood waiting for it. An employee from the consulate came aboard and waved a large envelope with papers and documents. "Mr. Giese, the Mexican officials are not coming on board, please bring this envelope to Captain Dähne. The clearance has been okayed. Ask him if there is anything else we can do!" I rushed to the bridge as fast as I could with the documents clasped to my side. Captain Dähne opened the envelope, checked the papers, and smiled. "Finally, finally we got it! Please tell the consulate agent that everything is in order and we thank them for their valuable help!" As the agent left the ship he called, "Have a good and successful trip, Mr. Giese!"

Our propellers began to move the ship steadily forward. The *Arauca* had already left on a northerly course in the early morning hours and was by now out of sight. It was a beautiful afternoon full of sunshine, wind, and choppy seas. We all felt as if we were newly born and inhaled the fresh salt air deep into our lungs. The big liner rocked slightly, boxing against the swell. War watches had taken over and alert commandos went through the vessel to check if all was shipshape. Double lookouts were stationed on all corners and wings of the decks. On the bridge we went to a two-watch system, while the third and fourth watch officers manned the crow's nest. Towards sunset the crow's nest suddenly reported the silhouettes of two warships approaching from a westerly direction. All binoculars on the bridge swung around. Friend or enemy? Captain Dähne ordered, "Mr. Ruppert, boats alarm, please! Mr. Kampen, check the typebook and find out the ships' nationality, U.S., English, or French!" The alarm bells shrilled through all quarters and within minutes the men stood ready at their stations, lifejackets around their chests and a small bundle of personal belongings in their hands.

They were U.S. destroyers. A sigh of relief ran through the ship. They were the same type of ship we had watched on previous days off Antonio Lizardo. They now paralleled our resumed course through the gulf, a so-called protective escort that was to remain with us through the 300-mile American coastal neutrality zone. That night myriads of stars and a waxing moon shone over us. The destroyers stayed with us in the darkness, their running and position lights leaving us dangerously exposed. We identified our escorts as the *Lang* (DD 399), *Benham* (DD 397), *Jouett* (DD 396), *Schenck* (DD 159), *Phillip* (DD 76), *Ellis* (DD 154), and *Cole* (DD 155).

The following day dawned with calm seas and beautiful weather. The sun was bright, sea gulls sailed behind the ship, and porpoises played their endless games around us in the warm waters. This seeming monotony was interrupted several times when our escorts left us and new warships appeared on the horizon. Boat alarms rang out, typebooks were consulted, and courses were changed until we were sure about the identification of those approaching us at top speed. This constant changing of "escorts" by the American navy and the fact that we didn't sight any other vessels gave us a feeling of confidence. In less than two days we were in the midst of the gulf stream cruising through the Florida straits. South of us was Havana and soon we saw the glow of Miami passing on our port side, where certainly at that very moment happy, carefree people dressed in handsome evening clothes enjoyed rich dinners and danced to soft music in the beautiful hotels that lined the beach. What a world of difference in sentiment separated us now. Just a narrow strip of sea, on one side peace and on the other the threat of destruction.

Northward we rushed, making a good nineteen to twenty knots. We began to sight ships of all nations, and if they didn't know that we were the *Columbus* they certainly saw that we were a German vessel by our national ensign, the swastika flag, which snapped briskly at the gaff. Most likely our position and course had been reported to the enemy by now, but we were still in American waters, safe for the moment. To our starboard were the British Bahamas, and as if to signal the seriousness of their mission our escorts now numbered six and were marching in formation line ahead, an imposing sight for vessels of other nations watching us. At night the illumination of the escorts' running and top lights was more brilliant than before.

We wondered what the English were planning for us. Certainly they were on the alert in Nassau, Bermuda, and in the far north at Halifax where the Canadians had a large naval base. The British must have been well informed of our movement. They had the capability to intercept the U.S. destroyer signals that were most likely reporting our position on a regular basis. While we weighed these possibilities, the U.S. coastline gradually disappeared.

We took our bearings by direction finder from Jupiter Inlet, St. Johns, and the Diamond Shoal light vessel and changed course to northeast, running in the center of the gulf current. Suddenly a plane appeared from our starboard, flew towards us, and then disappeared. It was 17 December 1939.

A short time later, our lookout in the crow's nest informed the bridge by phone that the destroyers were heading off. As they did we deciphered a flag signal from one of them: "Godspeed, Safe return, and Merry Christmas!" "Nice guys," I remarked to Third Mate Hans Falkenhahn, who was watching them with a grin. "These darned Yanks have a certain sense of humor and sportsmanship," he muttered. Then as quickly as they left, more destroyers approached at full speed. As we watched them, one of the wireless operators appeared on the bridge and handed Captain Dähne a long written broadcast from Germany. The captain turned to us and said, "Gentlemen, the pocket battleship *Graf Spee* has been scuttled by her own crew in the Río de la Plata and her commander Langsdorf has committed suicide! She had fought a gallant battle against superior forces and been badly damaged when she took shelter in that river. We need not be ashamed of her fate!"

By now we had reached the latitude of Bermuda, to the east of us, when several low-flying planes came towards us. They were U.S. aircraft and it appeared as if they were filming our vessel. At about this time our radio operators heard the news that two American heavy cruisers had left Norfolk, Virginia, with secret operating orders. We now estimated that we were about five hundred miles away from the area we had designated for crossing out of the American neutrality zone. The weather was much cooler now, and according to the radio bad weather was approaching us from the northwest. We decided to reduce speed slightly in order to slip into it as we passed from the neutrality zone into the free Atlantic.

Again and again, Captain Dähne called the ship's command to special meetings and informed all departments, demolition groups, fire brigades, messengers, and so forth of their plight and duties. We made certain that the engineers could flood the double bottoms and engine rooms as rapidly as possible with special devices, and that the demolition group and fire brigade could do their destructive job quickly and efficiently. There was some solace in the fact that all the currency and gold on board, the costly bed linen, the Persian carpets, and other valuables had been landed in Veracruz and given over to the care of the German embassy in Mexico City. At least some things from the *Columbus* were safe and could be returned to the Reich after the war.

At 0600 Eastern Standard time on 18 December we stood 240 miles off Cape Hatteras. Our lookouts were on intense alert. Suddenly our conversation on the bridge was interrupted by one of the lookouts: "Sir, three points on the port I see a warship, a larger one than those destroyers!" At that moment one of the wireless operators came running to the bridge and reported that in the radio station they had heard one of the two accompanying destroyers in a frantic coded exchange with another ship nearby. Our typebook clearly identified the silhouette ahead of us as the modern U.S. cruiser *Tuscaloosa*. She must have been one of the two warships dispatched from Norfolk a day or so before. The two destroyers hauled out of line and disappeared while the *Tuscaloosa* took their place. Evidently she was to accompany us on the last leg before we left the neutrality zone.

Three

We Scuttle the *Columbus*

On 19 December we broke into the Atlantic. We were now prey for the English hunters. The sea was getting rougher and a long swell rolled towards us. Dark gray clouds covered the sky. Rain was forecast; we hoped for haze and dense fog. All passed without incident that Tuesday morning. We plotted our position as best we could whenever the sun peered through the clouds. At 1200, the end of my watch, I left the bridge and went to the mess room to eat some salty *Lloydlabskaus,* a special north German concoction of corned beef, potatoes, onions, and spices. Afterwards I made a couple of rounds along the decks and talked to some of the crew. I noticed that at about 1400 the large gray hull of the *Tuscaloosa* was slacking off to our port rear. Perhaps she was about to leave us. I went to my room, undressed, and flung myself on my bunk to get a couple hours of sleep. After about an hour alarm bells sounded. I rolled out of my bunk, threw on my old uniform, and ran to the bridge. There was a warship approaching at full speed five points off our starboard bow.

The ship was still twelve to fifteen miles away, too far for positive identification. The third mate called, "Better get ready, Otto!" I dashed to my cabin, got my lifejacket and small bundle of belongings, put my two small diaries into a plastic bag, slung my camera around my neck, took the sextant and nautical books and, with a last glance around the cabin, rushed to my motorboat on the portside boat deck aft.

To my relief, all of my men were there. They had obeyed my orders to be punctual. It was my desire that ours be one of the first boats in the water, towing other boats clear of the ship. I had been tasked with the navigation of the boats should we remain in them for any length of time. We were to fix our position for the wireless operator so that he could signal any ships in the vicinity.

The *Columbus* about to be scuttled. The enemy is ready to seize her. We have to be fast about scuttling, putting our plan into effect as soon as the bulk of the crew mans the lifeboats. No one takes along more than a small bundle of personal effects.

I rushed back to the bridge to pick up the chronometer, sextants, and the sea chart with our exact last position, 38°02′N, 65°33′W. It was about 1530 in that zone. On the bridge all the nautical officers were assembled. They appeared calm.

We were pretty certain by this time that the ship approaching us at high speed was not of the U.S. destroyer types that had been shadowing us previously. We searched the horizon and sighted the *Tuscaloosa* far in the distance.

Most of the officers had gone to their boats while the ship's loudspeaker was calling out alarms and orders. After taking muster and ensuring that all men were accounted for, they ordered them into the boats and awaited further commands.

Captain Dähne, Chief Officer Ruppert, and Second Officer Kampen, in charge of the demolition and fire-brigade teams, remained on the bridge. The captain ordered, "Engine telegraph on attention please! Mr. Kampen, have the chief engineer come to the bridge." When the engineer appeared, Captain Dähne instructed him to wait for written orders, which would be delivered to him by messenger

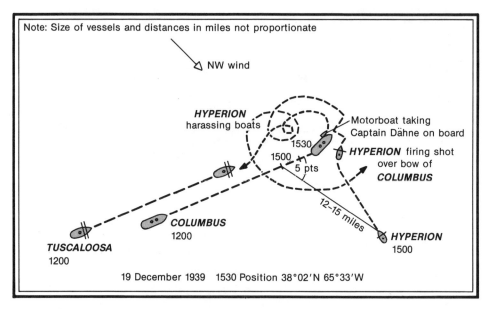

Note: Size of vessels and distances in miles not proportionate

NW wind

HYPERION harassing boats

Motorboat taking Captain Dähne on board

1530

1500

5 pts

HYPERION firing shot over bow of *COLUMBUS*

12-15 miles

COLUMBUS
1200

TUSCALOOSA
1200

HYPERION
1500

19 December 1939   1530 Position 38°02′N 65°33′W

The Scuttling of the SS *Columbus*

from the bridge. This way we could avoid any fatal mistakes that might be made on the telephone.

By now our turbines were humming at high speed, pushing the ship steadily ahead. "Hard-a-port the wheel, Quartermaster," called Captain Dähne, and when the vessel fell off, "Ease the wheel, steady! Let's see how our stranger reacts!" Up to this moment we had seen only the narrow bow silhouette of the warship, by now about three miles away. Just then she swung over to starboard, taking up a course to cross our bow. The English ensign went up on her gaff, followed by a muzzle flash from one of her fore guns. There was a dull report and a high fountain of water on our port side where the shell hit the water. It was a warning shot: We were to stop all engines. This we reluctantly did, since escape was now impossible. The bridge messenger was given the written order to deliver to the engine room. All sea valves and condensors were to be opened immediately. "Mr. Kampen, go ahead with your demolition and fireworks!" ordered the captain. The enemy destroyer hesitated for a moment before passing our bow on a zigzag course at high speed. Perhaps she thought we were armed, or that German submarines were in the area to protect us.

A flag signal went up on the British mast: "Here destroyer *Hyper-ion*. Please stop immediately. You are captured! Please lower gang-way!" The *Columbus* had stopped dead in the water now. She was drifting and showed her port side to the wind. An atmosphere of complete calm prevailed on the bridge and in the boats, which dropped quickly into the water. The disciplined crews carried out their orders. The motor in my boat started instantly, and it proceeded without difficulty in the long swell and choppy seas. Without delay we started to pick up crewmen hanging on rope ladders and to tow the rowboats away from the rocking hull of the ship. Everything went exactly as rehearsed. The rowboats soon formed into towing units, which our motorboats then pulled in the direction of the *Tuscaloosa* heaving to about two miles away.

When I looked back I saw that the last boat, which was to take off the fire brigade, was still hanging in the davits on the boat deck. While another motorboat took over our convoy, my boat returned to the ship and we tried to hold onto one of the foremost boat blocks. The *Hyperion* was cruising at maximum speed around the *Columbus,* still suspecting a reaction from us or any U-boats that might be lurk-ing below. She began to harass our boats by moving among them as they headed for the *Tuscaloosa,* by now steadily approaching. In spite of the loss of their ship, the many hardships they had endured over the past few weeks, and the rough seas they pressed through, the men were in high spirits.

In the meantime, Kampen and his brave men of the fire brigade did a marvelous job of fast and precise work. If the enemy was to board the ship, there was no time to lose. After the engineers had done their work deep down at the floor plates, double bottoms, and wherever valves could let in seawater, the men hastened from their stations. Then the fire brigade poured highly flammable benzine fluid on mattresses in the mess rooms, libraries, and other spaces. They threw large tanks of the liquid down the staircases so that the fire would reach deep into the ship. Torches were lit and the liquid ignited. With incredible speed the flames leaped from room to room, tearing down walls and quickly eating away the dry wood carvings. Explosions sounded in rooms where the overheated air had gathered, small at first, then massive. A high flame shot from behind smoke-stack no. 2, followed by another thundering explosion that ripped open hatch no. 3. I watched from my boat as the flames raced through

Manned lifeboats go into the water quickly, thanks to the crew's outstanding discipline.

The men who lowered the boats follow on rope ladders.

As soon as the lifeboats clear the *Columbus*, they form units under the command of officers.

the vessel as if by some magic mammoth hand, cabin after cabin engulfed in fire.

Another signal went up on the *Hyperion:* "Lower gangway! We send prize crew!" Captain Dähne immediately signaled, "Not necessary. Our vessel is aflame and sinking!" It was time for the remaining men on board to leave the ship. Boat no. 14, with the fire brigade, fell the last few yards into the water and cleared the ship. The sea had grown rougher in the meantime, and I could hardly hold my boat in position under the bridge. The captain was still there. I pleaded with him to come down, and finally, much to my relief, he jumped and grabbed a hand rope that was already smoldering and lowered himself into my boat.

I hoisted the boat's swastika flag, picked up boat no. 14, and towed it in the direction of the bulk of our lifeboats. We left boat no. 14 in charge of another towing group and headed back to the *Columbus,* by now engulfed in thick black smoke and flames. It must have been ap-

The last boat to leave the ship hangs in its davits on the port side forward. The crew is waiting to take on the demolition brigade and engine-room team, who are preparing to scuttle the ship. At this moment a tremendous detonation caused by trapped air is tearing open the deck before the second smokestack.

The last man to leave the ship was Captain Dähne. He follows the demolition team, who opened the seacocks and other outboard valves to let seawater pour in, and a group under Officer Kampen who set the vessel aflame. As Dähne lowers himself on a manrope into my boat, I order the German flag hoisted.

proximately 1700. Darkness gradually descended over the scene. There she stood to the east of us like a large flaming torch.

I saw the area where my own cabin had been on the flaming boat deck and thought of all the many valuable personal belongings I had left behind. But this loss was nothing in comparison with the sacrifices of our comrades in Germany, who had perhaps already given their lives to the cause.

We watched as the once-magnificent liner began to settle in the water. Thousands of industrious workers had helped build, shape, and decorate this beautiful ship during years of grave crisis in Germany. Once the pride of North German Lloyd, she had fallen victim to the war and, at this particular moment, to a small British destroyer. The thought seemed mildly ludicrous to us.

As if reading our thoughts, the *Hyperion* headed at high speed towards our boat. I called out, "Captain, I think it's time we leave. The destroyer wants something from us!" With these words I immediately turned the boat and steered towards the *Tuscaloosa*. The British destroyer soon paralleled our course and we could clearly see the officers on the bridge signaling us to come alongside. Some of their sailors had cleared part of the main deck from the stanchions of the railing where they intended to take us aboard. "Turn your heads away, boys!" ordered the captain. The destroyer then tried to steer us away from our course towards the *Tuscaloosa.* We both went into a circling action, with our boat making an ever-decreasing circle. Unexpectedly, as if tired of the chase, the destroyer veered off and left us alone.

Later, aboard the American warship, we learned of the message traffic between the two vessels:

> *Hyperion:* "Like to take sixty prisoners, among them the captain, officers, and fire brigade. Impossible to take more. Other destroyers have been called to take rest of crew!"
> *Tuscaloosa:* "Our orders, either you take all or none. We are warning, stay away from the boats. If you ram or sink one, we will have to commence firing at you. Please answer!"
> *Hyperion:* "Roger, roger, please take entire crew!"
> *Tuscaloosa:* "In order, we will take all!"[4]

Several hard explosions rip up the decks of our *Columbus,* turning this renowned and beloved ocean liner into an inferno of flames, steam, and smoke.

The *Hyperion* watches our movements and veers toward us. She follows us in a wide circle, then suddenly returns to the *Columbus.*

West of us the silhouette of the *Tuscaloosa* stands out against the evening sky, promising safe haven, at least for the moment.

It was dark when we arrived alongside the *Tuscaloosa.* We were surrounded by drifting lifeboats. Some of them had been wrecked by their crews as they began to board the cruiser. Nets and Jacob's ladders had been cast from the main deck of the ship for those crewmen who were disabled or too weak to climb up the side of the cruiser. The men jumped from boats bobbing in the rough sea and made their way up the nets and ladders. The American sailors helped in every possible way. Some jumped into our boats in order to attach ropes and lines, allowing our crewmen to get aboard. The latter stood on deck a bit forlorn and soaked, but nonetheless happy not to have been taken prisoner by the British.

Soon the first of our crewmen were called down into spacious mess rooms where they received warm and ample food. Captain Dähne remained with us on deck to watch the final throes of our beloved *Columbus*. Her flames reddened the dark rainclouds for many miles around. Although hundreds of tons of water must have entered the interior of the ship by now, cracked and burst open the bulkheads and decks, and rushed into the remotest corners, she was still afloat, listing about fifteen degrees to port.

I remember saying to myself, "Goodbye, dear old friend. You had a heart and soul, and everybody who had ever gone to sea on your planks had loved you, whether the tens of thousands of your happy passengers, who will soon read about you in newspaper headlines around the world, or the many crewmembers who served on you through the years. Forgive us for what we had to do to you. You died in honor, no enemy entered your decks. Farewell, old friend."

We stood silently watching the death of our ship, our home at sea, as the *Tuscaloosa* picked up speed to depart the area. There was no pathos expressed, no "Heil Hitler" calls with outstretched hands— nothing. We only had a sad feeling of emptiness in our hearts.

We were soon taken by some ship's officers to their quarters, where they urged us to take seats in large armchairs, offering us coffee and cigarettes. They were cordial to us and gradually the tension lessened. We began to talk about the last few days. There were no disparaging words about the deeds of the *Hyperion* or the *Tuscaloosa*'s role in the loss of our ship. The crews of all three vessels had done their duty, following the orders of their respective services and governments. We were touched by the candid words of Captain Badt, commanding officer of the *Tuscaloosa,* when he said, "Gentlemen, I sincerely hope that our United States will not be involved in this war and that this vessel will never be dispatched to a similar assignment!" Then we went to the officers' mess room, where Germans and Americans sat side by side. This was our first solid meal in several days.

In the meantime, all crewmembers had been assembled for general mustering and counting. With great regret we found out that two men from the engine department were missing. None of the crew had seen them. Perhaps they had not heard the general alarm and had been surprised by the flames, or they had managed to escape but were picked up by the British. On the request of Captain Dähne,

Captain Badt contacted the *Hyperion* by radio and received the information that no survivors had been taken aboard the destroyer.

We were most impressed when the officers of the cruiser doubled up in order to offer us their cabins. Before I lay down I went to the main deck of the heavy, laboring cruiser, which boxed into the high swell and rough seas, making slow progress. This was the weather we had waited so long for on the *Columbus*. Where was she now? Had she slid down to her eternal resting place? The horizon was dark wherever I looked.

Finally, the *Hyperion* signaled the *Tuscaloosa* that the *Columbus* had gone to the bottom at 2310 at latitude 38°02′N, longitude 65°33′W. The message from the *Hyperion* contained other news that we learned about later from the ship's officers. The *Columbus* had gone down on even keel. Upon hearing this I remarked, "Gentlemen, in life and death, she was indeed a proud old lady!"

Four

Distressed Seamen

· · · · · · · · · · · · · · · · · · · ·

The *Tuscaloosa* set her course for New York, where we were to be disembarked and quartered at Ellis Island. After anchoring off the Ambrose lightship for a short period we proceeded through the Narrows into upper New York Bay. Ahead and along the banks countless lights shone dimly through smoke and fog. Her engines stopped, and the ship inched astern into a designated anchorage at Tompkinsville. Reporters were allowed to board the ship and take pictures of the activities of both crews. We were soon taken on board tugs and tenders and transported to the island so well known to immigrants entering America. Ellis Island was also known as the Island of Tears.

It was dark by the time we entered the wide gates of the processing building on the island. The bright lights illuminating the assembly hall stung our weary eyes, still affected by salt water and the sea wind. We sat where we could and wondered what would happen next. Again, reporters descended on us asking questions and taking pictures. Captain Dähne gave an interview to a large crowd of reporters, telling them the story of the *Columbus* in a calm and precise manner. Later, after being assigned quarters and dormitories, he addressed us at an evening meal in the dining hall. We were guests of the United States, he said, and we were to act like guests as long as we remained in the country.

Thanks to the kindness of the officials on Ellis Island, we soon felt more relaxed. The accommodations were not what we expected as distressed seamen, but then one should consider that the station had probably not been prepared for an onrush of 576 Nazi seamen, as we were referred to by now in the local papers. It was especially difficult for our ordinary seamen, who had been crowded into quarters without sufficient beds, tables, and chairs. Most of them had to sit and sleep on bare floors. The rooms were not adequately ventilated and

Ellis Island, known to many immigrants as the Island of Tears, is for us distressed seamen a welcome haven. The large halls soon smell of cooked turkey and trimmings. Christmastime!

when the small window slots were opened, ice-cold air chilled the living areas. Many men were soon in the hospital with severe colds.

During the day crewmen stayed in the heavily guarded spacious hall, we officers in the brighter and more comfortable library. All of us enjoyed the hot and cold showers, where in addition to bathing we were able to wash our underclothes. Officers' shirts were taken care of by stewardesses from the *Columbus* who were still with us but living in separate quarters. Donations from the German community in New York gradually filtered in to provide our crew with additional clothing.

The representatives of North German Lloyd were trying to resolve our status with the U.S. State Department. In January 1940, we were told that negotiations were being conducted that would result in our being shipped to the West Coast by train, then taken by Japanese vessels or other ships of neutral nations to Japan. The plan was to return to Germany via Siberia.

On 10 January, the New York newspapers ran a story with this lengthy headline: "German Crew Going Home across Pacific. All *Columbus* Men of Military Age to Quit Ellis Island. May Avoid Capture by Trip via Russia. Nazis Confer at Embassy on *Columbus* Crew. Wiedemann Flies East to Plan Their Repatriation with Dähne also Present." And indeed, Captain Fritz Wiedemann, German consul general at San Francisco and former personal adjutant to the Führer, had arrived in Washington by plane and gone directly to the German embassy for conferences involving our disposition. Captain Dähne had also flown to Washington.

The conference, in which State Department officials participated, was held in the offices of Dr. Hans Thomsen, German chargé d'affaires. Though a decision was reached, the State Department did not issue any official details other than that we were to leave Ellis Island on Sunday, 14 January 1940. Details of our departure from the United States, it was explained, were to be kept secret and out of the press in order to prevent our capture on the high seas by British, Canadian, or French ships.

A heavy rainstorm whipped the Hudson when we left Ellis Island. It was foggy on the river and large ice flows made it difficult to dock the ferry at the desolate Erie train station, where six or seven trains were waiting for us. Armed guards urged us in the trains while the wind whipped around us. Soon they were rolling down the track, fifteen minutes apart, headed for Chicago. As we traveled west the

The crew of the *Columbus* is sent in two trains from Chicago to San Francisco. Here we are marveling at the beauty of the United States. Chief Officer Kurt Ruppert (*right*) stands next to Third Officer Heino Lampe.

At Omaha, about halfway between New York and San Francisco, the huge steam engines take on water. German settlers from Nebraska who have heard about us bear baskets of delicious native apples.

Daily Omaha Tribune carried an article saluting the brave crew of the famous *Columbus,* which was known to many of its readers in Omaha, Kansas City, and Denver. In order to make our trip more pleasant, citizens of German descent in Omaha met us with presents of cigars, cigarettes, and apples. Signs attached to the gifts read, "Good luck on your trip through the great West of the U.S.A. to which Omaha is the gateway," and "Good luck for an undisturbed trip back to the German homeland."

At Laramie, Wyoming, we reached the highest point on our trip, about eight thousand feet. We caught up with the other train that was carrying part of our group at Ogden and then both trains rumbled for an hour or so over the Great Salt Lake, which was partially frozen. We left the cattle town of Reno as the sun disappeared behind the Sierra Nevada, painting the sky in delightful pastels reflected a millionfold by the mountain snows. We passed a landscape of unsurpassed beauty with its dark lakes and blue and lilac valleys over which bright stars and a yellow moon were shining. I loved this place where once-proud Indians had hunted. Scenes from boyhood novels about the great American plains lingered in my mind as we traveled westward into the night.

On 18 January 1940 a total of 512 crewmen arrived in San Francisco during one of its worst cold spells in years. Of our original group of survivors, Second Officer Hinsch and Purser Hähne had stayed in New York along with five other men who had resident papers. An additional 57 crewmembers, which included boys, stevedores, nurses, and men beyond military age, were to sail back to Germany on the Italian ship *Rex.*

The rest of us, escorted by armed immigration service guards, were immediately taken to Angel Island in San Francisco Bay. (In its early years, Angel Island housed a large immigration station that processed foreigners who wished to live and seek their fortune in America. The island was used as a military base for almost a century, and during both world wars thousands of soldiers were processed through its quarantine hospital.) Part of the crew found comfortable quarters in the quarantine station, while I settled down with the rest in the main building of the immigration station. The conditions there were terrible. The bunks hung four high on chains, with mattresses caked with dirt and blood. There were no tables, chairs, or clothes hooks. During the night we were locked in by guards and had no place to relieve ourselves. There were only two open-air showers for two hundred men. However, we soon regained our spirits and set about to improve the place. We cleaned the quarters, helped the carpenter build tables, chairs, racks, and clothes hangers, and constructed a small writing room. The guards, seeing our misery, took pity and helped wherever they could. Gradually the head guard gave

The immigration and quarantine stations on Angel Island, across from Alcatraz in San Francisco Bay. The quarters are poor and the conditions unsanitary, so we take matters into our own hands and soon add many comforts of home.

us greater freedom and soon we were able to roam about the entire island.

Local newspapers reported that there were Allied warships waiting to capture us one hundred miles off the coast. On 18 January the Japanese liner *Tatuta Maru* departed San Francisco. Originally we were to have shipped out on that vessel. It appeared as if, for the time being, we were trapped in the United States. Other incidents were happening at sea that no doubt led to the decision to wait for opportunities to secure a safe passage for us. The *Asama Maru*, the flagship of the Japanese Nippon Yusen Kaisha (NYK) line, had sailed from San Francisco on 6 January with about forty German seamen among its passengers. The liner was stopped by a light Australian cruiser about thirty-five miles off Yokohama. A boarding party went on the ship and seized twenty-one Germans, who, it was said, were of military age. These Germans were brought as prisoners to Hong Kong. Rumors began to circulate that the Japanese were considering the use of their own warships to convoy their merchant ships sailing out of West Coast ports.

The *Asama Maru* incident, regarded by the Japanese as a serious and unfriendly act against Japan, created much unrest and resentment against the British. The British embassy in Tokyo had to be strongly guarded by police against the aroused ultranationalist Tokhokai party, which demanded that Britain surrender the German seamen and apologize for the alleged affront. Later, the nationalists expressed their sympathy to the German embassy in Tokyo. It was rumored that Captain Yoshisada Watanabe, master of the *Asama Maru,* was retired from active service by the owners and that he eventually committed hara-kiri. The general manager of the NYK Steamship Company in San Francisco asserted that in the future no Japanese shipping company would accept Germans of military age, especially technicians and mechanics who, the British contended, were being systematically recalled to Germany from the Far East. The British stated that it was their duty to prevent their return.

These incidents settled the question of our return in the near term, at least, and rumors that we would have to try to run the Allied blockade in small fishing vessels or other craft remained unconfirmed. Some of the men seemed content just to be on an island in the United States where they could eat and sleep and relax at the expense of their German steamship company. Others, however, and this was the majority, wanted to get home by any means.

At the beginning of March a group of thirty-five of our men left on board the Italian freighter *Fella,* which was bound for Salvador, the Panama Canal, Marseilles, and Genoa. All of the men were over fifty-two, a group that we thought would be passed through by the British and French naval forces. Our own chances of return seemed to dwindle further when we learned that the group of older men had been taken off their ship at Gibraltar together with another fourteen crewmen of the *Columbus* who had sailed with the Italian freighter *Rialto* on 16 March from San Francisco. A third group of twelve elderly men were intercepted by the Allies in late March on board the *Tatuta Maru.* This action prompted the Japanese to cancel the visas of fourteen other elderly crewmembers who were to ship out aboard the liner *Kamakura Maru* in the middle of April. Thus 451 men were left on Angel Island. The camps were now run by officers according to a strict daily schedule.

Shore leave, which had been liberal during the first weeks when men had been invited by local families to celebrate small parties, visit the World's Fair on Treasure Island, watch American films and roam around old San Francisco and Chinatown, had been suddenly restricted again, although not canceled entirely.

I became obsessed with thoughts of getting home to Germany and reaching the front before the war was over. I had an overwhelming desire to prove my manhood in a war in which so many of my sailing mates had already become successful naval officers. The idea that after the war men who had spent it on the front lines would partake of a glory all but denied to those who had passed it behind barbed wire only further depressed me.

The letters from my father and mother spoke of my good fortune. They told me not to despair about my fate, that even if I came home at that moment the war would soon be over. They said that after the war good and brave men would be needed to repair what had been destroyed in Germany and to build a better Europe.

Although my parents didn't mention the ongoing destruction of Bremen, we knew from American news reports that it was under heavy siege by British bomber aircraft. The only indication from my parents that Bremen was suffering the ravages of war was when my mother would mention how hard it was to walk to the bunkers at night.

The daily broadcasts of the Deutschlandsender kept us up to date about events in Europe and the world. The men also scrutinized American newspapers and compared their information with German broadcasts. They read what the famous American pilot Charles Lindbergh had to say about the conflict, that he saw no balance of justification on either side of the European war, declaring it merely a struggle for material gain by Western nations. They read about the struggle in Norway, the Netherlands, and France, of Hitler's announcement that the fighting in the lowlands of Western Europe would decide the fate of the German nation for the next thousand years. They read of the *Altmark* incident, Dunkerque, of false rumors of peace negotiations and a new era of U.S.-Nazi relations. They listened and read and hoped, yes, hoped dearly, that Germany's enemies would soon give up, because they didn't believe that England could hold out against the might of the German military forces. Not all, not even most, of the men wanted to fight. The sooner the war ended the sooner they would be on their way home. These were the topics of endless conversation as they walked the hills of the island. During the morning hours, when heavy fog rolled in from the sea through the

Golden Gate and over the hills of San Francisco, they thought of home and what perils lay ahead for them.

On 29 July Captain Dähne announced to us that the German embassy in Washington had contacted the U.S. government concerning another potential avenue home for us. The proposal was to ship us across the Pacific on board the U.S. liners *President Coolidge* and *President Taft,* if a guarantee of safety against British intervention could be received. The German government agreed with the proposal. However, the British were adamantly opposed.

Much to our concern, articles that accused us of spying began to appear in the *San Francisco Examiner.* Some of our men did boast about receiving invitations to the Mare Island Navy Yard, and they might have met with friends there and socialized in the clubs. And contact continued with the German consulate in town, where some of our crewmembers were engaged in office work. At no time, however, had anyone been involved in fifth-column or spy activities. The result of this publicity was naturally a severe setback for us, since it greatly curtailed our freedom.

Five

Escape to Japan

. . . .

I was convinced by now that I had to do something drastic if I was to return safely to Germany. It seemed certain that the United States would soon enter the war, that our camp would be moved inland and perhaps surrounded by barbed wire. Escape would be a fruitless then.

I had just come back to the island one day in early September from a visit to the World's Fair on Treasure Island when I stumbled on an article in the newspaper that detailed the escape of fifteen *Graf Spee* officers from Martin Garcia Island, where they had been interned. The Argentine Ministry of the Interior had ordered special police to hunt down the fugitives. That same night Hannes Kampen reported to us that Captain Fritz Wiedemann no longer had objections if we wanted to try to reach Germany on our own. With this news, I began to work on a plan for escape.

Since all Japanese vessels leaving U.S. ports on the West Coast were still searched and checked by Allied warships, I intended to board a Japanese or Russian ship in a Mexican port like Mazatlán or Manzanillo. My plan was to go by train or hitchhike down south, buy a horse, and cross the Mexican border at some remote and unguarded area.

I had some good friends who had a big ranch in Culiacán, Sinaloa State. The daughter of the owner had gone to school with my sister in Bremen. I wrote them a letter and communicated my plans, which were quite favorably received. My plan was set. I carried a few belongings ashore and hid them with friends in San Francisco. Since Captain Wiedemann was out of town, I had to wait for his return to inform him of my plan.

Although I kept my plan secret, I had an interesting conversation with Second Mate Konrad Pfennig. Pfennig had heard a rumor to the effect that at least four or five officers of the *Columbus* were developing plans for an escape. He said that under any circumstances it was advisable to inform Captain Dähne, who most likely would not give his consent. Captain Dähne reasoned that the U.S. authorities would take strong action against the captain and the rest of the crew if any of the men disappeared, especially officers. He was of the opinion that all officers had the moral obligation to help the captain and stand by him during these trying times. In fact, the captain would demand such support and would punish any man who attempted to escape and failed.

In mid-September Dähne spoke to the crew and stated in no uncertain terms that it would be much better for the men to remain in the camp. Our return was imminent, the defeat of England unquestionable. Also, he added, it would be ridiculous to believe that the United States was going to ally itself with the British at this late stage of the war.

Finally, Consul General Wiedemann returned. When he and Captain Dähne were informed of various officers' plans to escape they voiced somewhat differing opinions. While Wiedemann did not object "under certain circumstances," Captain Dähne argued that, unlike Consul Wiedemann, who was bound only to the German embassy in Washington, he was accountable to the U.S. government for the actions of his men. Any escapes would cause the gravest difficulty for the German government and him and the rest of the crew. No one was to leave the camps, and all existing orders were to be obeyed.

Since relations between Japan and the United States were steadily deteriorating, I felt that there was not much time left if I was to consider using a Japanese vessel for my escape. After much thought, I contacted Captain Dähne again and conveyed my thoughts about our situation, that there was little time left to act if we were to return home. To my surprise he answered that a plan was being studied by German authorities in Washington for smuggling eight officers aboard a Japanese vessel that was to sail on 25 October. Evidently eight of our men had undergone physicals and been found unfit for military service. The United States was allowing them to depart and their passports were ready. The German plan was that eight fit officers would take their place aboard the Japanese ship if all went well with the U.S. immigration authorities. Captain Dähne went on to say that if the plan failed, he would release us from our former obligation and we would be free to attempt escape by any possible means.

While we waited to learn who the lucky officers would be, a news headline dashed our hopes once again. On 23 October a San Francisco newspaper ran a story with the lead headline "Japanese Ship to Rush Nazis Home from San Francisco." It seemed that someone had leaked the plan to the press. Perhaps the U.S. authorities were already aware of our secret venture. At noon the same day Captain Dähne received an important call from the German consulate, after which he summoned Officers Kampen, Lampe, Falkenhahn, Sonnenberg, and myself, and Engineer Wille. "Gentlemen," he said, "I've called you because you have shown the most interest in escaping to Germany. Please sign these affidavits, which Mr. Lampe will bring with other papers to the consulate. We hope that the Japanese consul will issue visas for you and that American immigration officials will not object, as you will go on a special assignment of the utmost secrecy. Its nature cannot be revealed to you at this time."

We were overjoyed. That evening I snuck ashore to retrieve my clothes from my friends. The next day, 24 October, we packed our seabags and suitcases. The fever of expectation rose. Finally, Mr. Bernhard arrived from the consulate with our passports and papers. An hour later Captain Dähne called us together again. This time the medically unfit whom we were to replace came as well.

"Gentlemen," the captain announced, "our plan has been accepted by the Japanese and by American immigration officials. The *Asama Maru* will sail at about noon, you six officers will accompany the eight sick and invalid crewmembers to the NYK line pier and carry their luggage. How each of you gets on board will be left to your personal ability. Safe passage is granted by the British only for the invalids. No one officially knows about your presence on board except those few authorities who have secretly worked out the arrangements. You leave at your own risk.

"I reiterate that I have selected you because you young officers are needed in Germany today. Other officers will follow if this transport manages to get safely back home. Mr. Tielbaar, our chief purser, will disburse ten U.S. dollars to each of you for pocket money. By the way, there will be no shore leave for anyone but officers. I would appreciate it if this order is strictly observed. That is all for the moment. Thank you, gentlemen!"

During the early morning hours of 25 October we were busy preparing for our departure. The last utensils had been stowed away in bags and suitcases and the baggage was carried down to the pier of

Hans Falkenhahn, Heino Lampe, and I (*from the left*) before jumping on board our "escape" motorboat.

the quarantine station. Our eight invalids looked neat, cleanly dressed and shaven, while we officers had put on our oldest clothes, were unshaven, and wore fedora hats longshoremen style. At 8 AM we gathered around the small white cabin cruiser at the pier, where we were checked by a friendly guard. With lightning speed, rumors had spread through the camp that something was going on that morning there at the pier, and it seemed to me as if all the remaining crewmembers had assembled. Apparently by higher order, no guards had been posted at the pier. There were initial expressions of surprise, then hearty handshakes and fond farewells, for they knew that we were on our way home. We boarded the boat as the motors hummed and were put into gear. Our comrades ashore waved and cheered as we moved out into the bay.

Our boat docked at a remote spot at NYK pier no. 25. With great haste we carried the baggage to where other longshoremen were stacking suitcases for the ship's passengers. Here we deposited the heavy pieces, took light equipment under our arms, and helped our invalids up the steep gangways. Once on board they presented their passports, showed their visas, and were requested to go to a certain cabin in third class, located somewhere deep in one of the vessel's many passageways.

We urged the sick men forward as quickly as possible and soon found the cabin. No one had followed us so far. We pushed into the small cabin, locked the door, and kept silent. All the officers jumped into two bunks and the invalids piled the luggage around and on top of us. We ached from the weight, but it was the best hiding place should officials enter the cabin.

The time passed slowly. It was nerve-wracking. Then we heard footsteps. They came down the passageway and stopped in front of our cabin door. Someone started knocking, but we kept quiet and our light was out. The person jiggled the latch again and again. "Hello, is somebody in there?" No answer. Other footsteps could be heard approaching and they too halted at our door. The two strangers conversed in English. "Wonder where they are? It seems that these cabins are unused. Let's check again with the stewards." The two men left.

It was not long before we heard several more strangers approaching. "Hey, open up, we're friends of yours, we know you're in there, come on, come on, don't act silly!" No answer. We held our breath and didn't move. We heard them say, "Let's try some other cabins and search the decks too!" It was as if a stone had been lifted from our hearts, but we still didn't dare move or open the door. The same thing happened again; by now we suspected that reporters were following up on the rumors of escape by our crew.

It was about noon when we finally heard the bell signal ordering all visitors to leave the ship. I dared to peep through a crack in the door. Seeing nothing, I snuck out as fast as I could, taking only my camera with me. I rushed along the empty passage and around the next corner into a side arm, which led to a locker with a bull's-eye above. The locker held a couple of buckets, some rags, and brooms and had ample space for me too. I squeezed in and closed the doors from the inside and waited until I heard the ship's motors start. Then I crawled on top of the locker and took some pictures through the bull's-eye. My hands were a bit shaky, not so much from the excitement of the last few hours but from the tremendous feeling that I was free and on the first leg of my long journey home. I grew more confident that we had in fact made it when I didn't sight any boat or Coast Guard cutter following us. I returned to the cabin after a large sailing vessel picked up the pilot outside the Golden Gate Bridge. The *Asama Maru* gained speed and pushed on into the Pacific.

We were still trying to decide what to do next when a polite Japanese steward entered, made a deep bow, and told us in excellent English that he had received orders from the chief steward to conduct us to a cabin in the second-class section. It had been specially reserved for us and was removed from the rest of the ship's passengers. The idea was that, from now on, the invalids were not to know or talk to us. It didn't take us long to change our clothing and appear like normal passengers. As far as we could tell, nobody else besides the captain, the chief steward, and the table steward who had accompanied us to our cabin knew of our presence on board.

The *Asama Maru* was on "Voyage No. 60 Homeward" when she carried our group to Japan. Her "Souvenir Passenger List" brochure included our names and listed us as American students.

Naturally, any vessel that appeared on the horizon was scrutinized by us. Was it enemy or friend? Our first reaction was to find a good hiding place in cargo holds instead of ventilators, smokestacks, elevators, cabins, and wardrobes, which are usually the first areas searched. We tried to find out what orders the captain was under should the vessel be stopped by Allied naval units. We were told that any British ships would probably be dissuaded by the rumor that Japanese submarines would escort the ship from Honolulu to Japan. There was also another factor that played in our favor. There were several Japanese ambassadors aboard the *Asama Maru,* and the British were probably under orders to avoid any incident that might cause international repercussions.

On the evening of 30 October we tied up at pier no. 8 opposite the famous Aloha tower in Honolulu. The passengers crowded the gangways and flocked ashore. Who couldn't resist the magic of these islands, where millions of people spent their holidays away from a world growing evermore troubled? Although we felt lucky having made our escape from the mainland, we wanted somehow to get ashore and see Hawaii. This would be a once in a lifetime chance for us. Longingly we leaned on the rails of the promenade deck and studied the activity below, the number of officials, the gangways, looking for a way to sneak ashore without being discovered. Soon we had obtained some blank landing cards on which we scribbled some names. With the air of travelers of the world, three of us sailed past the Japanese and U.S. officials down the gangway and ashore.

The Japanese flagship *Asama Maru* at the pier in Honolulu. Following an urge to see the island and its people, we manage to get by the U.S. security guards with faked landing passes and leave the ship in a crowd of American passengers. For the next several hours we play the role of carefree tourists.

Naturally, we didn't dare go back on board again until shortly before the departure of the ship, which was scheduled for 1200 the next day. Although it was past midnight by now we found plenty of bars to visit. Sunrise found us on a beautiful beach where I filmed Hawaiian dancers. We had a relaxing morning surrounded by throngs enjoying this paradise. But our time was short. We hurried to the pier somewhat apprehensive. Getting back on board, however, proved as easy as getting ashore. We managed to pass up the gangway with the bulk of the passengers. Soon the liner moved her stern into deeper water while thousands of paper ribbons tore apart and beautifully colored leis drifted in the water as a symbol of farewell.

The master of the liner arranged a series of entertainments for the passengers. Garden parties, evening dances, and Japanese plays were held on the promenade deck. As for us, we tried to keep fit as possible playing Ping-Pong, running around the decks, or swimming in the spacious saltwater pool. One of our invalids was suffering heart attacks, so we decided to go on night watches at his bedside. The ship's doctor regularly injected him with camphor. We feared he would not survive the journey.

One of the German passengers reported to us that somebody had stolen a pair of shoes out of his cabin. Within an hour we found the culprit, a former German sailor of the liner *Europa* who had booked passage in the third-class section. Kampen, Lampe, and I called him into our cabin and gave him a sound licking in the presence of the owner of the shoes and another passenger. The honor of German seamen was upheld.

Everyone on board was of the opinion that the United States would enter the war now that President Roosevelt had been elected by a solid 59 percent of the American electorate. As we neared Japan the weather became rough and stormy. Rumors spread that a Japanese submarine was in the vicinity and that the liner was now in contact with Japanese warships by radio.

During the evening of 11 November, we could see the distant lights of the Japanese coast and were thankful that fate had brought

Back on board, many an eye sheds tears. As the last ribbons tied to shore tear apart, the ship's band plays Hawaiian farewell songs.

us so far unscathed. Early the next morning our anchor chains clanked into the water while ships' sirens and the horns of small launches made a hellish noise. We had arrived in Yokohama.

On shore, the Japanese officials were very lenient with us. For some reason, however, we remained under police escort. We learned later that the British had intended to take our liner but had abstained from doing so because of the threat of Japanese submarines. They sharply protested our presence to the Japanese government, but the Japanese refused to hand us over. Then the British tried to persuade them to keep us interned in Japan until the end of the war. So the Japanese decided to keep a police escort with us to give local spies the impression that we were in custody. A short time later it was thought best that we should disappear for awhile. We were transported to the Kaihin Hotel at the beautiful beach of Kamakura outside Yokohama.

A few days later we learned from the German consul that our invalids were to leave Japan in two transports on 22 and 23 November. Prospects were dim for our own passage aboard these transports. We were to be assigned to jobs on German freighters in Japanese and Chinese ports since most of their officers had been taken to work in embassies and consulates, or on vessels that acted as tenders for German raiders operating in the Pacific. These freighters were often left with only a captain and chief mate and some engineers to run them. These vessels were eventually supposed to travel to Germany with materials badly needed there. So we were all ordered to various freighters. My assignment was the 5,000-ton *Spreewald*.

Before we parted we had a small party and reminisced about the happy days on our beloved liner *Columbus* and the drama that followed. At first we were disappointed that we could not return to Germany as a unit and then join the fight together. We had to be happy finding a place where we could serve for the common cause. Each had a job to do. We vowed to do our best and to be men of strength and integrity.

....

PART TWO

Homeward Bound with the Blockade-Runner *Anneliese Essberger,* November 1940– December 1941

Six

German Freighters Galore

· ·

After I had checked in with Mr. Fredrichsen of Messrs. C. Illies and Company on 22 November 1940, agents for the Hamburg-Amerika line vessels in port, I reported to Captain Bull and Chief Mate Nitz of the *Spreewald*.[5] They were both goodhearted, able seamen. I quickly felt at home in my new setting.

There was not much to do but keep a variety of lists up to date and take care of an onboard dispensary that was placed under my charge. I had forgotten most of my medical training received at the nautical academy in Bremen, so much of my time was spent studying medical handbooks. The report book of sick crewmen showed that a high percentage suffered from venereal disease. Unfortunately, the medication needed to treat this disease was not available in Japan. I did my best with what I could find on board. Each morning the delinquents were mustered on deck, cold and shivering, to execute washings with calcium permanganate. I prescribed castor oil for pains of the belly with good success. This along with a couple of friendly words and some sympathy seemed to cure most of the men.

Since the *Spreewald* rode at anchor some four miles offshore, there was only a twice-weekly boat transport from the nearest landfall. We replaced this meager service with daily sailings of our little dinghy. Since there was no motor, it required more than ordinary skill to sail the small boat through the rolling and often tempestuous seas encountered from the outer anchorage to the inner harbor basin.

Ashore in one of the more popular clubs, the Betty Bar, I heard much gossip about German raiders operating in the Pacific Ocean and our freighters supplying them from Japanese ports. Apparently, if one wanted to acquaint oneself with the most secret details of such activity, it was only necessary to frequent restaurants and bars in

Tokyo, Kobe, and Yokohama. The cities and ports abounded with spies collecting intelligence on German ship movements.

One day the *Spreewald* positioned herself alongside the *Elbe* to deliver fuel oil. Soon thereafter the *Regensburg* tied up on the other side of the *Elbe*. Next the *Odenwald* went alongside the *Regensburg* and the *Havelland* positioned herself outboard of the *Odenwald*.[6] These movements were made to exchange or supply bunkers, provisions, and stores, and in some cases to receive prize cargoes brought in by raiders and their supply ships. No doubt the checkered pattern of movements gave the spies something to get excited about.

While I heard that Kampen had safely reached Bremen, I noticed that Falkenhahn was detached to the *Regensburg,* which according to bar reports was to leave Yokohama in mid-December. I envied my friend from the *Columbus;* he had a good chance of becoming a prize-boarding officer on one of our raiders, and perhaps of bringing a prize back to one of the ports in France.

Three weeks went by and our old German freighter remained in port. We hadn't moved a mile closer to Germany and the front in Eu-

The *Kulmerland* returning to Kobe anchorage from an operation in the Pacific Ocean. She has been supporting German raiders.

Blockade runner badge

rope, my sole purpose for escaping from the United States. In a wave
of disillusionment I went to Lieutenant Commander* (*Kapitänleut-
nant*) Bellstedt of the German embassy, who was in charge of manning the blockade-runners, and spoke bitterly of my situation. He
was understanding and responded that within a few days I would
travel to Kobe and be assigned as second mate aboard a ship that
would sail soon. A week later, on 17 December 1940, I found myself
on a windy train bound for Kobe and my new assignment on the
Anneliese Essberger.[7] Although the ship was fully equipped and ready
to sail, she needed some time in dry dock so that the barnacles and
growth on the bottom of her hull could be stripped off.

Captain Prahm and the officers and crew of the *Anneliese* were a
fine group of men who openly welcomed me aboard. I was given the
task of navigator, overhauling all equipment while bringing the sea
charts and logs up to date.

Christmas 1940 was as hearty as it could be with celebrations in the
German Club at Kobe. The entire crew enjoyed fine meals, a Christmas tree, and presents. What a difference between Christmas at Ellis

*Royal Navy ranks are given throughout the text.

As second officer of the *Anneliese Essberger*, I am in charge of navigation, coding and decoding messages, and camouflaging the vessel. I also serve as a watch officer.

Island the year before and here in Japan. The *Columbus* story, as old as it seemed to me by then, was something that none of her former crewmembers could readily forget. Wherever I went, to the German Club, German schools, aboard other ships, I had to promise to make a speech. And so it was on this Christmas. Amid the lights and splendor I reminded my listeners not to forget those of the *Columbus* who were sitting behind barbed wire in a lonely camp in the United States.

During the last days of December, the *Elsa Essberger* returned after three weeks of operations in the Pacific.[8] There was no traffic allowed to and from the ship for a couple of days, and leave was canceled for crewmembers of all German ships. This latter measure was to ensure secrecy for the departure of the fully loaded *Ermland,* which weighed anchor in the early-morning darkness of 28 December.[9]

On New Year's Day, 1941, I woke up in a hotel room in Kobe bathed in sweat. Rats were making a terrible noise, whistling and jumping behind the walls. I had a hangover and was drained from the previous night's celebration. I thought about where my life stood right now. Behind me was a year full of excitement and adventure. It had started out dull and ended full of sunshine. Was it true that someone born on Sunday always had luck in life? Or had the prayers of my dear mother been granted by God? Ahead of me lay a new year, unknown yet, the future obscure. But somehow I knew that I would sail safely through the tempestuous days ahead. I welcomed a life full of fight and hardship.

On 10 January, the *Münsterland* began to prepare for departure. Sampans and barges came alongside her daily, while the tanker *Winnetou* gave her oil and our own vessel joined in bunkering the ship.[10]

A few weeks later all shore leave was stopped for the crews of all German vessels in port. Six of our crew were shipped to the *Münsterland,* and the next morning, 26 January, her mooring was deserted.

In early February I visited the Hankjo-Cine theater and watched the film "Broadway 1940" with Eleanor Powell. I was fascinated with her dancing skill. Afterwards, I trained in the Koshien swimming pool, in the 100- and 1,000-meter swimming events that were part of the German government's silver-medal sports program. Later I went over to the German Club, where I settled down with a highball, two Americans, one of them the U.S. consul in Osaka, and a couple of artists who had come from preparing a big theatrical show, "Parkstrasse 13." Later that month I was invited along with our chief mate to attend the opening. Dressed in uniforms, we secretly smiled at the stiff promenades in the passages of the theater at intermission. There were nods and bows, gallant hand kisses, the showing off of dresses—a show from another world, so much different from the rough and open manners of our life at sea. Still, it was nice to be a part of it all.

The week of 8 March I had my watch in the German general consulate. Every week one officer of the German vessels in port stood watch in order to answer calls, receive telegrams, and see that no outsider entered the premises and the house at night. During my first watch, an excited Japanese man appeared at midnight and reported that an officer from one of the German ships had been jailed by the water police of the Kanoche District; it was my duty to go with him and search for the man. After we received special permits from the main police station, we hailed a taxi and went from one police station to another looking for the man. Unsuccessful in our venture, I returned to the consulate and went to bed.

At breakfast the next morning, the wife of the consul asked if I had not heard the bell ringing the night before. Because I was not there she had had to get up and receive several important telegrams. I felt terribly embarrassed and in the course of apologizing spilled some eggs on my pants. The kind lady forgave me for my behavior, and when I brought her and her husband a loaf of bread baked the German way from our ship, they became most cordial. Not long thereafter the consul hinted that my vessel would soon be assigned to an operation. "And, by the way," he said, "one of my sons is an officer on an auxiliary cruiser somewhere in the Pacific. If perhaps you should meet him, please convey our best regards!"

Finally orders came on 25 March. We were to proceed to the dry dock at the big shipyard in Harima. To establish the right draft, we had to lighten our ship by pumping part of our fuel oil, lubricating oil, and fresh water into the tanker *Winnetou*. Customs came on board and cleared the vessel for departure.

A fresh wind was blowing and it was a marvelous feeling to be at sea again, if only for a short trip. The barnacles on our hull slowed us so that we could barely make nine knots. Our pilot slept most of the way on a sofa in the chartroom. I had my hands full taking bearings to navigate us through the treacherous inland sea and into the bay. The naval shipyard appeared suddenly, nestled in a beautiful, peaceful-looking landscape. Nearly all of Japan's wartime plants, industries, docks, and yards were situated in such inaccessible places, surrounded by mountains and heavily guarded.

Normally no foreign ships were brought into these docks, probably to prevent espionage and sabotage. The *Elsa Essberger* was already in one of the docks undergoing repair. We were permitted ashore only by special permission and wearing armbands, and then only to get to the water closet. Rivet hammers rattled around us night and day. Huge cranes shifted loads while men and women toiled alike. Not far away, deep in the mountains, blast after blast could be heard. The Japanese were opening wide gaps in the mountains for a new dock. Hundreds of industrious hands were engaged in carrying off the rubbish.

On 26 March our second engineer fell sick with appendicitis and local peritonitis. We whisked him to one of the hospitals in the shipyard. I had my uniform on and was respectfully saluted, while constantly watched. It was some time before the operation could start and the poor man had to be continually sedated by injections. The operation was performed quickly and without complication. As soon as the patient was moved to a recovery ward, I returned to the ship.

Waiting for me was a letter from my beloved American girlfriend, Pat. My exuberance faded as soon as I read her words: "I will get engaged soon . . . but let us be friends no matter what the future brings. . . ." I knew in my heart that our worlds were growing farther apart and that there was little hope for a life together. I silently wished her well and immersed myself in my duties.

We returned to our anchorage at Kobe a few days later and noticed that the *Münsterland* had returned from her operation. Up to this point we had watched so many ships come and go while we remained moored in the harbor that we began to despair of ever sailing for Europe. But when the captain told me to go on board the *Elsa Essberger* and get advice about camouflaging our vessel, our prospects appeared to improve.

According to our calculations, the *Elsa* would probably operate in the Indian Ocean, which was still dominated by the British, while the *Anneliese Essberger* would return to Europe via Cape Horn and the Drake Passage carrying provisions for ninety days and 1,890 tons of diesel oil. We would disguise our ship later as a vessel of the Kawasaki Kaisha line, since she closely resembled its ships. Our hull would remain gray, with a Japanese national flag painted on both sides. The upper part of the smokestack would carry a red and gray

Celebrating May Day 1941 in Kobe, on board the *Elsa Essberger*. Captains Bahl and Prahm stand at the far right. There is good food and drink, speeches, songs and deck games to entertain the crews of the *Anneliese* and the *Elsa*.

ring with a large capital K on both sides. On the bow and stern would appear, in Latin letters and Japanese characters, the name *Daishi Showa Maru Kobe*. Since there was not much flammable material on board and it would take too long to scuttle the *Anneliese* should she be discovered by the enemy, we intended to place dynamite in the portside engine room. This would destroy the valves and tear a two- to three-square-yard hole in the hull.

We waited for final orders to sail. Barge after barge brought provisions and stores. Twice, shore leave was canceled for all crews. I had brought my sea charts for the eastward voyage up to date and had written numerous letters for the captain. Privately, I had deposited all my film and documents with friends and requested to have them shipped to my parents via Siberia.

We were excited. Everything pointed to our weighing anchor on 3 or 4 April.

Suddenly an order came for all vessels to report how many of their crewmen could be replaced by Chinese. What could this mean? We could only surmise that German seamen were needed to bring prize ships captured by raiders back to Germany. At the same time we received news about German and Italian vessels being scuttled in Central American ports and their crews interned. Would this action have any impact on operations in our area?

And so we waited on. Riding at anchor in Kobe at the time were the *Scharnhorst, Winnetou, Münsterland, Kulmerland, Regensburg, R. C. Rickmers, Burgenland, Ramses, Elsa Essberger,* and *Anneliese Essberger.*[11]

The early days of May came alive with electricity as rumors began circulating that the *Elsa, Ramses,* and *Anneliese* would soon weigh anchor. The *Elsa* had been pumped full of fuel and the *Ramses* was loaded with stores from a continuous stream of barges. Then one evening the *Elsa* weighed anchor. She was to sail into the mid-Pacific to meet and refuel vessels coming from South America, probably the small NDL freighters *Quito* and *Bogotá,* so that they could reach Japan. Was this a sign of American entry into the war?

A week later, on 16 May, the *Ramses* weighed anchor and left for an unknown destination. Were we next? Day after day I sat in our wireless station and listened to telegrams directed at German raiders and transports in the Pacific. I heard that the raider *Pinguin* had been sunk after a heroic battle with the British heavy cruiser *Cornwall* on 8 May near the Seychelles in the Indian Ocean.[12] Three hundred forty-one of her gallant crew and 213 prisoners were lost with the ship when mines she carried blew up. She went down in less than a minute.

Now messages to the *Elbe* and the *Regensburg* directed them, if necessary, to be scuttled rather than fall into the hands of the enemy.

Seven

Anchors Aweigh!

. . . .

At 2300 on 8 June, leave was canceled for crewmen of all ships. Two days later Mr. Kehrmann and a Mr. Pippon from the German embassy in Tokyo came on board the *Anneliese* to give the captain our last instructions. After a hearty good-bye and handshakes all around, they departed. The following evening Captain Prahm assembled the crew and declared, "Gentlemen, we are finally free to start our journey. Our ship's name is *Daishi Showa Maru*. If you should be asked by somebody where we are bound, you will answer Vladivostok. You are obliged to obey military law!" He then briefly explained that disciplinary punishment, in most cases, equated with imprisonment.

We had already darkened ship; not a beam of light could escape. At long last we weighed anchor. It was 2030 hours. The heavy chain clicked link over link into its locker and the telegraph was put on slow ahead. With utmost care we made our way through the other vessels. No doubt their seamen stood at the railing watching our dark hull disappear, just as we had with so many other ships before us, and probably with the same feeling of envy in their hearts.

A slight drizzle had started to fall, gradually growing thicker and thicker until it laid a dense veil before the lights of Kobe. Finally the last contact disappeared. As my watch was from 2400 to 0400, the dog watch, I went below deck to get some rest. While dozing off I thought back on the many events I had experienced since leaving Bremerhaven on 20 June 1939 with the *Columbus*. Now I was halfway around the world heading home.

When I came on the bridge at 2400 the drizzling mist had become dense rain. During the previous watch they had had to let the ship drift as they waited to find the lights at the bay's entrance. Double lookouts were assigned, and I had to be on the utmost alert for coastal lights. Though I was wet to the bone, it felt great to have a good ship under my feet and a willing crew with me. We would soon be on the wide ocean, surrounded by enemies that had not been able to sweep the seas free of German vessels. The words of the U-boat song of World War I came to me: *"Denn wir fahren, denn wir fahren gegen Engelland"* (Still we fare against England). Although our ship was no submarine, and she carried no torpedoes or arms, we would bring a valuable cargo back to Germany that would be needed for our war industry.

It was my job, as camouflage officer on board, to see that our Japanese name was painted on the stern, and as it was doubtful that anybody on deck would be able to sketch these difficult characters, I set about to do it myself. Armed with brushes, paint, and a small drawing, I went over the side and sat on a boatswain's chair, swaying wildly, a couple of yards above the turbulent wake thrown up by the propeller. After two hours of painting, the work was done and the Japanese name stood out in brilliant large letters.

The weather had improved and the sun was warm. Only a large, long swell was still running from the southeast making the vessel roll. How happy everyone was. We talked about home and dear ones whom we would see in about three months, perhaps the latter part of September. The sea watches were enjoyable after the long period of idleness in port. There was always something to be done. Bearings had to be taken continually, especially in the narrow passages among the small islands hugging the southwestern coastline of Korea and Japanese Kyushu.

We sailed along the coast of Korea at about twelve knots. At 0200 on 16 June we dropped anchor off Dairen, China. Later that morning a pilot brought us to a reserved space at the navy pier where we docked in complete isolation from other vessels. No one was permitted to enter the area, including patrolling Japanese soldiers who walked up and down the quay with steel helmets and fixed bayonets.

Soon the pier around us came alive. Stevedores, tallymen, soldiers, Japanese foremen, and a colorful gang of Chinese workmen swarmed over the pier and ship. Hatches were uncovered, booms topped, beams put beside the hatches on deck. There were huge piles of raw rubber bales and automobile tires and in the sheds and warehouses on the pier, endless rows of drums with sweet oil—in all about 5,000 tons of products worth several million marks, destined for Germany.

When we finished loading on the first day at about 1900, the officers and engineers found time for a beer or two in my cabin. The next

Our Japanese ship's name, painted by yours truly while en route from Kobe to Dairen.

few days we worked late into the night amidst the never-ending rattle of winches, the yelling of stevedores, and the cursing of Japanese foremen who treated their Chinese workers harshly, driving them with rods and whips. While our holds filled gradually and the sheds began to empty, our crew was busy painting the ship a bright gray. Soon she looked more like a yacht or a warship than an old freighter.

Early in our stay in Dairen, Captain Prahm introduced me to our mission. I read the sailing order that explained how a blockade-runner was to carry out her difficult mission. Apart from running the enemy blockade, we had to supply the German raider *Komet*, near the Tuamotu Archipelago in the South Pacific, with extra provisions, stores, fuel, and lubricating oil. For the sake of safety, two rendezvous points had been selected with a five-day loitering period at each. We were at liberty to choose the way from Dairen to these destinations; however, if we wanted to avoid a long detour we had to run pretty straight through a confusion of small islands that were more or less British possessions. I was tasked with choosing the routes and determining the arrival times at both rendezvous.

Following our contact with the raider, we were to follow a route around Cape Horn. Once past it, we were to intersect certain geographical points until we entered a zone along the north coast of Spain, which was regularly patrolled by the German Luftwaffe. From there we were to proceed to the mouth of the Gironde River in Bordeaux. I felt that we could complete this operation within sixty-eight to seventy-eight days, if everything went smoothly and we were not thrown off track by enemy convoys or warships. I was quite proud of having gained the confidence and trust of the captain in these calculations.

Shortly before our departure from Dairen, our plans and dates of arrival were handed over to the German consulate, which in turn passed them on to the German embassy in Tokyo. Our calculations would be all that German authorities would have to track us, since we had been strictly forbidden to use our wireless unless we were in need of fuel or water, or if we were attacked by enemy forces.

At 2100 hours on 20 June, fully loaded and ready to sail, our ship weighed anchor in a torrential rainstorm. Rain had covered our departure from Kobe and rain veiled our sailing from Dairen. Double watches were assigned as before. Soon we were in the midst of the Gulf of Bo Hai. We proceeded down the west coast of Korea, cruising the Korean Strait to a point in a bay off Nagasaki only known by

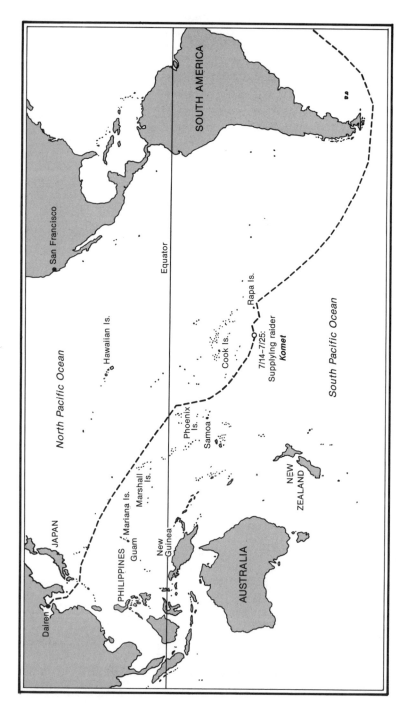

Track of the *Anneliese Essberger* in the Pacific

the naval staff in Tokyo, the captain, and myself. Soon a motorboat came alongside with two high-ranking Japanese officers who conducted us into Sasebo, a base hidden in the mountains. The moment we anchored, a large navy tug with two barges in tow approached us. Aboard the barges were several large cases. Officially, these boxes were declared as *Dauerproviant* (durable provisions). What they actually contained was torpedoes and their accessories, all greased and tightly packed. Indeed, they were the first torpedoes for the German Luftwaffe, which so far had only used bombs in attacking enemy vessels at sea. The Japanese had used torpedoes for some time now and gained considerable experience with them.

It was of paramount importance that our ship not fall into enemy hands. For this reason, large boxed mines were placed in hatch no. 2 and the engine room. The fuzes were cut to about seven minutes' burning time. At the end of each fuze we placed a signal torch to light the fuzes.

After the Japanese officers had bade us farewell, we waited for darkness, weighed anchor, and sailed out of the small and idyllic bight after a magnificent sunset. We had about six thousand miles to cross before meeting our raider.

Eight

Across the Pacific

. . . .

The following morning, as soon as the Japanese coast was out of sight and we were free of foreign vessels, I continued camouflaging the ship. Our task was supported by fine weather and a slight southeast trade wind. Although the boatswain and several sailors helped me, it took about two days to change the old camouflage at the bow and stern from *Daishi Showa Maru* to *Terutoyo Maru*. Then we painted a large Japanese sun flag on a white background on each side of the hull, as well as a capital K, representing Kishen, onto the red and gray smokestack.

In the meantime, we listened to radio broadcasts over the loud-speaker. War had finally broken out between Germany and Russia. We heard the speech of the Führer, which was read by Goebbels, and we listened to the accusations of von Ribbentrop against Russia. We believed that Hitler had tolerated a great number of abuses by Moscow of existing agreements and that the time was therefore ripe to clear up the situation by force. We were thrilled to hear that the German army had been so successful during the first few days of battle and wondered if the United States would now enter the war. In any event, we had to take these and other changing events into consideration as we planned our mission.

I disregarded any misgivings I might have had about fighting Russia. I was angry at the Russians for entering the war against us, thrilled by the successful strategy and operations of the German army and the Luftwaffe. I didn't give the severe Russian winters much thought. We had beat the Russians in World War I and I thought that they probably hadn't improved much since that time. Whole armies were surrendering to our forces. Our military seemed invincible, at least judging by the news reports.

Measuring the large K on the smokestack, which stands for Kishen or K line. I also change the name on the bow and stern to *Terutoyo Maru* and paint a large Japanese flag on each side of the hull amidships. This new camouflage is necessary after we sail from Sasebo, Japan.

During the first nights we occasionally sighted larger vessels crossing our track. We carefully avoided being seen. Since our ship was sailing in the warm southeast trade winds, large numbers of porpoises accompanied us and countless flying fish tried to avoid us, often in vain. They would land with loud flapping noises on the hot decks. The calm waters, dark to bright blue, reflected a sky of the same vivid colors. Large cumulus clouds drifted around us. Off in the distance we could see rain pouring from darkened clouds, trailing a veil of mist over the water.

The air was buzzing these days with orders and directions for *V-Schiffe* (*Versorgungs-Schiffe*), or supply vessels and blockade-runners. At first the telegrams contained only notes about positions and so forth. However, when these ships entered the area around the Bay of Biscay, the wireless traffic increased, ordering changes in courses and routes to avoid enemy air patrols, warships, and convoys.

Something had gone wrong with the *Elbe*. Apparently she was forced to use her wireless despite orders to remain silent. More and more promises came that Luftwaffe reconnaissance planes and German warships were en route to accompany the vessel to her destination. We figured that the *Elbe* must be in real trouble. Then we received a telegram saying that the *Regensburg*, which had been sailing astern of the *Elbe*, would soon be in the vicinity, probably to render assistance. The usual pilot information for ships did not arrive. In fact, telegrams about the vessels stopped altogether. [13]

With deep regret we heard about the sinking of the Hamburg freighter *Alstertor*.[14] This had been a successful supply vessel for German raiders under Hamburg-Südamerika line Lieutenant Commander Block, who had at one time sailed to the remote Kerguelen islands in the south Indian Ocean to supply the raiders *Pinguin* and *Komet*. One piece of information that lowered our hopes was the recall of the *Ramses* to Japan. That freighter had already neared the Horn; we could not understand why she was turned back but figured it was too risky to run the blockade. In that event, we might get the same orders after meeting and supplying our raider. The days passed quietly, without incident. No other ships were sighted. Only now and then we heard radio transmissions of some foreign vessel nearby.

A long and high northwest swell made our vessel draw water over her main railing. A landlubber would have despised the eternal rolling, but we loved it, only cursing occasionally when vases, glasses, pictures, and pens slammed into the corners of our cabins. The porpoises played and jumped all around us. Now and then gigantic whales would push their dark shiny bodies to the surface and exhale high fountains of hissing spray. At night we marveled at the brilliant constellations which, however, with the exception of the Southern Cross, couldn't match the dazzling lights of the northern sky. Often, much too often, our thoughts raced ahead, towards home and those who awaited our return. We could not give these thoughts too much room; if we failed to arrive at our destination the disappointment would be that much greater.

Nine

Rendezvous with the Raider *Komet*

· · · · · · · · · · · · · · · · · · · ·

From about 7 July 1941 on, after passing the east corner of the former German Marshall islands, we pursued a more southerly course so as to feel our way through the confusion of the Phoenix, Tokelau, Samoa, and Cook islands. Our route was leading directly through enemy territory, with the exception of Samoa, which was a U.S. possession. Generally the islands were well populated and regularly called on by vessels in the San Francisco–New Zealand services. Still, up to this point we had not seen any foreign vessels that could have given us away to enemy warships.

A rough sea was by now running south-southeast, and we had to box hard against it to keep up a planned daily run of about three hundred miles. Owing to delays caused by periodic engine repairs, strong winds, and swelling seas, we arrived at our first meeting point on 14 June, a day late. Our orders were to be at the rendezvous point, 28°30′S, 15°20′W, at 0800 and 1600 daily. Though heavy weather had played havoc with the ship and interfered with our navigation, we were confident that we were within three miles of our rendezvous point.

We cruised the area at reduced speed with all watchstanders intensely scanning the horizon. Finally, at about 1430, a lookout called, "There's a vessel at about two points on the port side." I swung my binoculars around and saw the other ship steaming a parallel course over the horizon. When the stranger veered and headed towards us I called the captain to the bridge. Then she changed to a course that would bring her directly across our bow. We could see her more clearly now, as she appeared occasionally at the top of a long wave. She had extremely sharp lines with a raking bow and a cruiser stern. Since both ships were running at top speed and closing fast, we decided to hoist our recognition signal. A black cylindrical object was

First Officer Koch and Third Officer Wietholter "shoot the sun" to get our noon position. At the right is the helmsman. We are about to rendezvous with the raider *Komet.*

raised on our foremast. The other ship answered by searchlight, signaling the letter B.

In salute, we hoisted our real call letters and signals for *Herzlich Willkommen* (Hearty Welcome). When the vessels were close to each other, I flag-signaled another salute and apologized for not being at the rendezvous earlier. Gradually both vessels stopped, then drifted slowly past each other with all hands manning the railings. Jokes and questions went back and forth, and I discovered quite a few acquaintances from former times.

Germany had sent auxiliary cruisers into battle during World War I. Ships such as the *Emden, Möwe, Wolf, Kronprinz Wilhelm, Leopard,* and *Seeadler*, under the command of Felix Graf von Luckner, plied the seas, attacking Allied merchant ships and battling enemy warships.[15] Likewise, auxiliary cruisers disguised as freighters were released to raid and harass enemy ships at sea during World War II.[16] Our raider, the *Komet*, was the smallest of eleven raiders active during the war. Built in 1937, she was a former fruit vessel of North German Lloyd operating between Bremen and the Canary islands. She was camouflaged as one of the more modern Japanese-type ships of the Osaka Shosen Kaisha line and carried a slightly illegible name, the *Ryoku Maru*. Her home port was Osaka.

Originally she had had an Arado reconnaissance plane on board, but the aircraft was out of action due to a hard-water landing. She also carried a small armored speedboat for minelaying. All told, there were 270 officers, petty officers, and men on board. Her commander was Vice Admiral Robert Eyssen.

Her operations in the Pacific were generally successful, and at times her commandant acted as the leader of a squadron of German auxiliary cruisers consisting of the raiders *Orion* and *Komet* and their supply ship *Kulmerland*. On 7–8 December the raiders attacked and destroyed four phosphate ships off the island of Nauru, northeast of Australia. Following that action the squadron dropped anchor off Emirau Island and landed over five hundred prisoners.[17] The *Komet* then returned to Nauru on 27 December and destroyed the island's sizable phosphate-working pits, loading facilities, and oil tanks. Admiral Eyssen warned the administrator of the island to abandon the targeted facilities prior to the attack. This was done and casualties were kept to a minimum. Great Britain and Australia swore to do everything possible to hunt the *Komet* down. The former prisoners had given a fairly accurate description of the raider, and much was written about the *Komet* in the world press.

In the early morning hours of 14 July, we started to load provisions and stores into the raider's fast, efficient motorboats. Although we had well over two months of provisions for her, the admiral was disappointed with provisions like meat that were no longer very fresh. Nor were there fresh vegetables on hand, so vital to the well-being of a crew. In general, the food provisions did not compare with those that other supply ships brought from Germany. We had about 1,200 tons of fuel for the raider but no fuel hoses. She had had no hose since leaving hers on board a Norwegian prize tanker that had to supply the raider *Orion*. Since we were scheduled to supply the *Orion* at a later date, we hoped that we could pick up the *Komet* hoses at that time. We would need them then, for the rendezvous area was usually engulfed in bad weather and under constant surveillance by enemy aircraft. Transfers under such conditions have to run quickly and without incident.

Thus we were compelled to use the raider's fire hoses, of which she had an ample supply. It was decided that the *Komet* would tow us

We finally meet the *Komet*, under the command of Admiral Eyssen. The smallest of the World War II German raiders, she has made her way into the Pacific via the northeast passage around Siberia. In the southern Pacific she has operated successfully with the raider *Orion* and the supply ship *Kulmerland*. We start provisioning the *Komet* using her fast motorboats.

with a 200-yard-long, 6-inch-thick manila line shackled to our anchor chain. The swell, however, proved too high, so both vessels just drifted while the oil was pumped with a pressure of about four atmospheres (one unit of pressure is equal to 14.69 pounds per square inch). To prevent a collision, the raider had rigged up tarpaulins as sails so that she would drift faster than us.

During the night the wind died down completely, and the raider towed us again after we had turned out about fifty yards of anchor chain. At first, we tried to pump oil on into the evening. But usually the hoses got fouled up and tore, causing numerous leaks. Since it was strictly forbidden to switch on lights, the hoses could not be repaired at night. Thus fueling stopped when darkness fell.

Soon the big, heavy manila rope broke too, and several more lines had to be brought out. By now the raider had developed a refined towing system, three minutes stopping and ten seconds running ahead slow. This went on all day and throughout the night, until the wind shifted and got stronger. Then our vessel was unable to obey rudder and we had to be towed again, with constant dead slow ahead by the raider. Thus it went for days, towing, stopping, oil hoses out, oil hoses in, repairs, endless work during which I usually had duty on the bridge. To keep up this constant activity, the raider had sent some of her sailors over to help us. They often reported to me for duty. I had served previously with many of them while aboard the square-rigger *Schulschiff Deutschland*.

Often during this time we could hear across the water the bully voice of Admiral Eyssen, who had a personal interest in everything

The *Anneliese Essberger* towed by the raider in calm seas. The heavy manila towline and the fire hose used to transfer fuel are visible.

The raider assists us by sending over a signalman during provisioning.

happening aboard his vessel. He kept his ship in fine shape and his men in the best of trim. In spite of the long time they had been away from home, the discipline and spirit of the crew were impressive. I had a great desire to join them, which would have been possible if there had been space for another officer. Such was not the case, for several other merchant marine officers had recently been taken aboard from various supply ships.

The *Anneliese Essberger* camouflaged as a Japanese K liner, as seen from aboard the *Komet*. The latter, which lacks fuel hoses, receives about 700 tons of fuel through fire hoses. This is a difficult and time-consuming operation.

The raider's chief navigator delivered the basic plans for a new sailing route for us. I was surprised at how well informed he was about naval activities in both the Pacific and Atlantic theaters. He apprised us of the positions of the British auxiliary cruisers *Queen of Bermuda*, *Alcantara*, and *Asturias*, and marked out areas on our charts that were frequented by enemy convoys. Our new route was therefore based on the latest intelligence available. Barring any surprises, we should make it safely to our next rendezvous. I figured that we would make contact with the raider *Orion* by the end of August if all went well.

After the oil hoses had been taken in with the towage gear, the raider sailed a short distance away while we watched with interest. Suddenly she hoisted an alarm signal, German war flags rolled down the sides of her hull over Japanese camouflage flags, and another German war flag went up the gaff. Part of the bulwark dropped away, superstructures and deckhouses were rolled aside, and threatening heavy-caliber guns could be seen all around. Small antiaircraft machine guns were hoisted on the two masts. It was an unforgettable and grand scene when the proud raider passed us at full speed with her guns trained on us. "Please regard us as sunk!" we signaled the raider. The admiral signaled back, "You are still my friend!"

We were cruising now at a speed of seven knots and on course 130 degrees, while the raider had echeloned to our port side, ten miles distant. During the night she would echelon back into our wake, keeping us in sight at all times. We had orders from the admiral to hoist our signal and head for the raider in case we saw another vessel. Then we were to watch the other ship and try to ascertain her course and speed. In case the raider should see something, she would go after it and we would follow her. If we should lose sight of each other, we would receive an order to meet, which she would communicate to us after fixing her position by astronomical observation.

On 21 July the wind died down and the sea grew calm. We stopped and drifted stern to stern, quickly rigging the oil hoses and pumping fuel. Up to that point we had pumped 620 tons of fuel into the tanks of the raider. As the admiral did not want to release us so soon, knowing he would need more oil, he ordered us to join him in search of booty along the Australia–New Zealand–Panama shipping lane towards the Galapagos islands. If no targets were found along this lane, he intended to check for traffic on the Los Angeles–Manila track, where there might be some Dutch vessels laden with tin, wood, minerals, or rubber destined for England or the United States.

We stopped often as we searched the sea lanes, and when weather permitted we pumped more oil. Finally, on the twenty-second, after transferring some 700 tons of fuel to the *Komet*, the admiral seemed satisfied and ordered that the hoses be taken in for the last time. Shortly before we separated, a flag signaled me to the raider to receive final instructions. I was lucky enough on this occasion to meet and talk with Admiral Eyssen.[18] He along with his staff and crew wished us a safe and successful return home and warned us to be ever on the alert. The admiral gave me a copy of his up-to-date war journal for delivery to German naval authorities. As I stepped over the railing and climbed down the pilot's ladder into the waiting motorboat, I turned for a last glance at my friends on the deck. The *Komet* accompanied us until the twenty-fifth. At about 0700, after we had exchanged flag signals wishing each other a safe journey, she disappeared.

Ten

Passing the Horn

· · · · · · · · · · · · · · · · · · · ·

Gradually it became colder. The temperature dropped to 10°C, which was quite cold for a crew that had spent so much time in the tropics. Our course ran along the great circle down to Cape Horn. This would be my first experience rounding the cape. I don't believe that there were many sailing ships in the "good old days" that passed it in good weather. Most of the reports I had read mentioned strong westerly winds and storms that often lasted for weeks, sometimes months. Many a brave captain had to give up his attempt to pass the Horn. Most of them, however, had been successful after strenuous week-long work, perhaps losing part of their rigging and some of their crewmen. There were others that never made it into the South Atlantic. For steamers and engine-powered ships there was no giving up. They had to somehow cope with the elements and plough their way through mountainous seas.

The first signs of our approach to the horn were albatrosses and other storm birds. With them came rain, hail, steadily dropping temperatures, and then the first snow! Heavy, dark-gray clouds skimmed over us as if chased by a fierce enemy. Now and then the dark curtains were torn open and a whitish sun would burst through onto seas as tumultuous as a Wagnerian opera. The wind had veered southwest and increased on the twenty-seventh to force 7, while the barometer dropped to 745mm. The thermometer showed 5°C. Woolen clothes, oilskins, and cold-weather coats had long since replaced our tropical clothes.

Early on the twenty-eighth the weather began to worsen, at first with moderate intensity, pressing the seas ahead so that their tips became white collars streaking foam behind them. The next day winds started to howl and scream in the stays and rigging, at first dull and rumbling, then increasing to a high, frantic pitch. The white collars

As we approach the latitude of Cape Horn, the lookouts on the "Monkey's Island" have to keep sharp watch for foreign vessels. To see but not to be seen! as the motto goes.

In the fangs of the Horn, running up from the rear. Our lifeboats, which have been swung out in case we encounter enemy warships, have to be doubly secured in these rough seas. Of course, here the boats wouldn't have been much help to us.

flew from the mountain tips toward the dark clouds and the swells grew higher and heavier. During the afternoon our small vessel rolled and heaved while breaker after breaker covered the decks. The seas thundered towards us, often reaching the height of a two-story building and threatening to bury the entire vessel. Somehow she always managed to escape. The giants would roll beneath her and she would slide back into the water valleys with her bow deeply dug in and her stern pointing at the sky. The ship groaned and rumbled tremendously. Often the strain on her structures became so great that we had to reduce speed by night. There was no sleep to be had, not even when one had stowed his tired bones into his bunk. The resonance of the breakers hammering against the hull was deafening. One could only lay awake hoping the ship would hold together and make it safely through the raging seas.

On the morning of the thirtieth it brightened: A violet-gray light allowed us at least to see our hands. We instantly put the telegraph on full speed. Then fate struck the next night: During my watch the

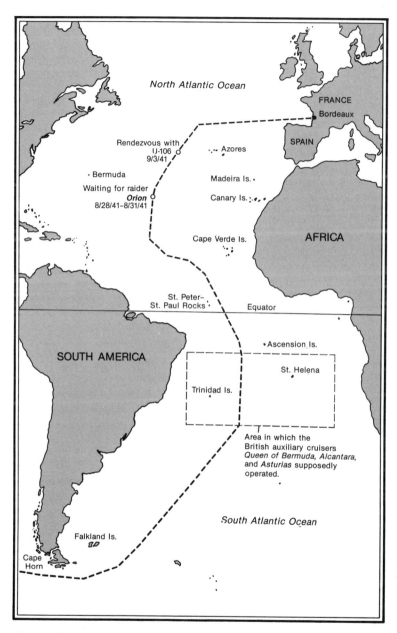

North Atlantic Ocean

FRANCE
Bordeaux

SPAIN

Rendezvous with
IJ-106
9/3/41

Azores

Madeira Is.

· Bermuda

Waiting for raider
Orion
8/28/41–8/31/41

Canary Is.

Cape Verde Is.

AFRICA

St. Peter–
St. Paul Rocks

Equator

· Ascension Is.

SOUTH AMERICA

St. Helena

Trinidad Is.

Area in which the
British auxiliary cruisers
Queen of Bermuda, *Alcantara*,
and *Asturias* supposedly
operated.

South Atlantic Ocean

Falkland Is.

Cape
Horn

Track of the *Anneliese Essberger* in the Atlantic

chief engineer appeared on the bridge and asked me to stop the engines for repairs. I reduced speed and tried to keep the stern of the vessel into the wind as long as possible before stopping the engines. After fifteen minutes the seas gained the upper hand and we were soon rolling helplessly. More than once I lost my grip on the railing and slid across the deck, hitting the compass and landing in the scuppers, collecting black and blue marks and cursing like the devil.

Eventually we gained control of the ship and moved forward at slow speed. On the bridge the barometer had dropped to 737mm. With the temperature at 0°C, we ran around like gray, bearded mummies. When snow or hail thundered on our heads, we played turtle and dug deep into our oilcoats, glancing only now and then at the sinister lights of Saint Elmo's fire scurrying over the mast tops and antenna.

At last, on 4 August, the weather calmed down, and it so happened that we rounded the famous cape in the finest *Mützenwetter* (weather mild enough to keep on one's cap). Having chosen a more southern route, we did not actually see the cape. However, we did make out the island of Diego de Ramirez some thirty miles to the north. This occasion was, as in the old days, a special one. That evening the captain invited us to have a couple of rum grogs with him in our mess room. This was indeed welcomed, since the temperature had dropped to minus 4°C.

Eleven

Searching for the *Orion*

· ·

For about two days we steered an easterly course between the Falkland and Georgia islands before daring to head northeast. We had to be extremely careful in this area, for an enemy warship could be waiting in the Falklands. Also, we were wary of meeting one of those small Norwegian whale catchers that could not be trusted to remain silent upon sighting us. The weather remaining calm, we lowered the heavy cargo boom at the foremast and built a small platform for our lookouts at a height of about twenty-five yards.

It also became convenient at this time to re-camouflage the vessel. She would be the Norwegian freighter *Herstein*, owned by Herlofson, Sigurd and Company and with Oslo as a home port. I had to change the design on the smokestack, change the names and home port on the bow and stern, and paint huge Norwegian flags on the sides. Additionally, I designed large Norwegian and German flags to be rolled out on the fore and aft hatches respectively, in case we should be overflown by enemy or German aircraft.

Our radioman became more active now than ever, listening on the wireless to the ship traffic around us. Twice daily he copied reports of German newscasts so that we were well informed of political and military happenings. The meeting between Churchill and Roosevelt was the main topic. We wondered what the outcome would be. If Churchill requested the expeditious transfer of the treasure of England's banks to Canada, it could signal imminent danger for the British empire. On the other hand, if a proposal emerged that aimed at the complete destruction of Germany, the United States might soon enter the war, giving our number one enemy much-needed hope. One had to credit the British—they were tough and persistent.

Days passed without us seeing another vessel. A large whale mother and her offspring swam with us for some time. On 14 Sep-

Here I am with helpers, outlining our new letter on the smokestack. H for Herlofsen, Sigurd and Company, a Norwegian outfit. Our new name is the *Herstein*.

tember we entered the area where three British armed merchant cruisers reportedly patrolled between South America and Africa. We were told that they operated by moving at certain times from one to another of four designated squares. All three vessels were former passenger liners, fast and heavily armed. One of the ships, the *Alcantara*, had already had a brief encounter with the German raider *Thor* and been seriously damaged.[19] These three cruisers were superior in all respects to our small *Anneliese*, so we had to make sure that we were prepared. Day and night we called the crew to general quarters and demolition and boat maneuvers. It is little wonder that the crew could soon respond to these drills in their sleep.

The main work, however, always rested with the officer on watch. Whenever a ship was sighted, he was responsible for calling the captain to the bridge, giving the general alarm, alerting the engine room, climbing the crow's nest on the foremast to identify the ship, and passing the exact position of the ship to the radio operator for immediate transmission.

If escape was not possible, the two free watch officers would take command of each boat where the crew, with lifejackets and a few of their belongings, awaited further orders. The captain and the officers on watch were to stay on the bridge, watching the enemy and deciding when to slow down and lower the lifeboats into the water. The captain would then enter one of the lifeboats with the rest of the engineers. As soon as the boats were ready to push off, the watch officer on the bridge would give the watch engineer a signal through the speaking tube, whereupon both men would arm themselves with storm signal lights and hand grenades and scuttle the ship.

Once in the zone of the British cruisers, we had to decide which course to choose, one that would circumnavigate the zone or one that would carry us directly through its center. We decided to take the most direct route on the grounds that it might in fact be the safest. Perhaps the enemy would least expect us there and as a result be negligent in his surveillance.

We received a coded message that we were to meet a German U-boat during the morning of 3 September. We were deeply thankful: It was certain by now that we were being traced according to plan. More messages came telling us which signals to hoist and which courses to sail in case we should not make contact with the U-boat.

On the evening of the twentieth, while in my cabin writing my log, I could hear the sound of our national anthem coming from the mess

Lifeboat drill aboard the *Anneliese Essberger* in the South Atlantic.

room through the humming of the motors. I don't know why the radio played the solemn song, but I was in a holiday mood. It was my dear mother's birthday. Earlier that day I had written her a letter conveying my love and thoughts. She was no doubt asleep at that moment. Perhaps she was dreaming about her only son who had been away for so many years. She could not know that I was coming home. In celebration, I opened a bottle of beer and lit up a German cigarette. It was so very hot outside. Before going to sleep I took a bucket of fresh water and poured it over my head, read a couple of pages of Paul Keller's *Waldwinter*, and soon fell into a deep and restful sleep.

Prior to leaving the British operational area, we had a bit of excitement. One morning, shortly before 0600, our lookout in the crow's nest called, "Mastheads port side ahead!" We called the crew to general quarters while the officer of the watch jumped up to the lookout and checked the course and movements of the other vessel. She seemed to be sailing from north to south. Instantly we changed course to starboard and listened to the radio to see if the other ship would use her wireless. We heard nothing. The officer of the watch called down from aloft. "She's a large vessel; the tips of the masts are far apart." And that was the last we saw of her. Soon she disappeared into low-hanging rain clouds on the horizon. This area was generally devoid of ships other than British warships, German raiders, and blockade-runners. We reasoned that she must have been one of the three enemy cruisers—in which case we were darn lucky.

Shortly another vessel appeared out of a rain bank on our port side. She was close enough to us that we could make her out to be a tanker. We could clearly see her bridge and superstructure. She was running on a course approximately opposite ours, so we figured she was on her way from the Gulf of Mexico to Cape Town.

"Hard starboard, boy," called the captain to the helmsman. And when our *Anneliese* came around like a good steed, "Ease the wheel, steady as she goes!" For some minutes we watched the tanker with anxiety. When she too disappeared without causing trouble, we slapped each other on the shoulders and resumed our course. The whole area around us and towards the coast seemed to be humming with ship activity. Quietly our radioman placed a slip of paper on the chart table. He had scribbled that about twenty ships were near, judging by the intensity of their wireless traffic. Most were Brazilian, Spanish, and American.

We were now sailing with the southeast trade winds, which came from our stern and brought few fresh breezes. The interior of the ship felt like a baker's oven. During the day all activities took place on open decks. Soon everyone looked like a South Sea islander, suntanned and leathery. We measured the temperature in the sun at about 50°C and in the wheelhouse at over 33°. Sleeping in our bunks meant waking up bathed in sweat. So most of us spent the nights on open decks watching the sky's glittering northern constellations. My favorite was Orion, with the brightest of fixed stars, Sirius.

During the day it was as if we were in the Pacific trade zones. The scene was familiar to seafaring men of the world, something we would always carry in our hearts: a deep-blue ocean reaching as far as the eye can see to rich blue skies and white, billowy cumulus clouds, all woven into a thing of beauty and peace. Surely we were witnessing God's work. Thus we sailed on, bow waves splashing their monotonous song and the ship lulled back and forth in the long, soft sea swell.

Northward, then westward and again northward we sailed—tracks crystallized out of necessity. We passed the nights without seeing other vessels or being seen by them. The trade winds changed from southeast to northeast as our journey continued without incident.

On 28 August we arrived at our next rendezvous, Point Corona at 28°00'N, 43°00'W, where we were to meet the *Orion*. We were two days early.

Since the weather was calm we let the ship drift during the night. We returned to the contact point again on the twenty-ninth, hoping that the raider might be ahead of schedule and not cause us to linger in this dangerous area. But no ship was in sight. Would the raider perhaps have new orders for us, or maybe a load of prisoners to be offloaded somewhere ashore? We were back again on the thirtieth. Still the *Orion* was not to be seen.

To ease the tension we set out fishing lines to catch bonitos circling around the ship. The water was crystal clear and the movements of the fish were watched and followed by our boisterous crew along the railing.

The sun bore down on us mercilessly. In the evening we watched a brilliant and colorful sunset. From somewhere appeared a gramophone; everyone listened to romantic music and thought of home. A telegram arrived, but it did not say clearly whether to proceed or wait

Our brave ship runs day and night at utmost speed to reach our rendezvous point with the *Orion*. The drums on deck (*starboard aft*) contain our reserves of lubricating oil.

awhile longer for the raider. We decided to remain in the area for another day or so.

I arrived on the bridge fifteen minutes before midnight on the thirty-first to relieve the third mate of his watch. After he had briefed me about his watch, he remained on the bridge to chat. I had just hung the binoculars around my neck when one of the lookouts yelled, "Sir, isn't that a ship over there?"

"What?" I put the glasses hastily to my eyes. "Damned, indeed! Hard starboard!"

And what a ship it was, a mighty fellow moving along at high speed a few miles off our port side. "Easy, boy, easy, steady at 180 degrees!" The third mate had jumped down to inform the captain and radioman. I called the engine room. "Two times full speed ahead please. Give us all you can. We may be in trouble!"

I called out "General quarters!" summoning everybody on board. The other vessel had not changed her course. Incredibly, it appeared, she had not sighted us yet. Within seconds the captain was on the bridge in pajamas and a robe. "Where, Mr. Giese, where is she? I see absolutely nothing."

"Here's the glass, sir, over there!"

Captain Prahm was wide awake now. "Bring the confidential papers to the bridge fast and keep them ready!" he ordered. "Does she use her wireless!"

"No sir, all is quiet," the radioman answered.

The moon shone full now on the other ship, a freighter, and we could recognize practically everything on her deck. Suddenly she turned into our wake. The *Anneliese* trembled and rumbled from the enormous strain of her engines as they pushed her through the water. Then, unexpectedly, the other ship turned to our starboard. She turned again and ran to our port.

We couldn't figure out what she was doing. Perhaps it was she who was afraid of us—although she seemed to have a big gun at her stern. It could have been that she had seen us long before we had made her out, and that she thought we were neutral since we had kept on course. She held hers, but when we suddenly veered to starboard she might not have seen from her position that we were heading away; perhaps she thought we were heading straight for her. She therefore started to zigzag, not knowing which way to run. Whatever her reasons might have been, she finally escaped with incredible speed towards the northeast while we resumed our course, also northeast. Thank God she didn't use her wireless.

After this incident we decided to proceed on course and not wait any longer for the *Orion*.[20] We wondered if we would successfully rendezvous with our U-boat. Would she be at her position after our bad luck with the raider?

Twelve

On the Home Stretch with the *U-106*

· · · · · · · · · · · · · · · · · · · ·

On the night of 2 September, I handed over the watch to the chief mate with some lighthearted words to the effect that he not ram the sub, as we were nearing our rendezvous at 37°55′N, 37°24′W. We had set out our recognition signals for the U-boat, a mast with a boat sail hoisted in a lifeboat starboard aft, and a Jacob's ladder over the side forward of the bridge.

Shortly after 0500 on the third, someone knocked anxiously on my door and poked his head inside. "Sir, please come quickly to the bridge! The U-boat will soon be alongside." I jumped out of bed with a loud shout of joy. I ran as fast as I could to the bridge. There she was, quite near us and stopped dead in the water. It was exciting to see this long, narrow tube of steel and iron pitching and rolling in the long swell. On her conning tower I could see a couple of sun-tanned boys with unshaven, laughing faces waving to us. What a magnificent picture! The U-boat arm of the German navy brought much pride and glory to our military forces. I stared at the *U-106* in awe.[21]

The commandant, Lieutenant Commander Jürgen v. Oesten, was a blunt, dashing fellow. As he talked with our captain his manner made a deep impression on all of us. After such a long and lonely voyage, we were thrilled to be with other German seamen out on the wide ocean.

They had no idea what our future orders from Berlin might be. As for now, however, we were to steam home together. Since we were the bigger brother, we would dictate speed and course and the *U-106* would follow. If we saw enemy planes or warships or perhaps a fat freighter, we should instantly give notice by "wagflag," *S* for ships, *F* for planes, just a couple of times. He would have one of his men watching us. If he saw the enemy first, he would play duck, an expression U-boatmen used for going into a dive, while we were to act as a decoy, gradually changing our course towards England.

The good weather did not last long. Dark clouds rose over the horizon and soon covered the sky. Strong winds brought a storm and it became bitterly cold. Our good ship bounced and pounded into the heavy seas, the deck drowning in a rush of swirling water. Although we ran at full speed, the U-boat was much faster and usually forward of our bow. What a sight! All we saw, when she boxed against the seas, was a white, foamy spot, bow cutting under the waves and tons and tons of water rolling over her deck, pounding her conning tower, cascading fanlike in the air, then falling in a heavy deluge on her aft deck. Sometimes she would rise on the saddle of a breaker, listing badly, and water would pour out of the many slots of her deck, streaking like milk along her sides.

We could clearly see the men on watch over there. They were dressed in thick oilskin, sou'westers tied to their heads. Each one had a broad belt around his breast through which he was secured by a wire strap to the socket of the periscope or the handrail of the conning tower. They must have cursed about their current task, protecting a damned freighter and guiding her home; they could do much better submerged, less speedy but calmer and certainly drier. But orders were orders and there they stood, stoically doing their job, ducking whenever the seas thundered over them, grinding their teeth, spitting salt water. They wore fixed binoculars, removing them only when they ducked or had to wipe the glass clean again.

In the meantime, we received more telegrams urgently warning us to look out for British planes and warships. There was no need to warn us—after all, we were in the area where other blockade-runners like the *Alstertor* had gone down. We maintained full alert. For reasons of simplicity, Guidance Group West sent orders and instructions direct to *U-106*, which signaled the information to us. We received word that the British battleship *Rodney* was cruising nearby to protect convoys assembling at Gibraltar. We took a wide detour, only to run up against a huge convoy en route from England to Gibraltar. Another wide circle was necessary. When we resumed course we could still see the tail end of the convoy on the horizon. I felt certain that the U-boat commander was itching to go into action. But he had just come from a long operation, and an attack now would probably bring enemy warships quickly down on us. So we continued on course, heading home, together.

U-106, a type IXB boat, under Lieutenant Commander Jürgen v. Oesten, has orders to escort us to the Spanish north coast.

We couldn't do much to ease the lot of the crew of this small wolf of the Atlantic, but we did manage to send over some fresh rolls from our ovens by means of a heaving line that ran to their conning tower. They returned the gesture by providing us with fresh cigarettes, not stained like ours, and a bottle of good, clear schnapps. The exchange between comrades at sea filled our hearts with joy.

Our course was set to the western cape of Spain's northern coast, Cape Finisterre. Rain and haze continued to affect visibility. However, on 8 September, while standing my dogwatch, I sighted the lights of the coast.

When the first rays of the morning sun groped over a still-sleepy September sky, we were on full alert. We instinctively felt that attack would come from the air, this particular area being well patrolled by enemy warplanes. No ships were sighted on the horizon.

My thoughts went out to our brave, good U-boat. I turned in her direction and discovered that she was gone. There was only a choppy sea, nothing else. My heart stopped for a moment. Hadn't I been watchful enough? Why had the U-boat suddenly disappeared? I sensed danger, something imminent and realistic. "Watch out for planes!" I called to the men on lookout. "They must be coming from somewhere." Without experience in meeting enemy aircraft attacks, we had no idea from which direction or altitude they might suddenly spring.

"Have the Norwegian and swastika flags ready on the hatches," I ordered crewmen on the fore and aft decks. "And wait until I tell you which ones to roll out." I yelled to the helmsman, "Port the wheel, but let her come easy, go on 10 degrees." I directed another man to call the captain to the bridge. Hardly had I finished that order when from about two points to starboard three streaks rose over the horizon and proceeded steadily in our direction. "Ready for maneuvers," I called down to the engine room. Then I dashed to the starboard wing of the bridge to watch the aircraft, which were now off the beam.

There was nothing else to do now but wait. I wondered if the boys in the U-boat had seen the planes earlier than we had, but then only a few minutes had passed since they went under. The minutes seemed to run into hours as we waited anxiously to see if friends or enemies were maneuvering in the distance. Our most recent cable traffic had alerted us to expect German reconnaissance planes along the north coast of Spain.

German Heinkel He-115s, wagging their wings at us and displaying their black cross insignia. Our hearts beat faster in the realization that Germany is expecting us.

Low over the water they came, lower than our masts. Now we could see their round bellies and the bulges on each side of the wings where the engines were mounted. Their droning, like the sound of hornets, was dull and threatening, and still we were unable to identify their nationality. For a moment we stood glued to our positions. Then there came a loud jubilant cry from all, mixed with a tremendous roar of motors skimming just a couple of yards over the tips of our masts. There on the wings for all to see were the broad and mighty black crosses of the Luftwaffe. The aircraft were Focke-Wulf 200 Condor long-range bombers.

"Roll out the German flags on the hatches," Captain Prahm ordered. But the crewmen had already done that by themselves. They stood and laughed and waved at the planes. The pilots returned their salute, wagging the wings of their planes a couple of times. I was busy tapping "Welcome" on the key of our hand searchlight. In a matter of minutes they were headed away from the ship on a course for Bordeaux.

While all this was happening, the U-boat had surfaced again and a smiling commander appeared on her conning tower. He signaled to us, "You will make it now alone. The planes will check on you regularly, but keep your eyes and ears open. It has been a pleasure to be with you. Have a good trip!" With that he put his gloved hand to his shabby and wrinkled white cap in salute. We waved thankfully and signaled, "Hope to see you again, somewhere, sometime, good-bye and return safely to your base." I was to meet Lieutenant Commander v. Oesten again the following year on board the *Tanga*, which served as a floating repair ship for the U-boat arm.

While we cruised along the coast, just on the border of Spain's three-mile neutrality zone, we could see the ruins caused by the civil war in that country. Two or three times a day German aircraft, Heinkel 115 floatplanes, checked on our progress and communicated our position to Bordeaux. Although we were still in dangerous waters, we began to feel relatively safe.

We passed Santander and Bilbao the last night, and the lights of these towns shone warm and friendly on our crew as we sailed onward in a completely darkened ship. When we arrived at a position off St. Jean-de-Luz during the early hours of 10 September, six German minesweepers approached to escort us into port. This was a mighty big welcome for a little freighter, we thought, and it showed that we were at least of some importance to Germany.

Bordeaux coming into sight. The piers on our starboard side are crowded with all types of vessels, a colorful armada into the midst of which the pilot will squeeze our ship. Our journey covering half the globe has finally ended.

As we steamed northward off the coast, we could see the white beaches of Les Landes with the beautiful dunes of Pyla, the highest shifting dunes in the world. Soon the mouth of the Gironde River lay before us. The afternoon was warm and sunny as we entered the estuary of the river. We anchored at Arcachon, where the first officials came on board. We had endless questions for them. Tension and expectation of the next day's events meant a sleepless night for all hands.

The last day of our "blockade run" was spent steaming upriver with the assistance of a pilot. How lush the scent of the plush meadows, lawns, and fields around us! We saw farmers and their cattle peacefully grazing. Houses began to appear, typical French country houses with their long and narrow windows, which always looked a bit sad, and the rain-washed shutters covering them like eyelids. More and more houses appeared along the embankments. We were full of joy as we moved under the hot sun. Soon we would be with our dear ones.

We tied the *Anneliese* up alongside many other vessels docked on the west bank of the river at Bordeaux. We watched as a stream of uniforms representing all arms of the German military service came aboard. They were led by Admiral Harry Menche and his staff. He shook hands with every man on board, praised the discipline of our crew, and congratulated us for bringing our ship safely to port. He

One of the first naval officers to come on board is Admiral Harry Menche, accompanied by his staff.

ended his visit by wishing us all a happy vacation with our families at home.

Our first day in Bordeaux was unforgettable. After the visitors left the ship we sat on the boat deck and enjoyed a festive drink. The sun set behind the towers and houses of this old town, casting its blood-red, nearly violet rays against a cloudless sky. Slowly the river pushed its way past our dark hull towards the distant sea. Suddenly all was quiet around us. The landscape breathed peace and comfort. It was all over now; we had sailed halfway around the world and survived the perils of war.

I realized that I stood at another crossroads in my life. It had hurt to be away from home when the war started, and although what I had done thus far was not glorious, nonetheless it was nothing to be ashamed of. I had lived by the slogan, Make the best of any situation wherever you are. I would not have wanted to miss the events of the past few years. I had loved and enjoyed those times. Some of my friends had already fulfilled the Latin proverb *Dulce et decorum est, pro patria mori* (It is sweet and decorous to die for your country). Alas, who knew when it would be my turn?

A few days after making port, I was granted leave to visit my family in Bremen. Before departing Bordeaux, I bought some nice cloth and textures for my mother and two sisters, also cigars, tobacco, and good cognac for Dad at the base commissary.

The vacation was wonderful and can hardly be described in words. It was one big festival with parents, sisters, and relatives who wanted to know all the details of my adventures. Bremen had not as yet suffered too much from air attacks by the British, although here and there craters and ruins could be seen. In general, life continued at an easy but restrictive pace. Visits filled my days; many a good bottle of Rhein and Mosel wine was opened and many a cheerful and confident toast rang from our lips.

Back in Bordeaux, the crewmen of the blockade-runner *Anneliese Essberger* were all decorated with the Iron Cross Second Class, while Captain Prahm received the first-class medal.

I was personally invited to spend a few weekends at Admiral Menche's chateau outside the city along with members of his staff. One evening by the fireplace he said, "Dear Giese, I think I know you well enough to tell you that we would like to have merchant marine officers such as yourself in our navy. Would you perhaps like to join the *U-Boot Waffe?*" That was the navy's U-boat arm.

Admiral Menche has decorated Captain Prahm with the Iron Cross First Class and all other crewmembers with the Iron Cross Second Class. Here I proudly display my new decoration.

I responded immediately and with conviction. "Yes, sir, the sooner the better, sir!" In all haste we completed the necessary documents and applications, which Commander (Korvettenkapitän) and bearer of the Knight's Cross Hans-Rudolf Rösing sent to Berlin.[22]

Early in the morning of 8 November 1941, my twenty-seventh birthday, Admiral Menche's limousine stopped at our gangway. The driver brought a letter from the admiral: "Congratulations on your birthday! May the new year of your life, as I confidently hope, bring the fulfillment of your wish to serve your people and the Führer as a U-boatman. I expect you to join me this evening for dinner at my chateau."

The admiral's chateau was an eighteenth-century brick and stone building with tile shingles on the roofs, high windows protected by shutters, many chimneys, and a wide portal of old oak or mahogany. In comparison with German castles, it looked elegant. There were several bedrooms upstairs, some with balconies. The bathrooms had been modernized but still used old fixtures. There were large halls on the ground floor with huge fireplaces. On this occasion the admiral had invited several other naval officers, and it was around one of these fireplaces that we enjoyed fine wine and food while we spun lively seamen's yarns.

That evening the admiral gave me a birthday present: confirmation, through Admiral Dönitz, commander in chief, submarines, of my official transfer from the merchant marine to the U-boat arm. With a grateful heart I will always remember those cordial hours with the admiral and his staff in his chalet.

Back on board the *Anneliese* I was up to my neck in work, representing Captain Prahm and the other officers who had gone on vacation and taking care of the many visitors who boarded the ship daily. During the evening hours I followed the lure of such places as Tourney and Lion Rouge to sip some of the rich southern French wines with beautiful and charming local women.

When the other officers had returned from leave, we invited the ladies of our navy command, the German equivalent of Waves, for dinner on board our blockade-runner. In general, it was strictly forbidden for them to come aboard vessels in port but with our good reputation and some official manipulation we were successful.

Captain Prahm objected to my passing over to the navy. He told me the head of the shipping company that owned the *Anneliese*, *Staatsrat* (state counselor) John T. Essberger, would do everything through the traffic ministry to sabotage my plans because of a severe shortage of merchant marine officers. My orders had not come through yet, and I worried that I would have to go to sea with the *Anneliese* before they arrived.

In mid-November 1941, Admiral Menche suggested that I take leave again since I would soon be assigned to a front-line boat in the Atlantic as watch officer with the rank of lieutenant junior (Leutnant zur See "S"). The hour of departure from my old "battleship" had really come. My last words to my comrades of so many days were spoken to the accompaniment of genuine Martell cognac.

I was, of course, pleased to be assigned the rank of lieutenant junior. It was normally given to officers assigned a special commission in the German navy, not active naval officers, and in some cases merchant marine officers serving on board ships in various unique capacities. This was the transfer route that Admiral Menche attempted in moving me from the *Anneliese Essberger* to U-boat service. I assumed that other merchant marine officers had joined the U-boat arm in a similar manner. Unfortunately, as I was to find out later, such was not the case. My situation was unique and became somewhat political. Admiral Dönitz had decided that if I really wanted to become a U-boat watch officer and was that eager to be on a front-line boat, I would have to start from scratch. I was to learn the trade on one of his operating boats as a seaman, without the benefit of basic U-boat training. My mettle would soon be tested.

Sitting in the train homeward bound once again, I thought what a beautiful and free life I had, not forced to stay in one place but pushed on into an ever new and changing world.

Towards the end of November I was summoned to a radio station in Hamburg to send some words to my *Columbus* comrades during the program "Blinkfeuer Heimat" (Revolving Light Homeward). As I had not yet received a cable from the U-boat arm, I continued on to Berlin and other towns to visit friends and relatives.

On my return to Bremen I picked up a newspaper at the train station. The headlines screamed, "Japan at War with USA and England! Warmonger Roosevelt has reached his goal: The dollar imperialism has been victorious! The Japanese Military Headquarters announces that from Monday morning on, 0600, a state of war exists between Japan and British and U.S. forces in the Pacific."

I could hardly believe it. Then I recalled all the student demonstrations I had seen in Tokyo and I remembered the numerous articles in the newspapers in Kobe. This moment had probably been in the making for some time and was unavoidable. I went on reading: "Mutual war against USA and England! Up to final victory!"

On 11 December Hitler held another of his *Reichstag* speeches in which he stated that Germany henceforth regarded itself at war with the United States and that passports had been issued to the American ambassador and his staff in Berlin. A new agreement between the Axis partners, German, Italy, and Japan, had been signed. It stated that the three partners would bring this war, forced on them, to a victorious end by any means possible and that no peace or armistice with the Allies would be made without the consent of all three Axis partners. Additionally, the partners would agree to work jointly after a victorious war to forge a just new deal as set out in the pact signed on 27 September 1940.

Hitler went on to express Germany's disdain for the deceptions carried out by the United States under the camouflage of neutrality. He mentioned the betrayal of the *Columbus*, the reporting of many other German merchant vessels to the British fleet, attacks on German U-boats by American warships, the confiscation of German freighters in American ports, the occupation of Iceland and Greenland, the convoying of British ships, and the surveillance and betrayal of German operations, all hostile acts committed before a declaration of war. [23]

The sudden realization that we were drawn into a war with the United States, so to say overnight, had a very sobering effect on me for two reasons. First, we were now confronted by three of the most powerful nations in the world, the United States, England, and Russia, with a fighting potential in men and material that far surpassed Hitler's ambitions on land and at sea. Although Japan's expansion was impressive, it was not of much immediate help to us in our struggle at sea and against Russia. Also, having to fight on so many fronts would work against us as the war went on.

Second, the history of my family was closely tied to the United States. In about 1886, when my father was six years old, his family had emigrated to America. As I remember the story, they settled in Wisconsin, where some members of the family were already farming, and bought land. Several years of drought destroyed the crops and their investments. They were forced to sell out and return to Bremerhaven on the Weser, where they settled in Lehe. My father eventually became manager of the large bunker department of North German Lloyd.

When I was a boy he often told me about his time in America, of Indians and trappers, hunting parties and cold and snowy winters. During one he nearly froze to death after losing his way home from the country school. There was a German author, Karl May, who wrote novels about Indians like the Winnetou, trappers such as Old Shatterhand, and life in the wide territories of America, books I devoured as a small boy. Nearly all German youngsters with a mind for foreign countries read his books.

In old Bremen it rained throughout December while I waited and waited. I received a letter that month from the Essberger company stating that the owner would not consent to my discharge from the *Anneliese*. Admiral Kehrhahn, in charge of the naval command in Bremen, advised me to return to my vessel in Bordeaux to prevent charges of desertion. I telephoned Admiral Menche, who insisted that I stay in Bremen. Finally, in the middle of December, I received a cable ordering me to report to Naval Command No. 4 in Hamburg and from there to proceed to Wilhelmshaven and U-boat training.

PART THREE

. . . .

With the Gray Wolves in the Polar Sea, 1941–43

Thirteen

An Unexpected Beginning

. . . .

I arrived at the Moltke barracks in Wilhelmshaven on 22 December 1941. After a brief look at my letter from the second commander of U-boats, the guard at the gate let me pass. As I walked into the complex, it hit me that my civilian life was now over. I found the clerk's office without much trouble and was not greeted very warmly. In fact, I was informed that I was overdue. I was given an *Essensmarke* (mess check) and told that I would be issued a uniform and undergo further processing the following day. Since all of the barracks were crowded, I was directed to sleep in the *Schuppen* (shed). After being told to get a cardboard box to ship my civilian clothes home, I was curtly dismissed.

I was somewhat mystified by this strange reception and thought that there might have been a misunderstanding. I politely explained my situation. I assumed that I would enter the navy then and there as a lieutenant junior "S" and be accorded the amenities accompanying such status. I was quickly informed that mine was the rank of a seaman, and that perhaps later, in accordance with the letter of the second commander of U-boats, I might become a watch officer on a submarine. I was quite upset over this turn of events, but my complaints were ignored and I quickly made my way over to the shack where I was to sleep.

What I found there was miserable. I would never have believed that a German barracks, even its shed, could be so dirty. I had to lay down in my good civilian clothes on one of many entangled straw mattresses and cover myself with foul-smelling blankets. In the open lockers I saw remnants of food, bread in great quantities, moldy and dry, and sour-smelling marmalade. Angry and uncomfortable, I could find little sleep and listened for hours to the restless nibbling of large rats feasting on the residue of the food.

The next days were spent receiving uniforms, utensils, and filling out *Laufzettel* (calling slips). The room to which I was eventually assigned had only old-timers in transit. Christmas was near so we had to "clean ship" from morning till night, wiping, mopping, scrubbing urinals. In the beginning this was hard for me; during my merchant marine years we had not been required to do such tasks. Words of reprimand from a bossy corporal didn't help matters and I became depressed, taking everything personally. Once I had been an experienced and talented marine officer; now I had to play the role of "Sailor Giese," new, stupid, and inexperienced.

Christmas passed joylessly. I felt ill and listless, disinterested in everything. I grew defensive and possessed of a rage that could only be controlled with great difficulty.

During this time the British began intensive air raids over Germany, especially over Wilhelmshaven. Attached to the fire-fighter command ashore, I had to drive through the town at night to help extinguish catastrophic fires. Thus I experienced the inferno of destruction first hand.

One night I had crawled up to the loft of a high apartment house engulfed in flames, nourished by a strong wind. I didn't feel the pain of my bruised and slashed body—all I wanted was to help people who might still be in the house. However, with a gas mask on I could hardly see my hand in front of my face. I was alone. Suddenly I heard above me a noise louder than the crackling and breaking of burning wood. It was a bomb dropping. I thought that my final hour had come. I had the momentary feeling that a huge, ice-cold hand was closing around my neck and I was struck with a gripping fear.

Within seconds there came a tremendous explosion that threw me to the charred floor. The filter of the gas mask jammed and ground into my teeth. The floor was shaking and giving way while a sea of sparks showered down on me. Beams, bricks, and cement began to fall on me and then I was falling through the floor to the level below. Choking and spitting into my mask, I crawled on all fours through dark rooms and passages filled with dense smoke and flaming curtains. I finally made it to a staircase and dropped down the collapsing structure out onto the street, numbed by the explosions and spreading fires.

Three houses down from us a heavy-caliber bomb had scored a direct hit, leaving a huge crater where the homes had been. The street was ripped open and uprooted trees lay scattered about. We did what we could to help, carrying the dead out from the rubble and comforting the hysterical *Hausfrauen* (housewives) of the neighborhood. Then we moved through other streets, where fires reignited and wind carried the swirling flames to other houses. The whole town seemed to be ablaze. High above we could hear the droning of bomber motors, the continuous popping of light antiaircraft guns, and the deep barking of heavier artillery.

The train station had received two direct hits by heavy bombs. A long train filled with soldiers ready to go on leave had fallen victim. There were many dead and dying men in the wreckage, the first casualties I had seen in the war. The stench of blood and burnt flesh was overwhelming. I will never forget the screams and whimpering of the wounded and dying, the nerve-wracking sirens of ambulance cars, the piercing noise of ships' sirens coming from the direction of basins in the port area. This was war with a difference. I had heard many a bemedaled soldier mention that war was easier to bear at the front than at home. Standing there in all that chaos and devastation, that truth reached into my soul.

Good news came just before the beginning of the new year. A friend of mine in the clerk's office at the barracks gave me a message that read, "It is requested to appoint HSO (*Handelschiffsoffizier*) merchant marine officer Giese N 284/38 ES for the purpose of instant operation with the U-boat arm to C.P.O. 'S.' He will participate in a course for U-boat watch officers in order to be dispatched in that capacity on an Atlantic boat."

After the New Year holidays with my family I reported to my new command in Neustadt/Holstein, where I was attached to the fifth company with the explanation that my being there was only temporary. An understanding chief petty officer put me in the clerk's office to save me from work in the barrack's yard. However, weeks passed and nothing happened. I began to feel that somewhere there must be someone causing these delays and obstacles. Perhaps someone from the *Essberger* office.

I was granted a trip to Hamburg, where I went to the John T. Essberger offices. When I asked for an explanation of my situation, I was told that the traffic ministry had done everything possible to sabotage my career with the navy. It was just as Captain Prahm had said: The merchant marine service needed officers, and it would do everything possible to retain experienced ones. Although I made a point of objecting, in a way I was happy to be going back to a job that meant action after all of my depressing experiences with the navy.

Fate, however, held a different card for me. One sunny day in the middle of January 1942, I received orders to report to the commandant of a submarine that would soon be ready to leave for operations in the Atlantic. Not having had the benefit of watch-officer training at Neustadt/Holstein, I reported aboard as a seaman.

Arriving in Kiel, the famous German naval port, I had to pull my uniform tightly around me because of a biting cold wind. A thick layer of ice covered the bay and ships could hardly make headway unless they kept in the passages that icebreakers had opened up. The *U-405*, to which I had been assigned, had just arrived from Danzig, where she was built, after a hazardous trip through thick ice floes (see appendix A). Heavily damaged, she had to dock immediately for repairs.

Fourteen

Life aboard the *U-405*

. . . .

On 4 February 1942 I reported to the *U-405* as a sailor, without the training and expectations that every other recruit had upon reporting to a German man-of-war. I had had no pre-military training with the Hitler Youth, no extended basic training in the use of arms, and none of the special instruction offered in the standard six-month training course during which recruits were acquainted with submarines and their functions. I came aboard as an ordinary human being with some *Lebenserfahrung* (experience of life) but otherwise ignorant of the environment around me.

One most important asset I did bring with me, though, was the firm will to be a comrade through and through, and to appear and feel as young as possible with these sailors who were no more than twenty years old. I realized here again, as before, that if I wanted to be successful I had to forget what I had been and learn all I could in the shortest possible time. Most of all I had to ask questions, over and over again. The young sailors were pleased to prove their knowledge to an older comrade, and with their help I was able to learn about the boat quickly and without direction from my superiors. Soon even the petty officers approached me on their own, in friendship and confidence.

During this time, while the boat was in dock, the young men crawled with me through all her corners. One day when the captain, Commander Hopman, saw me looking through a slot with a sweaty, dirty face, he commented laughingly, "Well, Giese, seems to be a bit different than manipulating every day with sea charts and pencils! Do you enjoy this trade?" Upon which I answered enthusiastically, "Yes sir, very much!" And this was true, because the boys drilled me relentlessly to master the peculiar routine of a submarine crew, the frank but disciplined attitude towards superiors, and the enormous speed with which all actions had to be taken and executed. Speed was the lifeline for the crew of a U-boat—the petty officers verbally pumped that into me all hours of the day and night.

On board they concentrated on a "sport" called *Kreisen* (circling). I and another greenhorn who had signed on at Danzig were quickly initiated into this critical procedure. Two orders made a submarine disappear from the surface within seconds, "Alarm" and "Duck." One day First Watch Officer Lieutenant Horst Willner called the two of us onto the conning tower while several petty officers posted themselves at various positions in the boat and on deck. We stood there harmless and ignorant, with hammering hearts, sensing something bad. The officer, smiling, had a stopwatch in his hand and was looking somewhere up in the sky. Suddenly he yelled in a high-pitched voice. "Alarrrrm!" and when we looked at him in deep surprise, wondering if he had seen something terrible coming down or fallen sick, he yelled at us, "Down there through the round hatch, you idiots, get moving!" Well, we thought, an order is an order but he could have told us in a calm voice. So down we went, one after the other, taking care not to kick each other's head, clinging to the handrail on the sides of the stepladder as we made our way to the central room. We arrived, panting in our heavy coats. We thought that we had done quite well. Full of pride, we nodded to the waiting petty officer and wondered why he and the others around laughed so much. Lieutenant Willner appeared through the hatch several yards above us. "Excellent, gentlemen. Now come up here again and we'll do it once more, only a bit faster this time, please!"

We clambered up to the conning tower, where we politely saluted and reported back to the lieutenant. He looked us over from top to bottom, smiling sarcastically. Alright, I thought to myself, this time we'll please you and do it a bit faster, but don't get so excited yelling this bloody alarm, it only makes us nervous. Say it calmly and you'll see how fast we sink down through this narrow hatch of yours.

"Gentlemen," said Lieutenant Willner, "you seem to think that this is all a great joke [I did not at all]. But imagine there are five to six men on the conning tower who would like to get into the boat when an enemy plane or destroyer suddenly appears from nowhere. And, naturally, this enemy politely waits, pulling the trigger of his machine guns or the release of his bombs until all of us have gradually climbed down, closed the hatch cover, and brought the boat into the cellar. No, gentlemen!" He raised his voice threateningly. "The enemy will start shooting at us from afar because he knows that we will be down within seconds!"

It was hard to believe that someone could get down two narrow hatches into the central room faster than we had and be followed by several more men without hurting one another. I looked down the hatch again.

We were told to watch the performance of a particular petty officer. When the alarm bell rang out a second later, there was a hiss where the officer had been, followed instantly by a thud as he landed on the deck below, then a short shuffling of feet. Seconds later someone tapped my shoulder, and thinking it was the other greenhorn, I said, "Yes, that petty officer sure must have hurt himself. Serves him right for showing off!" Again, the tap on my shoulder. "You'd better turn around Giese. I hope that you saw how I did it." I hadn't, nor could I figure out how he had made it back up to the conning tower so fast.

The alarm sounded again. "You first, Giese!" Lieutenant Willner barked. Some strong hands grabbed my back and lifted me off the deck, then down I went, banging against the sills of the hatches, barely touching the handrails with my hands, just sliding along them with my heavy booted feet. I crashed onto the deck of the central room. Before the other greenhorn fell on me, I was grabbed again by strong fists and thrown aside. I stumbled into the petty officer room, squeezing through the round, narrow bulkhead hatch, and slid across the deck between a table and some bunks. Panting and heaving, I grabbed the rail of the small ladder leading to the hatch on the afterdeck and pulled myself aloft. With a couple of racing steps I made it across the open deck to the platform where the antiaircraft guns stood. I climbed another few steps and reached the conning tower, followed by my exhausted comrade. "Fine, gentlemen, but much too slow," the officer said, reading his stopwatch.

We went through the drill again and again, until my big, strong comrade sat down on the rail in the *Wintergarten* (antiaircraft-gun platform), hands hanging slack at his side, lungs pumping like an old bellows, and cried. With this, the game ended. It was the first and last time I had to "circle" in peace. I was quite thankful to Lieutenant Willner later.

All this served to bond an old merchant marine salt with the young, able, and vigorous sailors on board. Like all young men who face the hardships and hazards of going to war in U-boats, they lived life to the fullest while ashore. When they strolled into canteens and bars, girls had to be conquered and liquor "destroyed" by drinking. Indeed, one had the impression that U-boat crewmen enjoyed privileges far beyond those accorded members of other German military services. Perhaps this is understandable, for enormous discipline and courage was expected of these young men who had to fight a fierce enemy in hazardous seas far from their homeland. No wonder their few hours or days ashore were crammed full with the delights denied them at sea. Joining the boys during their escapades, I almost felt that I had found the fountain of youth.

Towards the end of February 1942 we made trial runs. These hectic days were typical of the routine of boats preparing to go to sea on patrols. Torpedoes were stowed with an ingenious device into the bow and stern compartments and into deck tubes or cylinders. Stores and provisions for at least eight weeks came on board. The food on the U-boats was usually ample, nutritious, and tasty, the meals prepared by specially trained cooks. No wonder I gained seventeen pounds on my first cruise.

During our trial runs the tension on board grew. Where would we operate? In the Atlantic, or the ice-covered seas to the north? Finally the orders came. We were to operate in the North Sea, then proceed to Drontheim, Norway, to await further orders.

Fifteen

First Patrol: Forging the Team

. . . .

The sun was bright white when our boat made ready to leave the pier, where the commanding officer of the flotilla, his staff, and some relatives of our crew had assembled. The lines dropped into the water and the E-motors (electrical motors) pulled the boat away. When the diesels started humming their lively song we passed the liner *St. Louis*, which served during the war as a houseboat or hotel for U-boat crews.[24] Many had lined the railings. They called out "Hip-hip-hurrah!" three times while the bands played the U-boat anthem and other marches. We waved to our well-wishers and afterwards turned to the routine of the submarine. It was 3 March 1942. In the Holtenau locks we entered the famous Kiel canal, and when we left it at Brunsbüttelkoog we saw the clean white houses on the dykes bidding their farewells to us.

A submarine chaser serving as protection against enemy planes conducted us to Helgoland, the strongly fortified German island in the North Sea that housed huge U-boat bunkers. Here in the deeper waters we performed our diving and trimming trials, compensated our auxiliary magnetic compass and radio direction-finder, then proceeded alone northward. The weather turned rainy and foggy, typical North Sea conditions.

Our orders were to guard an operational grid in the North Sea, off the Norwegian coast, and to form flanking protection for heavy German naval units such as the battleship *Tirpitz* coming down from the north. With the exception of many fishing boats and drifting mines, we only saw several English PBY Catalina seaplanes, which would shadow us continuously later on. Although this operation lasted but three weeks, it gave me a taste of what life aboard a submarine was going to be like, squeezed into a small tube 73 yards long and 6.8 yards wide.

The *U-405* on her way from Kiel to Trondheim. The bow waves of the minesweeper escorting us are visible to port and starboard.

On board I found it best to bear all privations with good humor and forget the usual day-to-day comforts of life, like washing hands and face, taking a hot shower, brushing teeth, and shaving. During operations in the Atlantic or Arctic one simply could not escape becoming crusted with dirt. At first, I thought a man could get scabies or some other skin disease if he didn't wash down at least once a day. To my surprise, I soon learned that we could make do by just rinsing off our hands and faces a couple of times a week with salt water. Afterwards, we splashed "Cologne 4711" onto our faces and distributed any remaining dirt with ointment, vigorously rubbing it into the skin. Our hair and beards soon got filthy and clotted from the salt water breaking over the ship, and even the best comb broke when we tried to disentangle the hairy mess. So it was left as it was and sprinkled with birch water to neutralize the odor, which seemed to differ with each man.

However, it was absolutely necessary to take at least some care of our teeth, because there was no dentist on board. We used a special toothpowder to ward off scurvy. In spite of our efforts we often de-

During our first patrol, the boat running close to the Norwegian coast without escort, the bridge watch has to keep a sharp lookout. It is sunny but frigid and the men wear their thickest clothes.

The quick-firing 8.8-centimeter gun at the foredeck, as photographed on our arrival at Trondheim.

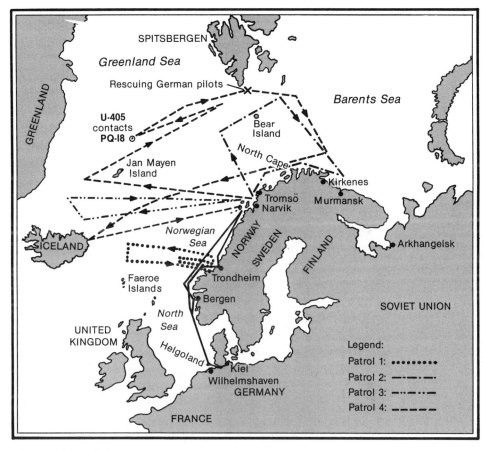

SPITSBERGEN

Greenland Sea

Rescuing German pilots

GREENLAND

Barents Sea

U-405
contacts
PQ-I8 ⊚

Bear
Island

Jan Mayen
Island

North Cape

Kirkenes

Tromsö
Narvik

Murmansk

*Norwegian
Sea*

ICELAND

NORWAY

SWEDEN

FINLAND

Arkhangelsk

Faeroe
Islands

Trondheim

Bergen

*North
Sea*

UNITED
KINGDOM

SOVIET UNION

Helgoland

Kiel

Wilhelmshaven
GERMANY

Legend:

Patrol 1: • • • • • • • •
Patrol 2: — • — • — •
Patrol 3: — • • — • • —
Patrol 4: — — — — —

FRANCE

Track of the *U-405*

veloped sore gums and loose teeth, which caused considerable pain.
And although all of the crew underwent careful physicals before and
after each trip, we had many sick men during this first cruise. So
many, in fact, that the commandant had to treat them during regular
sick call hours. One of the boys had angina, which could hardly be
cured on board with the continuous cold and humidity. We eventually handed him over to a patrol boat near the coast.

One of the worst problems for crewmen of U-boats was trying to
maintain regularity. Castor oil and pills were frequently used with
mixed results. Constipation was caused by the lack of space available
for movement and the considerable amount of time spent sitting or
resting in bunks. With only one or two water closets on board (one on

At Trondheim after our first patrol, Admiral Karls visits the flotilla. Commander Hopman, at the foot of the gangway, salutes the admiral and his staff.

The *U-405* in Trondheim. Commander Hopman is reporting the crew ready for inspection to Admiral Karls. *From left to right:* Engineer Lieutenant Senior Dewald, First Watch Officer Lieutenant Willner, Second Watch Officer Lieutenant Niesta, and our three chief warrant officers.

smaller boats, two on larger boats, of which one was used for storing provisions), the long lines and the difficulty of working the lever device to flush the bowl made the whole process of relieving oneself a major undertaking. But like everything else, we mastered it and lived with the situation.

It was a pity that the media seldom told about the life of an enlisted U-boat crew, who lived in a single, messy, greasy room in the fore part of their boat. Most of what the public saw was officer and petty officer quarters. The *Bugraum* (bow room) was where sailors passed their spare time, where they slept and ate, and where torpedo personnel, the "mixers," carried out their greasy work checking and overhauling their weapons.

One of our favorite pastimes during evening hours was listening to reports of auto races on the Nuerburg Ring or the Avus. The calls were unique, since the sailors used naval expressions instead of racetrack lingo: ". . . Carraciola drives into the starboard bend and races

17 miles an hour along, when suddenly his port diesel breaks down and he has to switch in the E-motors, so that in the meantime he can grind his exhaust gas traps, then he chases on with strong smoke development and giving ample oxyhydrogen sounds . . ."

Operatic songs were popular with the crew. Greenhorns had to deliver three, preferably women's roles, over the boat's loudspeaker system. The worse they sang, the more jubilant the crew became. The loudspeaker crowed in high soprano tones all day long. In between, if no radio stations could be had, we played records, preferably English jazz.

Not all was spare time and watches. Potatoes had to be peeled, the boat had to be kept as clean as possible under the circumstances, and we performed exercises, maneuvers, and drills on a continuous basis, operations that the men enjoyed.

And naturally we had to sleep, which was near impossible when the boat rocked in heavy seas while running surfaced. Often men were thrown from their bunks onto the floorboards or into the bunks of neighbors. Sometimes an entire bunk broke loose and went sliding back and forth across the deck, its occupant clinging to his mattress. Vegetables, bread, and tin cans that were stacked up in the bow room would frequently come tumbling down on men trying to find rest in the lower bunks. A few unlucky ones were drenched in scalding coffee. It was no small wonder that the crewmembers were a bit frazzled when they woke up after such fretful experiences.

It was during this rough, accelerated training period that I came to know the life of a U-boatman and the hardships one had to endure. We had forged into a unique band during this maiden voyage, and I must admit that during the ten months I served aboard the boat there was never serious trouble or a fight. As bow-room senior, it was to a great extent within my power to influence the men. Although I had only indirect disciplinary power, they obeyed unconditionally, which was a matter of pride with them. Comradeship was of the utmost importance to the entire crew. Adherence to iron law, as well as trust and confidence in our ability to meet any challenge, was the rule. With my personal dedication to these simple principles, it was easy for me to pass my sailor's time in a manner at times enjoyable.

Also, I was glad to be among men who like myself cared little about politics. U-boatmen were seamen first and foremost, concerned with fighting the elements and an unrelenting enemy. I remember once hearing a humorous story that perhaps sums up our feelings regarding the political situation. One of the U-boat aces was approaching a pier in a French base port after a successful cruise. The pier was crowded with people of all sorts. There was a band, a reception committee, party members, and so forth. The boat was running with E-motors towards the pier. When he was within calling distance, the commandant asked through his megaphone, "Are the Nazis still in power?" The good folks answered, "Yes, Yes!" At this time the boat was close to the pier, and the commandant ordered in a voice loud enough for all to hear, "Full astern, both engines!" Of course, the order was given to avoid hitting the pier, but we still had a lot of fun telling the story in U-boat circles.

Returning to Trondheim on 22 March, we found the town and surrounding mountains deep in snow. We traded some cigarettes for the use of skis owned by the German mountain police and made our way by electric car up to the large ski hotel at the foot of the Kralloen, where the slopes were crowded with Norwegians and Germans. We decided to move onward, along well-worn snow tracks through dense forests, deep ravines, wide plains, and deep slopes into an El Dorado of white snow. We stopped at various ski huts where Norwegian skiers, German mountain troops, and a few navy types like ourselves joined in the local fun. Here we were all sportsmen who had been brought together by a simple love of the outdoors and the pleasures of a skiing holiday. We were in a wonderland that allowed us to escape the distant realities of war.

Sixteen

Second Patrol: Combat!

On 25 April 1942 we received orders for our second patrol. It was on a Saturday and I was sitting that evening with a bunch of our sailors in the Trondheim Deutsches Haus enjoying a film. The projector was suddenly turned off, the lights went on, and an excited voice called, "All comrades of *Feldpost-Nummer* [field post no.] M 35435 assemble instantly at their base point!"

At 2400 we brought stores and provisions on board, and before the first rays of the morning sun appeared over the horizon, the *U-405* stood ready at the entrance to the Trondheim fjord with her bow pointed northward. After a short call at Narvik, we proceeded to our new position in the Polar Sea. The spring storms had whipped up the water, which boiled and bubbled around us. Our bow dipped deep into the white foam of the sea only to be thrown skyward, then dropped back hard and heavy. Momentarily she seemed to stay still, trembling with exertion, shaking her nose indignantly, before rushing against the next mounting wave in a sudden, explosive jump.

Fighting an angry sea required continuous maneuvering and constant vigilance by the bridge watch. The men would be drenched, spitting salt water and cursing the unyielding elements. We had to be particularly alert to spot drifting mines in the heavy seas, mines that often passed only a few yards distant, causing our stomachs to tighten and churn. Contact with them in these icy and desolate waters would have meant certain death for all. Gradually, however, the seas calmed, and when we reached the ice barrier a brilliant polar sun reflected the splendid ice floes that began to surround us. The colors were of the purest blue and lilac to the palest pink. Some icebergs had the shape of small castles, others of animals or sailing ships. One late afternoon while we were deeply absorbed in the beauty of this panorama, the call "Alarm!" rang through the boat, followed by the shrill sound of the bells, "Destroyer ahead!"

Through the conning tower hatch we tumbled as the boat plunged to 300 feet. The chief petty officer on watch had seen the enemy some miles ahead of us. "To battle stations, flood the torpedo tubes, course 15 degrees, bring her to periscope depth," ordered Captain Hopman. Carefully, he and his officers watched the destroyer.

The enemy stopped. No propeller noises could be heard. But a wisp of smoke was rising from her stack and she trailed a low bow wave.

Captain Hopman ordered the chief petty officer to study the enemy through the *Spargel* ("asparagus periscope"). After a while the officer, shaking his head in disbelief, burst into laughter. "Sir, I beg your pardon, but I think we're mistaken. This is no destroyer, it's a lousy iceberg in the shape of a ship!" Everyone looked through the scopes again and again. Up we went and there we saw our destroyer peacefully drifting along. What we had thought was smoke was a few dainty clouds, and the bow wave we had noted was a long swell running higher on the flat and submerged side of the iceberg. Later this incident would be memorialized by wags in an illustrated pamphlet.

The weather had changed, the barometer dropped deep into the cellar, and a heavy swell started to run up when we were ordered to set course northeast into the Barents Sea. The message indicated that an enemy convoy, QP-11, in company with the British cruiser *Edinburgh* and eleven other escorts, was heading west from Murmansk. Other boats, under the commands of Dietrich v. d. Esch, Karl Brandenburg, Heino Bohmann, Heinrich Timm, Hans-Joachim Horrer, and Günter La Baume, were already engaging the convoy.[25]

With her motors putting out maximum power, the *U-405* raced towards the action. As she drew near we could hear the loud detonations of depth charges. Before we sighted the convoy we met some other U-boats of the wolf pack, but we didn't linger long together since there were Russian submarines reported in the area.

Onward and onward we pushed, while heavy breakers whipped over the men on watch aloft. The water was ice cold and the watchstanders had to hold their breath as the blue-green seas crashed over them. Presently we saw the first smoke clouds rising faintly on the horizon. The hunting fever grew, but before we reached the convoy and had come within torpedo firing range, one of the lookouts on the rear quarter shouted that he saw a destroyer sweeping towards us at high speed.

She must have detected us with her hydrophone long before we had seen her. Down we went, to the hissing sound of destroyer propellers growing louder and louder until it seemed she would cut right through our hull. And then it was quiet. The destroyer had stopped, trying to detect us with her hydrophone gear. We stopped our electrical motors and silenced our trimming pumps.

Then the depth charges came, the first ones we would experience on this boat. Luckily they were poorly aimed, though the noise they generated was fearsome. I had been told by others, warriors of the old front line, that depth charges often affected the morale of the crew more than they damaged the boat. Now I saw the truth of that observation.

Soon our radioman, "Sparks," who operated the hydrophones, reported that the destroyer was departing at high speed. Up we went, cautiously, to contact the convoy, by now zigzagging through the water. Suddenly enemy planes were over us and we were forced down again, and then again later. Much time was lost with these tedious and exhausting maneuvers. We saw the convoy one more time, far off on the horizon, before it disappeared into a dense cloud bank.

In an attempt to intercept the route of our bounty, we sailed through dense fog straight into Kola Bay, where we took up a waiting position near the Murmansk coastline. We waited and waited, cruising up and down, listening for sounds in the moving fog. Hearing nothing, we decided that the rest of the convoy must have avoided contact by proceeding to Arhangelsk. At last, we turned towards Narvik to take on fresh supplies and receive new orders, knowing that at any time Russian planes and submarines could bear down on us.

Meanwhile our attention was turned to a more immediate problem. The seas turned thunderous as we passed Kirkenes, the famous North Cape and Hammerfest and Tromsö. As long as the seas came from ahead, they crashed against the plating of the conning tower and we could duck until the boat had wallowed through. But gradually they came from abeam and then later from the rear, changing course frequently. For days we wore heavy canvas belts lashed by strong steel straps to the boat. At first, we laughed at this precaution as unnecessary and inconvenient; it hampered our jumps through the hatches during alarms. But I soon realized the necessity. More than once we had to pull lookouts from the top of bulkheads, where they lay, breathless and in pain. Comrades of other boats had not been so lucky; some whose straps broke were found missing after the water subsided.

Since my task was to guard one of the boat's rear quarters, I had a good chance to watch the spectacular scenes, which reminded me of those days off Cape Horn. Only this time there was a difference; now I was almost part of the sea, immersed in water so much of the time. The tremendous rollers were like the fangs of hungry wolves snapping at our small boat. As long as the fangs closed in the wake or on the afterdeck of the boat, their greedy tongues could only lick us up to the waist. But when those fangs closed right on top of us there was a thunderous crashing and bursting that snatched our breath away. A tremendous weight forced us onto our knees and tore at all our limbs. Above us a bright-green watery vault foamed and hummed before gradually subsiding. It became brighter and brighter while we fought against the draining water, spitting, choking, and cursing.

A glance at other comrades and short smiles from salty red faces gave us comfort that all was okay again. Well, sometimes. Once I found the sailor next to me kneeling on the grating as if he were looking for something. "Where are my teeth?" he cried out. "My teeth are gone, look!" He raised his head and I saw blood pouring out of his mouth. There was nothing left but a few scattered, broken teeth. In terrible pain, he was released from his watch.

The strain was just as hard on our aching, wailing boat. The hatch was closed at all times to prevent water from entering the boat. There had been incidents where other boats had been pressed underwater by heavy seas from the rear. And incredible as it sounds, there had been some cases where boats had run for hours after the entire watch was washed overboard. Thus we reported in the central room about every half hour to signal that all was okay aloft.

We chose the north passage into the long Narvik Fjord and felt relieved when the sea became calm. Soon we were in the midst of a magnificent landscape that reminded me of scenes in the "Flying Dutchman": the calm and deep waters of the fjords surrounded by high pyramids of rock, white waterfalls cascading down in transparent veils, clean, snug villages, and houses scattered amidst narrow patches of green. Serenity at last.

Our slender boat shot along the old battle sites where our destroyers had engaged superior British forces. Here and there we could still see the wrecks from those days of quiet heroism. Narvik lay ahead of us, with its large ore pier not yet reconstructed. Around us many mastheads peeped out of the water, vessels waiting to be raised from the icy waters.[26]

It was 9 May 1942. Ahead was the *Tanga* with Admiral August Thiele and his staff and the yacht *Stella Polaris* waiting to welcome us. I proudly recalled the time Admiral Thiele had made an instruction and inspection trip with our sailing ship *Schulschiff Deutschland* to South America while I was in my last term as a cadet. He had requested that I box with him for exercise and training every evening. Although many times my senior, he was in excellent physical condition and had me on the floor many times after delivering a couple of hard, fast blows.

The *Stella Polaris*, once the yacht of the Norwegian king, was the dream of all U-boat men after a rough tour at sea. Awaiting the crews were delicious showers, untimed baths in white tubs, beds with thick, soft mattresses and snow-white linen, rest, sleep, and celebrations. She was efficiently managed by a staff of stewards and other seamen

Returning from our second patrol to Narvik, Norway, we pass the wrecks of German destroyers, which put up a brave but futile fight against heavy British forces.

Ahead of us lies Narvik, our northern base. The large ore piers destroyed by British artillery have not yet been repaired.

from North German Lloyd. Among the crew I found to my great surprise a former member of the *Columbus* who had returned from the United States on a diplomat's pass and now acted as the ship's chief purser.

Unfortunately, our stay was short. In three days we sailed down to the town of Bergen to settle in a clean, comfortable new base compound.

Seventeen

Third Patrol: A Formidable Enemy

· · · · · · · · · · · · · · · · · · · ·

Within a week the *U-405* was on her way once again, this time to Kiel for repairs. We cruised with our escort vessels through the connecting fjords of Skagerrak and Kattegat and arrived on a beautiful day in May 1942. We all lined up on deck, pale white and bearded, for the jubilant reception. Decorations were awarded and we were given time off to join our families.

Soon I was in Bremen with my loved ones. It is difficult to put into words the emotions I felt as I rang the bell on my front door, that old familiar sound, saw tears of happiness in my parents' eyes, then grasped them in a warm and lingering embrace. Our terrier Bobby jumped high in the air, his stumpy tail wagging with joy. After we had settled down we sat in front of the fireplace, opened a bottle of wine, and feasted on my mother's delicious cake. We talked for hours. The days passed much too fast, filled with visits with friends, concerts, theaters, movies, parties, and bathing in the Weser River.

All was not to remain peaceful. One week, British aircraft attacked Bremen with bombs of all calibers, air mines, and phosphorous projectiles. Many of our friends' houses were hit. We all helped in whatever way we could. In the streets we found leaflets that included propaganda on our U-boat arm. It was strictly forbidden to pick up leaflets and keep them; I did so anyway and kept them hidden in my log. One claimed that a U-boatman would only last sixty days before "biting into the wet grass." This was naturally meant to scare our families. Other pamphlets said that this attack was only journeyman's work, and that Bremen would "enjoy" the masterpiece of a bomb attack during the next few days. Since we had learned that the British generally meant what they said, we waited out those next few days with great concern.

During a visit to my sister in Schweinfurt while the *U-405* is tied up at Kiel, I pose with my nephew, Peter. The rank on my shirt is that of seaman.

On 23 July we stood out to sea again towards Bergen and Narvik, where nature had already put on its autumn dress. The fjords shone in brilliant colors vividly reflected in the calm waters. At night dense veils of fog arose, clinging to the steep rocks and shredding as they lifted towards a pitch-black sky. The first days of August found us plowing through the waters of the Norwegian Sea on our way to a patrol between Iceland and Jan Mayen Island, at the border of the Greenland Sea. We were directed to find a large enemy convoy that had reportedly been assembled.

Thick fog, "pea soup," made our work extremely difficult. The eyes of lookouts burned as they strained to penetrate the white mass, which only seemed to get thicker each day. Often we heard the humming of planes nearby. It wasn't clear whether they were friendly Bv-138 patrol craft or enemy Catalina bombers. In any case, we felt quite safe under the prevailing conditions and did not bother to dive each time. The monotony was wearing on our nerves, the continuous humming of our motors at slow speed sickening as we wandered along in the wide, smooth swells. We went as far north as the ice bor-

Back in Bergen, Norway, the crew enjoys lunch on deck. It is a happy-go-lucky gang, despite the tight living conditions on board. The 8.8-centimeter deck gun can be seen on the left.

A Bv-138 three-engine reconnaissance plane checks on us. We call these planes *Entartete Kunst* ("degenerated art") because of their strange outlines.

der, since most often convoys were routed through this area. But we found nothing. Where was the convoy?

The activity in operational areas far to the north could not be compared with the activity and tremendous battles of the Atlantic, although the patrols were no less strenuous, dangerous, or perhaps important. But it seemed to us that we were lost here, disregarded by the big and lonely "wolf" in Berlin, Admiral Dönitz. We were his stepchildren, a few boats with bases in the northern reaches of Norway.

Our history was young; it had not actually begun until Germany went to war with Russia. Then the northern flank became a new operational area for the German navy, and U-boats were stationed from July 1941 on in Kirkenes to support patrol boats and minesweepers. These lonely wolves patrolled endlessly, guarding the coast of the Kola peninsula and the entrance to the White Sea, and battled doggedly with Russian destroyers and corvettes protecting their freighters. Gradually the enemy built up a convoy system in a large

At Narvik the crew of the *U-405* airs out the bunk blankets alongside the tender *Tanga*.

and sweeping arc from England by way of Iceland to the Russian ports Arhangelsk and Murmansk. In December 1941, three boats that formed the group Ulan attacked convoys PQ-7 and PQ-8. An eleven-ship convoy, PQ-7, lost one vessel, while PQ-8 suffered one ship damaged off the Kola inlet. All eight PQ-8 merchant ships arrived safely at their destination.

Because of repeated carrier raids, the shelling of the north Norwegian coast, and a British commando operation on the Lofote islands, Hitler guessed that the British might try to land in Norway. He directed Dönitz to base more than twenty U-boats in Norwegian ports. There were long in-port waiting periods for the U-boat crews, and needless to say they were more than happy when they got orders from Dönitz to leave their ports and wage attacks on the Murmansk convoys. The signal "Red" was on! But first we had to find the enemy.

This was done by U-boat "patrol lines" between Iceland and Jan Mayen Island, supported by Focke-Wulf-200 Condor long-range reconnaissance planes and Bv-138 flying boats. The first boat that sighted a convoy acted as *Fühlungshalter* (contact boat), hanging on to the prey and reporting the number, course, and speed of its ships to

The *U-405* rides alongside another type VIIC boat with their distinct, cigar-shaped hulls.

the headquarters of the BdU (*Befehlshaber der Unterseeboote*), or commander U-boats, Admiral Dönitz and his staff, located in Kernevel near Lorient and later on in Paris at Boulevard General Maunoury.

It was no easy job for contact boats to watch each movement of a convoy and relay it precisely by code to the BdU. Though they were often in position to launch successful attacks, they were ordered to wait until headquarters had summoned numerous other boats to the convoy. Then the order would come: "Ring clear, fight, and attack and attack and attack!" But more often than not, immediate contact was lost, not only because of rough weather and blinding fog but also often because a boat was forced underwater by carrier or land-based planes, destroyers, corvettes, and frigates. Destroyers were often called sweepers or chasers, according to their positions in the convoy. They moved back and forth with other escort vessels like dogs around a herd, trying to get the U-boats to dive and subject themselves to depth-charge attack.

Many times the efficient German intelligence service deciphered British reports and operational orders to convoys, which were sent out from the British convoy headquarters in Liverpool after a German U-boat patrol line had been discovered. This gave the BdU a further means of bringing boats into positions before an incoming convoy. If an enemy course deviated, the BdU had to calculate enemy movements like a chess player and give orders to individual boats, such as "Convoy PQ-17, grid square XY 2355, course 45, 9 knots." It would then be up to the individual U-boat commander to proceed to the grid quickly and smartly so as to engage the enemy.

The British headquarters staff was continually on guard and in the highest state of alert. Using intelligence from a variety of sources, it would react to developing situations by diverting convoy routes, changing courses, and ordering evasive maneuvers to ward off enemy attacks. Individual convoy commanders, "washed with many waters," were old salts and smart as foxes. During pre-departure conferences, they would instruct all ship captains of their convoy about future courses, necessary actions in all situations, safety measures, escort service, communications, and so on.

As advantageous as it was for the BdU to get data about a convoy to U-boats, it was extremely dangerous for a boat to touch its radio key and transmit even the shortest code, which could be detected by the enemy with their "huff-duff," or high-frequency direction-finder (HF-DF). Using this equipment, the enemy could locate the position of a U-boat without detection and order air and surface units to that point for attack. Once submerged, a boat was not as safe as it had been, because now it could be followed and located by ASDIC gear, a submarine detection and locating apparatus that emitted sound waves under water; if the waves struck an object, they would give off an echo. Echoes could arise from fish schools, wrecks, and water pools, and the man at the gear had to be experienced in distinguishing between various echoes.

In fact, simple disturbances in the water gave off an echo. This led to the development on the German side of a special device containing a chemical solution that, once fired through torpedo tubes, could create a bubble field of great density, giving off echoes similar to that of a submarine. A string of bubble fields would form a curtain behind which a U-boat could escape. However, since the device, secretly named Bolde, did not move in the water, an experienced ASDIC operator would eventually detect the ruse. Once the ASDIC operator had picked up the boat again—it sounded like a ticking noise running over the hull or as if sand was being thrown against the boat—the hunt was on. Two or three subchasers would often be involved. One or two would keep the submarine located with their ASDIC gear, while the third would run over the U-boat's presumed position and drop carpets of depth charges. Other ships would follow in turn, until a kill was confirmed or the hunters became convinced that their enemy had escaped. Only very experienced U-boat commanders were able to escape such deadly hunter-killer operations.

Escort groups led by such skilled British warriors as Captain Frederic John Walker eventually turned the tide of the war in the Atlantic. "Johnnie" Walker made it his ambition to lead the most potent of all submarine hunting forces with sloops like the *Wild Goose, Wren, Stork, Blankney, Stanley, Gardenia,* and *Starling.* His battle banner read, "With discipline, valor, fantasy, fearlessness, and humility to fight the enemy to life or death." He was a master of tactics and would use all means possible to destroy a submerged U-boat. If he could not kill his prey on the spot, he would wait until it surfaced for lack or oxygen or damage; then he would destroy the submarine by gunning or ramming it. As a result of his heroic leadership, his groups sunk no less than twenty-one U-boats during the war.

An incident reported by German U-boats crossing the Bay of Biscay proved to be fateful for our boats. They had suddenly started being attacked during low visibility, heavy cloud cover, and at night by undetected planes with bombs and machine guns. Our secret service soon found out that the British Coastal Command had rigged their planes with air-to-surface radar gear, which could detect surfaced U-boats at a great distance. Eventually all U-boats were equipped with a radar detection system that we called Metox at the time. This equipment at least gave us some warning of detection by the enemy.

Meanwhile, we continued to patrol our area without success. No ships were sighted or heard. Endless fog enveloped us. Although we had been on the line for only two weeks, it seemed like months.

Then, in our third week, "Alarm!" sounded. The watch of the chief officer reported seeing smoke clouds in a sector free of fog. The boat submerged and we listened carefully. Indeed, it seemed as if there were ships passing in a wide stretch ahead of us. Up we went to make contact. But much as we searched the horizon, we saw nothing. It was very discouraging. Our radio traffic indicated that several U-boats had been alerted, and new positions were formed. Our suppositions about the size and whereabouts of the convoy were many. We strained our eyes and ears to penetrate the fog. It remained calm, and an eerie feeling filled the air. Tension aboard the other U-boats gradually grew, and there appeared to be some annoyance with us since it was our contact report that initiated the hunt. The sea still appeared empty. There is nothing worse for a U-boatman than to think that a fat prey is somewhere out there escaping. After four weeks of fruitless searching we were called back to Narvik, where we returned to quarters on the *Stella Polaris*.

It was now mid-August 1942. The weather had turned perceptibly cool. The first snow covered the highest peaks of the mountains like a fragile dress, while the age-old glaciers remained aloof in their worn, steel-blue and gray gown. Before bathing and trimming our shaggy beards, we celebrated. We recited in jolly verse the events of the last trip, teasing each other, especially the commandant and his officers, toasting to better luck during future trips, drinking and smoking to our hearts' content and singing new and old U-boat songs. In a joyous mood we sailors went onto the promenade deck, grabbed all the white caps of the commandants of the various boats, and flung them into the ice-cold water. Of course, we were caught and ordered to jump overboard and bring the caps back and hang them on their hooks again. Since the promenade deck of the *Stella Polaris* was too high above the water to jump in, we crawled onto the

The track of the *U-405*, which will soon disappear in the restless sea. On our third patrol we go on endless outpost and patrol lines, seeking convoys and single runners. The northern border of firm pack ice is never far away.

sterns of the boats tied up to the pontoon, took off our U-boat jackets and pants and shoes, and dived into the water from there. We retrieved the floating caps and returned them to the promenade deck, where they were hung once again, not quite white and dripping. None were missing. The alcohol in our bellies had made us immune to the cold. Luckily no one drowned.

Eighteen

Fourth Patrol: Attack on PQ-18

· · · · · · · · · · · · · · · · · · · ·

On 27 August 1942, our U-boats prepared for new operations. Fuel, torpedoes, ammunition for the guns, stores for the deck and engineering departments, and provisions and fresh water had to be taken on. Medical supplies were replenished. Our radioman revised his instruction books with the latest orders, and the navigator on board adjusted his newest nautical sailing books and maps for the patrol. The batteries were recharged, the guns prepared for submerged running with a thorough grease-down. Once at sea, a test dive would be performed to get the boat in trim. As boats completed their preparations they ran out to sea, one by one. The weather was splendid: A white sun shone brightly on us while a fresh wind blew from the north.

For two weeks we cruised up and down between Iceland, Jan Mayen, Bear Island, and Spitsbergen in checkered weather. Alas, the Polar Sea lacked the Atlantic's abundance of game. Goebbels had reason to start his propaganda machine rolling regarding our operations in the northern seas. Two months before, PQ-17 had been detected by our planes and U-boats shortly after passing Iceland. The German High Command ordered all units to attack with all weapons. When the British Admiralty found that even our heavy naval forces were making ready to enter the battle, it gave orders to disperse the convoy, thus making individual ships easy prey for our planes and submarines. Out of thirty-six merchantmen and three rescue ships in the convoy, twenty-three merchant ships and one rescue vessel were sent to the bottom.[27] The successful attack on PQ-17 lifted our spirits and made us more determined in our search for the enemy.

Then we received some heartening news: Another large convoy was on its way to Murmansk or Arhangelsk. Consisting of about forty ships, PQ-18 was heavily guarded with the escort carrier

At Harstad to take provisions on board, the boat camouflaged with nets. The picture on the conning tower of a polar bear on an ice flow is the boat's insignia, drawn by me.

Avenger and numerous other escort vessels, including destroyers, corvettes, frigates, and sloops.[28]

We were ready for a fight. It would probably surpass all other battles here in the lonely and icy north. Again, we had first to find the convoy. With our motors at full power we sped down towards Iceland. The weather was marvelous, sunshine, medium-strong winds, and a corresponding light sea. One morning we caught a small tit-mouse resting on one of our jumping wires and took her with us into the boat. When we were suddenly forced to dive, she passed with excellence. It was a good omen for us.

According to our log, we should have made contact with PQ-18 on 13 September. Feverishly we scanned the sky and horizon for smoke clouds until finally, in the far distance, we detected many fine and fragile veils over a wide range. We seemed to be the first boat to detect the convoy. To get the exact data for course and speed, we had to get much nearer while remaining undetected. Surprise was our best

Third Watch Officer Lieutenant Heins scans the horizon for smoke clouds from convoy PQ-18. He is also trying to find the float of a downed German plane.

tactic if we were to realize the greatest success with the least number of losses.

More and more clearly the smoke clouds stood in the blue sky. Soon we could detect the ships' mastheads pointing up from the clear horizon like small needles. We had long since radioed a message to AdN (*Admiral Nordmeer*, or Admiral Polar Sea) about sighting the convoy. Now, after zigzagging a couple of times with the enemy ships and plotting our findings on grid maps, we could give him further information about course and speed. Soon other gray wolves closed in, having been directed ahead of the convoy by the BdU.

For the present, we had orders to act as contact boat. Soon, however, we were forced by enemy planes and a destroyer to "go into the protecting cellar" for about five hours. When we finally surfaced, the convoy had moved some distance away and we had to search for it again. This proved easy: All we had to do was follow our friends in the air, the fat Bv-138 floatplanes and a couple of Ju-88s that droned over the wildly evading ships amid a barrage of heavy flak.

During the evening, running surfaced on a fairly straight course at its flank, we managed to overtake the convoy. We missed a large tanker, much to the disgust of everybody on board.

The following day dawned with a pale-pink sky on the horizon. Planes and destroyers suddenly pounced on us, forcing us under again. Up and down we went, one alarm maneuver after another. Finally we were able to surface undetected to the rear of the convoy. Suddenly on the starboard side we saw fine thin streaks rising over the horizon and approaching in a broad front. There were planes as far as the eye could see. Then we heard their deep droning and finally recognized the German crosses under their wings and at the flanks of their hulls. The sky was full of Ju-88s, He-111s, and He-115s. They had come to help us and to attack the convoy with machine guns, bombs, and torpedoes. It was a tremendous thrill for us when they thundered low over our heads. Full of pride, we waved our caps and cheered.

Words cannot describe the picture that now unfolded before our eyes. The enemy had seen the approaching planes as early as we had and welcomed them with a hail of steel whose flashes stained the sky red. By now we could clearly see the size of the convoy. Through our glasses we watched the planes roll over on one wing and dive towards their zigzagging targets, picking up incredible speed, releasing their deadly cargoes, then gaining altitude again in a looping arch. The

The *U-405* approaches a life raft with three German pilots. Their sinking plane can still be seen a short distance ahead of our bow. A Ju-88 has circled over the raft and we will soon pick up the men.

noise of bombs and torpedoes detonating on their targets penetrated our boat. Death had struck the leading ships of the convoy, casting a nasty yellow, nearly blood-red glare over the entire horizon. Fires and major explosions welled up in an inferno of vast destruction.

In the meantime we reached the islands of Spitsbergen, through which the convoy tried to squeeze. I'll never forget the scene ahead of us and around us in the clear polar weather with its radiant sun. Smoldering smoke clouds rose towards the sky. The calm and icy waters were littered with lifebelts, rafts, boxes, and casks. Many a seaman must have clung to the wreckage, until exhausted by the frigid water, he gave a final glance at the snow-covered peaks nearby and released his grip, lost to eternity.

In the afternoon we sighted a bright-yellow rubber raft. Not far away were the contours of a sinking plane. We raced to the raft and saw some German pilots waving frantically. After a short, lucky maneuver we had the men safely on deck. They waved to a Ju-88 that had been faithfully circling above them. The pilots had tried to land their hydroplane to pick up some other comrades of a downed Ju-88. Their plane had been severely damaged while trying to land in a long swell. We soon found the other men. They were in pitiful shape. I had photographed the first rescue, but I didn't have the heart to record this one.

After many maneuvers we managed to pull one of the men on deck. His face and hands were terribly mangled. His eyes were fixed somewhere in the distance and he resisted with inhuman power our attempts to put him on his back. Finally I forced him down with my entire weight while trying to comfort him with soothing words. Another seaman held his head.

The raft that had two other pilots attached to it by ropes had drifted away. Our commandant did his best to zigzag the boat to the raft, but the wind and sea had churned up too much during the past hour. The situation was delicate, with enemy planes a short distance away and the danger of destroyers appearing at any time.

On impulse, I pulled off my heavy U-boat clothes, took off my boots, and stood on the lateral bulge of our boat, calling to the commandant that I would go over the side and swim to the raft. It seemed the only fast way to save our comrades. The commandant told me to remain where I was; he would get closer.

The chief watch officer had already jumped down on deck and tied a rope around my waist. As I took another line between my teeth, I was washed away by the long swell running against our boat. The water was icy, but in my determination to cover the seventy or so yards I did not feel any pain. Soon I reached the first of the men. The whites of his eyes were strangely discolored and his lips were ashen and pale. There appeared to be no life in him anymore. The other man was floating on the opposite side of the raft, groaning terribly. Blood was washing out of deep wounds in his face and from his mouth. I grabbed the second man under the arms, threw myself on my back, and signaled those on board to pull the line. Since the pilots were both tied to the raft, I had the dead man in tow. The thin heaving line cut deep into my chest. I could hardly breathe, submerged in water and holding the groaning comrade above me.

Now feeling the intense cold, I was glad when my head bumped against the side of the boat. From the deck they tried to pull the pilot up, but his weight together with that of the entangled raft and his dead comrade, was too much. Our boat was picking up speed. Somebody let my rope go. Floating past the conning tower, I yelled "Stop the motors!" I was drifting rapidly towards the propellers.

Finally the crew managed to pull the pilot over the low stern and cut the rest loose. Then they pulled me out of the water. From the tower I heard the words of the commandant. "Well done, Giese, congratulations!" No sooner had we lowered our pilots into the boat than the alarm bells rang. A carrier plane had finally become curious about our strange behavior and approached for inspection.

For three hours we went to work on the badly wounded pilots while the two other pilots assisted. We injected lobelin and cardiazol into the muscles near their hearts. We did not dare take off their tight flying hoods, fearing their skulls might be shattered. We rubbed them with woolen clothes and massaged their bodies, and finally brought one of them around. He awoke in a trance and looked around with bruised eyes. "Where am I? What happened?" he asked faintly. "You're alright. You're safe now on a German submarine. We'll bring you home and get you well again." We asked him about his unit and base in Norway. He was married and had children. There were no papers or pictures of his dear ones on him, only the recognition medal tied around his neck, which carried his official number. Finally he smiled, relieved. Gazing beyond us, he talked haltingly about the battle he had just experienced.

He and his companions knew that the fight against this convoy would be hard because of the tremendous firepower of the armed freighters and their escort vessels. They also knew that the Americans and British were set on forcing their way through the area of Spitsbergen and around the North Cape by any means possible. The pilots had received reports since the early morning hours of 12 September from Luftwaffe reconnaissance planes that flew relentlessly over the convoy despite constant harassment by enemy fighters.

Although they had already flown many missions over London and other parts of the British Isles, attacks on moving targets, especially heavily guarded convoys, strained the nerves of even the most experienced pilots.

The pilot began to tell of their attack: "Steadily we flew towards the mass of ships. The tension grew, we could feel and hear it crackling all around us. Countless small flames shot up from the targets below and seconds later we were surrounded by dark puffs of exploding antiaircraft shells. Our plane was shaking and trembling.

The first hits tore into our glass domes and fuselage. There was a splintering and cracking, above the noise we could hear the groaning of our first wounded. But very calmly, as if nothing had happened, we heard the voice of the commander of the squadron through our earphones, giving formation instructions. 'Left wing advance more, right wing slow down.'

"The spectacle around us grew more intense as the middle- and light-caliber antiaircraft guns joined the heavy barrage of the aircraft carrier and escort vessels. These had formed a fire-spitting circle around the convoy. It was as if a volcano had burst wide open. Left and right of us planes tumbled down. We had been lucky enough to push our plane through a gap in the curtain of fire. Our plane was still intact, whereas many of the others were heavily damaged and flying on one engine. The carrier was now right in front of us. As we released our bombs, we were attacked by a swarm of enemy fighters. Shells ripped through the fuselage and shattered our controls. We worked feverishly to control the plane but we were losing altitude fast. All I can remember is hitting the water hard. The impact was deafening. I struck my head against the panel board even though I had braced myself for the crash. We managed to crawl out of the slowly sinking plane and pull ourselves into our raft, helping each other as best we could and tying our bodies with ropes to the handline.

"The sky was still full of yellow and red fire and dark smoke, but from our low position on the water we could not see any ships of the convoy. One destroyer came near but failed to detect us. Our clothes were wet and we could feel the intense cold. It was then that the pain from our wounds set in and became nearly unbearable. Gradually it grew dark and lonely. The time grew into an eternity, so very lonely, up and down, up and down we rocked in the small rubber raft. Someone moved, stood up, and cried frantically before he tumbled down and the raft capsized. I lost consciousness then and remember nothing more." The pilot said he felt safe now that all the horror and pain was over. He smiled faintly.

Then, after three or four deep breaths, he and his fellow pilot died at nearly the same moment.[29]

That night we sewed both bodies into bedsheets, and when we moved away from the convoy we heaved them onto the deck, tied some trimming weights to their feet, and covered them with the German war flag. All officers and the watch were on the conning tower when Captain Hopman spoke the words of farewell to our dead comrades. A silent salute was rendered, then they slid into their wet grave. The stopped motors started humming again and we proceeded back towards the convoy. Today it had been the pilots' turn. When would it be ours?

The weather changed, first rain, then snow, and finally fog, fog, fog. Again, fast-approaching destroyers forced us underwater. Later, while surfaced, we were attacked by enemy Catalina patrol bombers that managed to get some well-aimed machine-gun bullets into our deck. It splintered in several places. According to our calculations, we should have overtaken the convoy on Wednesday afternoon, 16 September. We spent that day in fruitless search.

In our wake we sighted several destroyers of the *Achilles* and *Afridi* class. Our eyes burned from trying to sight the enemy through the fog. Constant alarms frayed our nerves. Depth-charge explosions could be heard close by. Towards 1700 another destroyer heaved through the fog. We shot two torpedoes at her, then crash-dived. One crewman struck his forehead against the sill of the hatch. The skin on his forehead split wide open. He looked as if he had been scalped when he dropped like a heavy bag onto the plating in the central room. The others tumbled on him. There was no time to take care of the man now. A few minutes later two thundering detonations shook the boat. We surfaced a short time later to observe the effect of our torpedoes.

We had hardly taken up positions on the bridge when we saw several destroyers on our starboard side bearing zero. They came at top speed for us. We could clearly see their high white bow waves. Captain Hopman's voice was excited and tense. "Alarrrrrm! Down, down, boys, fast!"

We dived through the hatch and tumbled to our stations. "Flooding! Go to 180 meters, quick!" We all yanked valves and handles as we had done so many times before; but this time, we instinctively felt that our hour had come. The destroyers had been very close by. This damned fog! Wide-eyed, we watched the depth manometers. The hands moved so terribly slowly. God, why doesn't the boat drop faster? "Destroyers have stopped," called Sparks from his position at the hydrophone. They had probably done so to pinpoint our position. We were quite certain that they could hear us, for our aim was to bring the boat down as quickly as possible with the help of electric motors.

"Destroyers at 60 degrees, two propeller sounds are getting louder, fast," called Sparks. The boat was listing forward heavily. Tools, pots and pans, buckets, dishes, boots, and a thousand other things slid down the floor plating with devilish noise, easily heard by the enemy. The loud beeping and chirping of the destroyer's ASDIC gear gave off a peculiar ticking and hammering along our hull as the sound waves made contact.

Captain Hopman had hardly finished saying, "Well, men, now they start!" when we heard the first grinding, lapping propeller sounds from the attacking destroyers. One destroyer steamed at top speed right over our position. We heard a loud crunching, as if a huge saw was being drawn over our hull. This was followed by a faint splashing sound. Everyone on board knew what that meant! The ensuing uproar was infernal. Fortunately the depth charges detonated above us; explosions below would have been deadly.

It was as if a large hand threw stones and sand along the hull when the ASDIC picked us up anew. Within a short time another destroyer attacked us. The same uproar again, and again, and again. Who was counting? The electric current had been reduced to a low voltage. Now the lights began to flicker and sometimes they failed completely, leaving us in pitch darkness for seconds. Paint cracked off the bulkheads, manometer glasses burst, and the pointers of the depth meters jumped from their sockets.

We were busy trying to appear composed, while our hearts hammered away and hot blood pressed through our veins. The faces of my comrades in the central room reflected slight signs of weathered terror. Their eyes gazed at a spot above them, as if to follow the attacks. Some watched intently the slight, slow movement of the manometers. Nearly everyone held on to something, perhaps intuitively; I caught myself clinging to an iron rod with my hands folded behind my back.

The deeper we went, the more relaxed the men seemed to become, although the detonations still shook the boat. We managed to level our boat at about 240 meters, a great depth for a type VIIC U-boat. Although the enemy continued throwing depth charges, one of our men had kept his golden humor. He leaned against the round hatch protruding into the central room and was leisurely marking off the number of depth charges dropped on us. Each four he crossed out with the fifth, and after a while he called out monotonously: "Captain, sir, report fifty full!" All eyes turned to him and the tension eased. Years later I thought of this man during risky situations at sea and it helped me a lot to overcome tension.

However, all had not gone well in the boat. The two bow torpedo tubes, from which we had fired at the destroyer shortly before our crash dive, had sprung leaks under the great water pressure because their outer traps had not been closed in time. The noise of water escaping into the boat through valves was loud and nerve-wracking. One man in the bow room lost control of himself and started to scream in a high-pitched voice. The torpedo petty officer tried to quiet him with words, to no avail. When the man started to crawl up against the slanting door to get into the central room, he was overwhelmed and knocked unconscious to prevent a panic by others whose nerves might have been on the verge of breaking.

In the diesel engine room, one of the rivets had sprung out and a powerful, finger-thick stream of water jetted into the boat, filling the bilges rapidly. An old, proven expedient helped: one of our hams was placed with much ado against the hole and bolstered with iron spokes and plates. The leak was closed, the boat saved. Thus on this day, 17 September 1942, the *U-405* had both her first anniversary and her baptism of fire.

The two aviators we had picked up out of the first raft and who had recovered quite well were sitting in the officers' mess, pale faced and depressed. I asked them which they preferred, shrapnel in the air or depth charges under water. "We don't like either, but if we had to choose it would be shrapnel in the air. This feeling under water in a small steel tube is suffocating. The noise of the detonations is nerve-wracking!"

Suddenly the destroyer attack stopped. Either they thought they had hit their mark or they realized that by now we were far out of reach of the destructive power of their depth charges. However, they had left a frigate posted on top of us, and wherever we moved she followed. From then on we played mouse. The boat was balanced with air in tank no. 3. The crew was forbidden to move: We had to stay on station and use as little oxygen as possible. Soon the boat stopped rising and falling and the trimming pumps were no longer needed. There was no sound; we whispered if we had something to say.

When the propeller sounds of the frigate finally disappeared, the commandant decided to surface under cover of darkness. Everybody put on *outerlung apparatuses* (Davis-escape gear), knowing that if anything should go wrong aloft the boat had to be destroyed first before we could think of saving ourselves. The chief engineer officer ordered bundles of dynamite placed at vital spots, pistols and machine guns were laid at the ready, and up we went as quietly and quickly as possible. The hull plates cracked and ground as the extreme pressure the boat had withstood gradually diminished. We broke surface with one big, final leap. The commandant and the watch rushed through the hatch onto the bridge, ready for any action, shooting, gunning, ramming, anything necessary to destroy the enemy and fight our way clear.

The powerful diesels roared up and went instantly full ahead. It was pitch dark, a strong northeast wind had blown the fog away, only now and then some stars peeped through the gaps between fast-moving clouds. The enemy seemed to have disappeared. If the frigate was still somewhere nearby, she did not see us. We shivered from the cold.

A new order arrived directing us to steam westward in company with other boats to pursue and rake a fast convoy that had left Murmansk, QP-14. We soon made contact with the small convoy and tried to stalk it. Bombs from planes and depth charges from destroyers kept us in shallow waters off Iceland. We rested the boat on the rocky bottom while the rays of ASDIC gears searched our hull, slipped off and came back again. It was not so easy to detect a submarine here, and depth charges were seemingly thrown at random, sometimes dangerously near, sometimes far away. Needless to say, the situation was tense. As soon as the activity died down a bit, we surfaced again to continue the hunt. Finally we were called back to Narvik by the AdN.

Cruising through dense fog again while alert to the danger of swarming Russian submarines, we finally reached our base on Sunday, 20 September 1942. "Congratulations, Captain Hopman, for having kept the best contact with the convoys," called Admiral Klüver as we tied up under the gangway of the *Tanga*. Girls came on board with arms full of flowers and decorated each of the rough and unshaven men, distributing here and there a hasty and bashful kiss. After the initial enthusiasm died down, we heard about the U-boats that had been destroyed. We honored comrades we had come to know well with a silent prayer. Those men had died in one of the hardest fought convoy battles of the war.

That evening, Captain Hopman called the crew together for a big celebration on the *Stella Polaris*. Although deeply fatigued, we were

The *U-405* after arriving at Narvik. She has been boarded by girls laden with flowers to decorate the crew. Smiling and bearded, I am flanked by two seamen of my watch.

proud of our performance and grateful for having survived the ordeal. The white beds into which we fell afterwards seemed to be heaven on earth. A few days later the *U-405* went to Bergen for repairs.

The repair work to be done was extensive. Two days before, Captain Hopman had sent the following radio message to Admiral Nordmeer explaining our condition: "Boat limited dive clear. Air intake line, exhaust line, flooding pipe, quarter rudder, pressure hull flange tube V, leaking. Electro motor room ½ ton water per hour."

On the morning of 7 November, I received orders to sign off the *U-405* and be ready for U-boat officer training in Germany. I was invited by Captain Hopman and his officers to the Grande Café for an excellent lunch. That same afternoon the *U-405* set off on another patrol in the Arctic Sea and the North Atlantic. With many other soldiers of all arms, I stood at the pier and joined enthusiastically in the farewell calls. I waved and waved my cap. Several of my old comrades returned my salute. Sadly, I would never see them again.

North Atlantic storms, high seas, and constant attacks on convoys continued to play havoc with U-boat sailors. They were chased by

One of the rescued German pilots (*center*) bids farewell to the warrant officers of the *U-405*.

"hunter-killer" groups and planes day and night. By late 1943 the Allies had greatly strengthened their antisubmarine forces, and their new equipment and more sophisticated tactics had turned the hunter into the hunted. U-boat crews faced constant danger as they continued their attacks on convoys.

On 1 November 1943, the *U-405* battled the American four-funnel flush-deck destroyer *Borie* some seven hundred miles north of the Azores. In a ferocious night surface encounter the valiant U-boat was lost with all hands. The *Borie,* mortally wounded, went to the bottom the following day.

I was in Bordeaux during the battle and was saddened to hear of the loss of my dear comrades. I had a vivid dream that night. The once-merry faces of my brave shipmates looked tired and hopeless. I prayed that God would have pity on their poor souls.

The *U-405* at Bergen for repairs. I am on the left, chatting with two chief petty officers.

PART FOUR

· ·

Final Years, 1943–47

Nineteen

Reporting aboard the *U-181*

· · · · · · · · · · · · · · · · · · ·

Prior to November 1943 I had been sent through several U-boat officer training courses. These included the following: naval instruction department, Third Company, Glücksburg (midshipman/cadet course); torpedo school, Flensburg/Mürwick on the merchant ship *Patria*; torpedo shooting practice from torpedo boats; school for intelligence, signaling, coding/decoding, enigma machine, etc., Flensburg/Mürwick, promoted to lieutenant junior; school for antiaircraft training, the steamship *Cordillera*, Swinemünde; first tactical school, watch officer course, the steamship *Pretoria*, Pillau; ship's artillery school, the steamship *General Osorio*, Swinemünde; and watch officer on *U-1191*, Hela. The *Patria, Cordillera, Pretoria,* and *General Osorio* were former passenger liners used as hotel ships for course participants during the war. There had been much talk about the toughness of these courses. After becoming acquainted with the subject matter, however, I felt that they were not so difficult after all, and there was much time left to enjoy life in general.

I had tasted the beauty of being home in the fatherland and marveled at her breathtaking seasons. Now, as the war took its toll on our country, I feared that Germany's beauty might someday be a relic of the past.

On one warm and beautiful summer day in Swinemünde, on the German Baltic coast, I nearly got engaged to a girl from Thuringia. But when I returned for another course in the autumn, I felt suddenly unsettled, not able to socialize as before. Perhaps I had become a different man, a wanderer between worlds who now felt home neither in Germany nor abroad. I felt that I had to go back to the free world, where speech was free and ideas could be realized by deeds.

At the moment, this was only a secret wish. Doing my duty in the tremendous battle in which I played a part, no matter how small, re-

Here I am, a midshipman at the torpedo school in Flensburg/Mürwick.

Ship's artillery school, Swinemünde, during shooting exercises. I am waiting my turn (*standing, second from left*) with other course participants.

mained my sole ambition. After all my training I was hungry to get back to sea, to get a front-line U-boat and prove my worth.

After passing my last course in August 1943, I stood at attention during a farewell inspection by Admiral Hans-Georg von Friedeburg on the afterdeck of the great ocean liner *Pretoria* in Pillau. It was quite chilly, and I mused about those happy warm days before the war when I strolled along the decks of my beloved *Columbus*. If only I could get back to the tropics. But how? I had hardly finished the thought when an officer of the admiral's staff addressed me: "Hello Giese, still here? Cheer up, we know you're longing to get out to sea again. Perhaps you might see to it that your tropical outfit is, ah, well, I have to be off." And with that perplexing statement, he joined the departing admiral and his staff.

I felt my heart leap into my throat, and that afternoon I went out on a long, lonely walk along the beaches. I listened to my innermost thoughts: farewell, farewell to the old homeland, to my beloved Germany, to my dear folks. And when the full moon shone a rich gold through the pines that evening, it seemed that I had been trans-

planted into a magic Japanese landscape, sinister and delicately alluring. Was it a good omen?

Three months later my dream of a tour in the tropics became a reality. I was ordered to the *U-181*, a type IXD2 boat, experienced in
battle operations in the South Atlantic and Indian oceans (see appendix A). On 3 November 1943, I reported aboard as a commissioned
second watch officer in charge of artillery and wireless operations
(coding, decoding, working on enigma machines, and keeping current on radar-detection devices). The *U-181* had just returned from a
patrol in the Monsoon operational area under Commander Wolfgang Lüth, whose Knight's Cross had been recently decorated with
diamonds, the Third Reich's highest award for valor. He had just
been relieved as commandant of the boat by Captain (*Kapitän zur See*)
Kurt Freiwald, a former adjutant of Admirals Raeder and Dönitz.[30]

Our boat was in one of the large concrete bunkers in Bordeaux
that the RAF had failed to destroy. She looked liked a plucked hen,
with her crew and German and French laborers carrying a thousand

Tactical school, Pillau, watch officer course. Training is on type II boats. Passenger liners
serve as tenders for the boats and houseboats for the students.

Commander Wolfgang Lüth bids farewell to the crew of the *U-181* at Bordeaux. (*Left to right:* Lüth, former First Watch Officer Lieutenant Gottfried König, Dr. Klaus Buchholz, First Watch Officer Lieutenant Fritz Düring, Second Watch Officer Lieutenant Otto Giese, and an unknown officer.)

things back and forth. It was difficult to find one's way along the deck and onto the boat. I could see that she was battle worn after an operation that had lasted over two hundred days. However, from my first moment aboard I sensed that I had found a unit that simply loved their boat. They had been welded together by her former commandant into a happy band of brethren. I was lucky to meet Commander Lüth after he returned from Hitler's headquarters, where he had received the diamonds, and to join in a *Kameradschaftsabend* (evening of comradeship). I was most impressed by the enthusiasm with which his men celebrated him. His leadership ability was striking.[31]

The new commandant would have to be exceptionally good to replace such a man. If he measured up he would have a combat-hardened team under him that could overcome the most difficult situations. We all became skeptical when we heard that Captain Freiwald was a polished *Schreibtisch Offizier* (a "paper processor"), even though he had had some training on U-boats before the war and a couple month's of special commandant training recently. On the other hand, perhaps it was because he was so exceptionally qualified that Dönitz gave him this particular boat. While Lüth was on the small side, bald, wiry, tough, a bit cranky, and his movements regimental, Freiwald presented himself as an intellectual, tall, lean, graying at the temples, and every bit a gentleman. Later on we came to appreciate his many fine traits and grew to love him.

He was an innovative person who introduced numerous ideas that had never been implemented on German warships. On one of his last trips to Berlin he had sent to the boat a large film projector, one of the latest models, and some twenty of the latest films. When the boxes arrived we thought that the equipment and film were destined for the top people in Southeast Asia or Tokyo, so we carefully stowed them deep in the boat. What a surprise it was when ten days after departing our base we were told that our first big film would be shown in the bow room. The screen hung in front of the torpedo tubes while our boat was riding at 50 meters submerged.

Freiwald acquainted his officers with another surprise early in our long trip to the Indian Ocean. He had invented the institution of "the coward on duty," in German, *der Feigling vom Dienst*. With his scheme something like a democratic command was created aboard our U-boat. How did it work? Well, every day the officers took turns being the coward. When sitting around the table in the mess room with the commandant and other officers, the coward had absolute freedom to criticize, correct, and even grumble about matters such as the daily routine and orders from the commandant. At home or on other fronts such behavior might be regarded as insubordination and subject to court-martial. But here the coward could express those feelings, which fellow officers and crewmembers might agree with, without fear of retribution. This institution was a complete novelty within a branch of the German forces where tradition and standing forbade an officer to express the slightest doubt, criticism, or fear.

Admittedly, perhaps senior officers other than Freiwald could not manage the scheme. But Freiwald would quietly listen to what was said and give thoughtful, honest reflections on what changes should be made for the good of the officers, crew, and boat. He always displayed patience and understanding, yet was firm when he knew what had to be done. Our respect for him grew as we forged into a closely knit team under his leadership.

We also learned quickly that our new commandant knew something about seamanship. He was the only one of the U-boat com-

At Bordeaux, Lieutenant Commander Landfermann reports to Admiral of the Fleet Dönitz along with the crew of the *U-181.*

mandants who dared to move our large boat from bunker to bunker or through the narrow locks into the Gironde River without the help of supporting lines. The skill and risk involved in such maneuvering can only be appreciated by those of us who know how difficult it was to move these long, deep-draft steel tubes, and how easily the depth rudders and propellers could be damaged by the concrete walls.

The crew was a devil-may-care group, welded together by long experience and hardship at sea and in warfare. Their joint experience executing risky attacks and constantly facing death had forged a comradeship of mutual respect and consideration.

We had frequent trips ashore in gay Bordeaux. To us France was "wine, women, and song," and much more. Officials, businessmen, workmen in our bunkers, people in the streets and women, all with few exceptions were polite, obliging, and amiable. We visited Paris and her many historic sites. We enjoyed the beautiful French land-

On a short leave in Bremen, I witness the continuous bombing by enemy planes. The detonation of bombs, the thunder of heavy artillery, the constant barking of nervous antiaircraft guns, and the wailing of military trucks and fire brigades make me feel helpless. Life, it seems, has no value anymore. How will this all end?

scape. The delectable French wines and rich meals were memorable occasions for us.

Aside from these obvious delights, the occupation of France was important to us for several reasons. It protected our western flank, it positioned us to launch an attack against England, and it gave our U-boats and other German naval vessels additional bases from which to carry out operations against the enemy in the Atlantic.

I was given leave to visit home before we went to sea. Since my last leave, much had changed in Bremen. Day and night enemy bombers attacked the town's ports and shipyards. The craters left by heavy bombs and air mines were countless and much of Bremen looked like a ghost town. The people looked tired and hollow-eyed from little sleep and scarce food. Often when the sirens wailed announcing another attack and my family left for the air-raid shelter, I would stay home, sitting at my father's writing desk bringing my war diary up to date. Our windowshades were drawn. When I heard the droning of the attacking bombers I would turn the small desk light off and go down to our basement. From there I had a good view of the terrible spectacle.

At the foot of the dykes was a heavy wooden tower with big-caliber antiaircraft guns barking wildly. The night sky was crisscrossed with searchlights seeking out the high-flying planes. The noise of the heavy artillery was deafening and endless thunder rolled from the bombed sites.

The restaurant on the dyke across from our house was hit by incendiary bombs. "Our little restaurant," where we had spent many happy hours. I went upstairs when the clear signal sounded to peep through the big glass window partly covered with plywood. It appeared that the whole town was on fire. U-boat life was hard and often bitter, but then we were soldiers fighting for our country and this was our lot—it was expected of us. But here were civilians, men, women, and small children who were defenseless. My family and loved ones had not wanted this war and its misery.

Soon my leave came to an end. We said good-bye to each other at home. My mother was weeping bitterly. My father wiped away a tear before he put on his steel helmet and hung his gas mask around his neck. He insisted on accompanying me to the train terminal to help me with my luggage.

The trolley car did not run at night so we made our way through darkened, badly damaged streets. At the train station we had to wait in the air-raid bunker for the special U-boat train Kiel-Brest, which had stopped several miles outside Bremen to wait out a night attack by American planes. The sirens wailed, the artillery went into action, and enemy bombs exploded, making the bunkers tremble and groan.

There we sat, my father and I, exhausted from our long walk and too tired to talk. When the attack was over, the train rumbled into the dark and badly damaged station. I told my father that I loved him, and with a heavy heart boarded the train. The train guards blew their whistles and yelled, "Hurry up, get going!" The smoke and steam from the engine added to the general urgency of the situation. Hardly had I entered the train and found an empty place in one of the dark compartments when it lurched forward and started moving out of the station. Soon we were speeding along the rails towards France.

On our last leg to Bordeaux, and shortly after Tours, an axle on one of the cars ran hot, screeching terribly. Suddenly shots rang out, the train's emergency brakes were pulled, and our luggage came tumbling down on top of us.

Commando orders rang out: *"Alles raus, Waffen klar! Schnell, Schnell! Mit Beeilung!"* ("Get out, get out, arms ready! Fast!").

From somewhere out of the forest a machine gun stuttered. Bullets whizzed over our heads as we jumped out of the cars and took refuge behind a railway dam. I cocked my little Walter pistol, lit a cigarette, and looked on with amusement. The *Begleit-Commando* (officers and men assigned escort duty on the train) ran excitedly up and down the long train. I wondered why the soldiers did not return the fire. Later I learned that they had been ordered to take their guns with them but not given ammunition. Soon all became quiet and we were told to board the train again. We arrived in Bordeaux without further incident.

Shortly before our departure for the Indian Ocean in mid-March, I visited an old friend, a former petty officer and wireless operator of the *U-405*, at La Pallice, France. We reminisced about bygone days over some fine French wine. Later we walked down the middle of dark, narrow streets deeply involved in conversation, our holsters unbuckled and pistols cocked. Suddenly glass splintered a few feet behind us, then to our left and right. It all happened fast, and with threatening thuds. The penetrating stench of strong acid enveloped us. The glass vessels must have been wafer thin, since in the bright moonlight we did not detect glass fragments in the large and gradually spreading puddles of hot acid.

We jumped from the middle of the street into the darkness, pistols drawn. There was no sound of a moving door or window, only a menacing calm. We hurried from the area and reached the base safely. The next morning I detected some large spots in my leather pants where the acid had done its work. I could only wonder what would have happened had the maquis (members of the French resistance) scored direct hits.

A few weeks before we were due to sail from Bordeaux the crew was put on a train northbound for a visit to Paris. Shortly after our arrival at the Gare du Midi, we heard that the maquis had used a time bomb to destroy the train following us. Up to this point we had been convinced that our German guard and defense were impregnable. I was soon to learn the reality of our defense.

With half the crew I enjoyed a couple of sunny days in the white dunes of Moullo. The most famous of these was at Pyla, the first sign

of welcome when I had entered port on the *Anneliese Essberger* two
and one-half years earlier.

We relaxed on the beach and engaged in a merry "war game." Our
group split into blue and red teams, and using sticks as arms we proceeded to stalk and attack each other. My group could hardly believe
its luck upon discovering a wooden decoy of a heavy machine gun,
quite visible from the sea, in the saddle of some dunes. Thinking it
had been left there accidentally by some soldiers, we carried it off to
surprise the other party. We crawled along the beach, crossing
wooden horses or barriers, entangled barbed wire, and various other
strange-looking objects. When we thought we had successfully cir-
cumnavigated the other party, we entered the dunes once again to
prepare for a surprise attack.

Quite unexpectedly, there was a shuffling of feet around us and out
of nowhere there appeared several German soldiers, their guns
pointed at us. "*Halt, Hände hoch!*" ("Hands up, and don't move!").
We obeyed instantly.

"You idiots!" I yelled. "I'm Lieutenant Giese from a German
U-boat and these are my men."

One of the soldiers responded, "Don't talk. You don't look like a
German officer, neither do your men look like German soldiers. You
will have to prove it to our officer. All of you march!"

We took the wooden machine gun and staggered along until we
came to a hidden concrete shelter. It took me more than an hour and
various telephone calls to our flotilla in Bordeaux to convince the
stoic officer in charge that we were harmless countrymen. Actually, I
couldn't blame him for being suspicious, for I had no documents with
me and perhaps we did look like dangerous British or American
commando raiders.

We learned that we had not only made it through the beach defenses, but also avoided live mines hidden along our path! The officer told us later that there were many such wooden machine-gun de-
coys in the dunes, since few real weapons were available in this most
southern sector of the Atlantic Wall.

Back on base, our flotilla had received an invitation to a variety
show and dinner party from the famous seaplane-base Byscarosse in
the lonely coastal district of Les Landes. Based at Byscarosse were
the world's heaviest planes, the Bv-222, which flew surveillance missions over the Bay of Biscay. The commandant of our base responded to the invitation by sending a corps of U-boatmen who

were steadfast in their appreciation of drinking and partying. I was one of them!

We roared with laughter as we watched the show. All of the soldiers were dressed up like ballet girls with long hair, big breasts, and shapely legs. The dinner that followed was excellent, but not quite solid enough a base for the drinking bouts that were to come. I went secretly into the kitchen and asked the chef for some tins of oily Spanish sardines. I helped myself to them in the bathroom and slipped the rest of them to my U-boat comrades. Soon the windows were closed to contain the noise and the *Prosits* (cheers!) started. Towards morning the windows were opened again. We U-boatmen had won!

Ice-cold showers and a rich breakfast brought us all back to reality. We visited the base's large, powerful planes. Many of them showed the scars of recent battles with the RAF.

Next the commandant of the base showed us a novelty I had never heard of, "a house of love" solely designated for the benefit of his men. The base being isolated, the availability of prostitutes kept the men happy. The rule of the house was strict: Different ranks had their designated days of visitation. Doctors examined the girls and everybody stayed healthy.

Finally we were ready to go to sea. Our orders were to proceed to Penang, Malaya, for operations in the Indian Ocean, then to return to Germany with valuable Far East war materials. On 8 March 1944, the Twelfth U-Boat Flotilla commandant, Commander Klaus Scholtz, and his staff held a small farewell reception for us, offering a champagne toast for a successful patrol. The next day we made a deep diving trial and then proceeded to La Pallice for final preparations.

Twenty

On Patrol in the Indian Ocean

• • • • • • • • • • • • • • • • • • • •

On 16 March 1944 we said farewell to Bordeaux in company with the *U-196* (Captain Kentrat) and seven minesweepers. Captain Freiwald directed our departure smartly from the bridge. As we headed south we surfaced twice a day to charge our batteries, two hours shortly after sunset and two hours in the early morning. There was no sunlight for us anymore, only when we would glance through the periscope. At night the lights of the Spanish coast glittered. Numerous fishing boats caused us to proceed with great care. We ran a day routine at night and slept during the day. This was standard procedure for a long, submerged tour.

In the early morning of 23 March, while proceeding off Lisbon on a course for the Madeira islands, we heard the high revolutions of a passing destroyer. We were at a depth of forty meters. Luckily, the destroyer didn't detect our passage.

After long hours under water the air would turn bad, 2.5 percent carbon dioxide. When the boat was surfacing, the pressure stabilized; before the conning tower hatch was even opened, one could see the bad air escaping. Boiling water in the messman's pots would suddenly surge up and vaporize. We would get up and salute when this stinking mess passed out of the boat.

Apropos saluting, there was no such thing as raising the arm in a "Heil Hitler." Space was too limited, and the saluter might have hit someone, perhaps the commandant, and nobody wanted to run that risk. If we saluted Nazi style among each other, we just plugged the thumb of the right hand into the pocket of our pants and raised the hand. Otherwise we just stood at attention, leisurely, when we made a report to our chief. On the "bridge" we saluted in the old military manner, U-boat style, with slightly bent fingers to the cap, a grin on the bearded face, and some pointed joke on the lips. That's how it was

Our sister *U-196*, under Commander Eitel-Fredrich Kentrat, passes the *U-181* at the pier on her way outbound to the South Atlantic and Indian Ocean.

with us, and that's how it must have been with all the salt-crusted U-boatmen on other boats.

One morning Captain Freiwald appeared in the central room with a bucket of hot salt water and his dirty clothes. We thought that he would call his orderly, but no—calmly and without a word he sat down and started washing. What a commandant! This gave me the idea to have a hot saltwater hose-down for the crew behind the diesels during our next two-hour surface run. What a delicious feeling it was! What a life!

We were now off Gibraltar. During our last nights in the Atlantic we often heard depth charges detonating, but they were far away. On 26 March we watched our first film, "Val Parez," in the "bow theater." We closed the Madeira islands on the twenty-eighth, marveling at their beauty through the action periscope.

It was now stifling in the boat. The air was dull and sultry. Our perspiration wouldn't dry anymore and our beards began to grow and get itchy. Only "Tosca" and our *Köllnisch Wasser* helped.

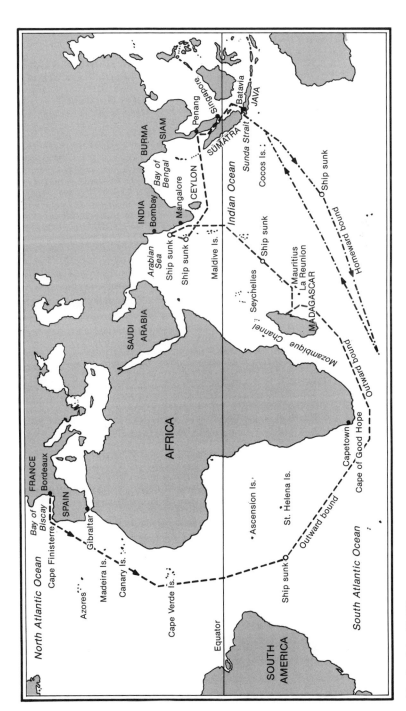

Track of the *U-181*

On 1 April we passed the Canary islands. That same day we received a message from headquarters directing us to operate in an area southeast of Madagascar. During our short surface intervals I had my men overhaul the antiaircraft guns. They suffered from the constant underwater cruising. I had to do each hand grip myself to guarantee complete operational readiness in case of an emergency.

We celebrated the birthday of our navigation chief petty officer that first week in April. The "special occasion" record was played, and in the central room the commandant and the officer corps congratulated the young man. A bottle of liquor was passed through the boat to mark the event. Surfacing, submerging, up and down we went to receive orders from the BdU regarding our forthcoming rendezvous with a returning Monsoon boat, the *U-188*. Our poor engineer, Hille, was near exhaustion with no rest in sight. The daily paper *Typhoon* kept us informed about events on the battlefields. The Russians were at the German and Romanian borders. How will that end? we wondered. Something had to happen soon!

We were sure that our dear ones at home had been informed that we were still alive. Prior to our departure, we had organized a communications system whereby the commandant's wife, who received nonsensitive information about the boat, would pass on the news by telephone or letter to families of the officers, who would in turn contact relatives of the crewmen.

We passed the Cape Verde islands at Eastertime and our thoughts turned to home and loved ones. The canteen issued chocolate, candies, and fruit juice. We listened to concert music and had a film showing in our bow room.

The interior of the boat was by now so moist that the lockers streamed with water. Leather surfaces were soon covered with a thick layer of gray mold. Nearly everyone had ailments—headaches, fevers, colds. We were now daring to surface for up to six hours at night. My dogwatch was exhausting because of little sleep, fresh air, and the strain of intense lookout duty. The night wasn't safe anymore in southern Atlantic waters. At any moment aircraft could appear from nowhere and toss a bomb down on our steel tube, which glowed in the otherwise pitch-dark tropical water.

On 22 April we rendezvoused with the *U-188*, a returning Monsoon boat. It was a memorable sight when two of the largest-type U-boats ran side by side, two ghostly shadows within calling distance.

After we received valuable information about our area of operations in the Indian Ocean, we parted and passed into the night with three short "Hip-hip-hurrahs!"

By wireless we heard that the *U-488* (Captain Studt) was no longer responding to calls from the BdU. His young wife in Bordeaux was suddenly a widow. We were all anxious to take revenge.

Several days later, while submerged, we heard propeller noises on our hydrophones. It was 1400, my section was on watch. Going to periscope depth, we sighted a loaded freighter ahead of us. We surfaced and gave chase but had to dive when a plane was sighted. An hour later we surfaced again. We caught up with the freighter and positioned ourselves about 6,500 yards ahead of her. We attacked as clouds covered the moon. Our torpedoes found their mark and the ship went down fast. Only a few of the crew managed to get into the ship's lifeboats. When we approached them, I asked one of the men the name of the ship. He mumbled a name that sounded like *Bena-van*. In fact, it turned out to be the British freighter *Janeta*.[32]

On 9 May we celebrated the two-year anniversary of our boat with a half-bottle of beer for each of the crew. We were now entering the area of Cape Town, and the seas were getting rough. The boat plunged through deepening waves that sent sheets of swirling water over the conning tower. Oilcloth and leather clothing were changed in quick succession. The happiest hours on board were those of the afternoon coffeebreak in the officers' mess when we played games, or those hours after dinner when we would spin yarns and sip a small jigger of rice wine, a gift from the crew of the *U-188*.

We thought we sighted a smoke cloud but were disappointed. It was only the blowing of a whale. More excitement came soon. Our boat was rigged with a *Bachstelze*. This was a small, single, piloted helicopter attached to a long steel cable and lifted into the air by the speed of our boat while the cable was gradually reeled out. From his position aloft, the pilot had a 360-degree view and could report any vessels. One day, as I was busy on watch keeping the boat running against a strong wind while our aviator flew aloft, the man at the hawser reel yelled, "Sir, sir, look, the cable snapped!" I looked up. Our hapless pilot was spiraling down toward the water. Eventually he hit the surface with a huge splash. The pilot seemed okay. However, a new danger quickly appeared. Thinking he was a wounded fish, several large albatrosses and numerous seagulls descended on him, trying to peck his head. Before serious wounds could be inflicted, we picked up the stunned airman, who was received with roars of laughter by the crew. Nobody was sorry that the helicopter was gone. It had been more trouble than it was worth.

We rounded the cape on 17 May, Father's Day.

Our poor "Doc" Buchholz had little hair left on his scalp, and to keep what he had and perhaps grow more, he used a tonic known in the German navy as Trylisin. The bottle stood quite prominent in his open locker. In a moment of recklessness, one of the crew suggested that some ingredients be added to it while Doc was busy at the radar station. This we did, enriching the potion with liquor, sugar, and glue. At night, when all of us watch-free officers rested in our bunks, Doc would attend to the remarkable work of massaging his shiny scalp with his fingers. That night everyone watched from behind their curtains, hardly able to restrain their laughter when he poured the sticky liquid into his hands and started rubbing it over his scalp. The grimaces he gave the mirror when he combed his few remaining hairs and watched them depart with the comb! We asked him why Trylisin had so many sediments in it; he explained that the chemical formula was such and such, and that naturally here in the tropics the alcohol would evaporate . . . poor Doc.

But, in need of a scapegoat, we were not quite through with Doc. Another plan was shaped one night during an officers' meeting. We ground some carbon pills to a very fine powder and poured it into his heavy U-boat boots. Although he wore socks, his feet soon turned black. The carbon was not easily removed, not even with soap and a brush. What a painful situation for the ship's doctor, known as the neatest man on board, to have to wait each night until his fellow officers were asleep to start scrubbing his shamefully dirty feet. Only when we told him of our experience with Bordelaise powder, which stained our feet gray, did he catch on.

It wasn't long before he got even. Within days our toothpaste had acquired the bitter taste of quinine, and when we urinated the stream was either red or green. Not knowing the cause, we mentioned this discreetly to Doc, who told us the most horrible things about kidney and bladder trouble. We were in shock until he confessed to his revenge.

We finally reached our operational area, some two hundred miles southeast of Madagascar, in early June. We patrolled the shipping routes between Durban and Colombo, Aden, and Australia with no

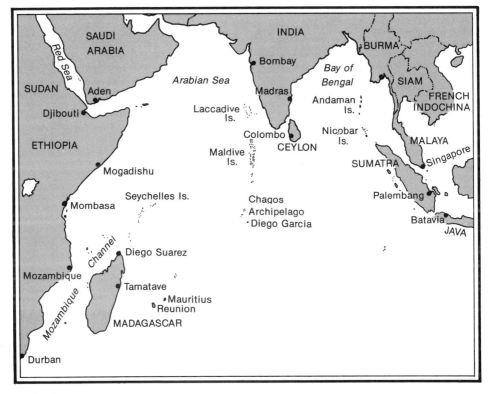

Indian Ocean

luck. The weather was almost too good, with beautiful sunsets and clear, moonlit nights. No smoke clouds appeared on the horizon.

Doc vaccinated the entire crew against cholera. My reaction was fever and the shivers.

On 6 June 1944 we received the depressing news that Allied forces had landed between Le Havre and Barfleur in France. They had launched an all-out invasion. But the reports added that the enemy had been thrown back, suffering heavy losses. The BdU ordered all U-boats to exert themselves to the utmost.

Finally on 19 June we sighted a distant freighter. The hunt was short. A single torpedo sent the Dutch ship *Garoet* to the bottom.[33] Safety lights flared in the water. Rafts and boats bobbed up and down around us. The men in the boats answered my questions willingly, giving the name of the vessel, its cargo (sugar and coal), departure port (Bombay), and destination (Durban). In return, we told them the shortest route to the coast.

The southwest monsoon was blowing with force now. The constant rolling and eternal spray over the conning tower kept us more than busy wiping our glasses. No sightings . . . We were in low spirits. During these days it was over 50°C in the diesel room, damp and hellishly hot. One day, at the end of my watch, it started raining in torrents. I kept the boat under the dark cloud, and part of the crew, including Captain Freiwald, appeared on the bridge naked as God made them to rub off their coats of grime.

We passed the northern cape of the Laccadive islands, some two hundred miles from the mainland of India. The sky was covered with dark gray rainclouds. Enemy planes might have attacked us at any minute, but we remained on the surface. I couldn't get rid of a certain tension inside me. Perhaps it was the climate of the monsoon which strained my nerves.

On 15 July 1944 we arrived at a position about thirty miles off the coast of India. At 1815 a ship was sighted. The enemy was automatically zigzagging, and we had difficulty getting to a forward attack position. The night drifted in around us. Our *Naxos* (radar warning) detection system sounded at about 2200. We stayed surfaced, close to our prey, not wanting to lose her in the darkness. Then finally we attacked with two torpedoes, scoring two hits on the British ship *Tanda*. The detection signal got louder and louder, reaching a force 5. If it was a plane, it should have been on top of us. We dived, leaving the sinking ship behind.[34] Two hours later we surfaced cautiously only to be driven down again by detection signals.

The next morning propeller noises sounded again. They were distinct, slow revolutions. Either a ship was running with caution or her crew was careless. We waited and listened as the sound grew. Freiwald decided to take a look through the periscope. He saw nothing.

A hunting fever came over the officers. We talked of precedents in such situations and decided to surface and attack. Freiwald went directly to the bridge with the watch officer and five men. The atmosphere was tense. Below, we waited. The propeller noises continued. We began to wonder if they were real or some phenomenon of the sea around us. Then came the terrifying call from above: "ALAARRMM!" The men tumbled down from the bridge and we went into a steep dive. The watch officer looked at me with a sweaty

face. "Twin motorplane out of the sun. Saw it too late." Everyone
looked up, waiting for the explosions.

Four hammer blows rocked the boat when we reached forty meters. All electricity went off. A high-pressure pipeline burst and blew
off into the central room with an incredible noise. Compressed air
streamed fiercely into the compartment. The hydroplanes were
jammed in a hard down position, giving the boat an increasing forward list; 20, 30, 35 degrees and still we continued down. The bottom
was now some sixty meters below. The electrical motors suddenly
stopped when a coupling failed to release. There was an immediate
overload, and all the fuses blew.

Our disciplined crew acted and acted fast. Within seconds, the
damages were pinpointed. The defective piping was turned off. Both
hydroplanes were shifted to manual operation, new fuzes for the
E-motors installed, emergency lights switched on. Minutes later the
heavily battered boat was under control.

On orders from Freiwald, our chief engineer leveled the boat at
eighty meters. Then, gradually, we began to repair the worst damage
as the boat crept along at three knots. The starboard fuel bunker was
cracked and leaking. We had lost about thirty cubic meters of diesel
fuel. We pressed the remaining fuel out and flushed the bunker with
seawater. Our gyrocompass was badly damaged.

Six hours later, still submerged, the boat was rocked again by thunderous depth charges too numerous to count. Finally we escaped, but
we remained submerged. Later we would discover that we had come
under attack by Allied aircraft and the Indian sloop *Sutlej*.[35]

After eighteen hours under water, we surfaced and headed for the
safety of the Laccadives, where detection would be more difficult
among the many islands. Freiwald masterfully guided the boat
through the maze of atolls. Although badly wounded, we were in
good trim again.

After a few days of surface running and continued repair work,
the boat returned to routine patrol. One morning while we were on
the surface and I was busy checking my sector ahead, Freiwald asked
me softly, "Giese, please turn around!" It was 1044 on 20 July 1944
and our defective, temperamental hydrophone had not signaled any
distant ships.

Pivoting, I watched as Freiwald and all the men smiled, then
ducked below the bulwark of the conning tower. One of them

We approach the coast of Malaya carrying the swastika on both sides of the conning tower. This, together with white paint on the front of the bridge and white cross-stripes on the foredeck, are signs for Japanese aviators that this is a German U-boat.

pointed his thick thumb in the direction of starboard aft, and there, not four thousand yards away, was the broad silhouette of a vessel. I looked open-mouthed at Freiwald. "Alarm?" I asked. He shook his head laughingly and said, "Let's try showing them our back side."

Undetected, we quietly maneuvered the boat into a forward position and waited to attack shortly after darkness. We fired two torpedoes, both hit, and the British ship *King Frederick* went down.[36]

We approached the men in the lifeboats and asked them the name of their vessel, their cargo, and destination. They were fearful and quiet. They appeared to have food and water and were capable of making their way ashore. We were mystified by their action. We learned later that they thought we were Japanese and feared for their lives because of harm done to other seamen by Japanese crewmen.

On 20 July 1944, the BdU declared a general alarm for the German navy following the attempt on Hitler's life. Hitler or no Hitler, we realized that the war was lost for us. Nevertheless, we were soldiers and bound to our oath. Our job was to sink tonnage and to fight to the bitter end. In fact, we hardly talked about the attack on Hitler's life. The

The men of the bridge watch scan the sea around the islands leading to Penang, a good hiding place for enemy submarines. The NAXOS radar detection device is in operation.

The *U-181* following the pilot boat on the way to Pulo Penang. Aircraft bombs and Indian sloop depth charges have damaged our aft deck plating.

radio messages were short. We felt that the sooner the situation calmed down, the better we would be able to prepare for the final fight and onslaught by enemy forces.

Freiwald sent a message to headquarters reporting our sinkings to date and our intention to proceed to Penang to repair our damage.

On our way eastward through the Straits of Malacca, we heard that Sabang had been attacked by British carrier planes and shelled from the sea. Furthermore, it was reported, a powerful British sea force of two battleships, two aircraft carriers, and several cruisers and destroyers was south of the Andamans, along our track. Hallelujah!

We heard by wireless that the *U-196*, which had left Bordeaux with us, was sending a series of short signals to the BdU. While the boat was in our vicinity, we worried that the signals would draw the attention of enemy forces, in which case we both might come under attack. Later, in Penang, when we met with Captain Kentrat (the *U-196*), we were told that he had tried at least five times to get a short signal through to the BdU before receiving a confirmation of his signal. However, he did exercise caution, diving after each signal and

The *U-181* approaching the islands as fast as the small pilot boat can run alongside. The men are wearing escape lungs, which inflate to lifejackets.

Even men of the free watch help keep a lookout while the German war flag merrily flutters in the breeze.

waiting for the following program time. He did not know that we were in the vicinity.

One night, in a dead calm, a long dark shadow loomed ahead. Our sharp night glasses revealed a conning tower. We watched each other for a few tense moments. Then the other boat dived and we departed at full speed.[37]

At long last, we approached Penang and radioed our estimated time of arrival. Captain Junior (*Fregattenkapitän*) Wilhelm Dommes, chief officer in the Southeast, responded, warning us to stay alert and await a Japanese escort vessel where "the Slot" led into the straits off Langkavi Island.

On 8 August a German seaplane, an Arado, appeared out of the early morning haze and circled a few times over the boat. The pilot clearly saw the two broad stripes across our deck and the big swastika on the sides of the conning tower. The plane dipped its wings a few times in salute while the crew cheered.

Soon the Japanese escort was sighted. It was not what we expected. Looking for something like a powerful minesweeper or even a sloop,

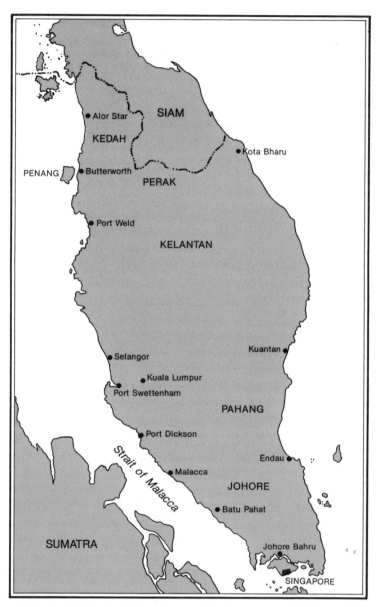

Malay Peninsula

we found ourselves welcoming a small motorboat that mounted a single small-caliber gun. Lieutenant Kölln, the German escort officer, stepped from the vessel onto our deck bringing baskets of fresh bananas and pineapples—precious cargo!

We asked Kölln to take off his lifejacket and invited him into the boat for a hearty brunch out of the last of our stores. He accepted reluctantly, declining to take off his lifejacket. We smiled, perhaps a bit too indulgently, as he strode around without much interest and appetite. It wasn't long before he told us in abrupt, rash words how it really stood with the "glorious and powerful Japanese navy" in the area. It had suffered devastating losses in recent dramatic sea and air battles in the Pacific, and as we went silently back on deck with him we mused that perhaps Goebbel's propaganda was nothing in comparison to the invention of victorious battles by our Axis partners down here.

"However, don't argue with the Japanese, gentlemen!" he warned as we stepped onto the deck. He left us then to take a long walk with Captain Freiwald on the sunlit deck. They were both deep in conversation while our boat zigzagged behind the small Japanese speedboat.

Luck was with us; nothing happened on the ten-hour trip. The crew enjoyed the fresh air and I had ample time to tell them about Japanese, Chinese, and Malayan manners and customs, which were so very different from ours. Most of all they wanted to know about love life in Asia.

The pier at Penang was filled with throngs of men, German and Japanese in white and khaki uniforms. The sun reflected from the glittering instruments of a large Malayan band. When a gust of wind blew music toward us, we were thrilled to hear German marches. In spite of a strong and unpredictable current, Freiwald brought the U-boat exactly where at the pier the Japanese admiral and his staff, the German officers and men, and the bandstand were positioned. As the German and Japanese national anthems sounded solemnly, all stood at attention. The German anthem was played a bit fast, like a foxtrot. "Banzai!" and "Hurrah!" rang out as the band played on. We had finally arrived at our distant post, anxious and excited about what lay ahead.

On our way to Penang, in company with the pilot boat, we flew pennants from our raised periscope to signify the tonnage of each vessel we sank. Underneath can be seen a mail pennant.

Third Watch Officer Lieutenant Hannes Limbach on bridge watch while the *U-181* approaches Pulo Penang, Malaya. Fresh fruit and some canned provisions from the liaison officer on the pilot boat sit on the bridge mantle.

The *U-181* preparing to approach the pier at Penang, where she will tie up. In the distance a large crowd waits to welcome the boat and her crew.

Captain Freiwald salutes the Japanese naval commandant at Penang. To the left of each officer is an interpreter. Dommes stands at attention behind Freiwald. The German and Japanese national anthems are played, followed by various German marches.

Twenty-One

Penang, Malaya

• • • • • • • • • • • • • • • • • • •

Our men were housed in the wide, airy Elysee Hotel, while we officers found quarters in a large villa that once belonged to a British doctor. This was a real palace, at least it appeared so to men who had lived for months in a small, hot steel tube. Our barman, Osman, could mix the best drinks to be found and our driver, Charley, had already faithfully served his British masters. For matters of concealment, all U-boatmen had to give up their bushy beards and don white shirts and shorts on which they wore a small cockade. No uniforms were worn except when working aboard the boat. The entire boat was shut down and each section started its hard work of repairs and maintenance with what assistance there was in Penang.

German shore-base personnel did their best with the help of the Japanese navy and civilian authorities to deliver all the materials needed to get the boat ready for sea once again. We were to be loaded at Penang and in Singapore according to a plan worked out by an enterprise called Roges Tokyo, a German company experienced in such work through our nation's blockade-runner operation. Our cargo consisted of about 130 tons of tin, 20 tons of ore (molybden), 80 to 100 tons of raw rubber, 1 ton of quinine, and some small amount of opium, all told about 250 tons. The tin was melted into small hollow bars into which the ore was poured. A tin cover was placed on top and sealed with tin. These bars were then loaded in the bilges and placed tightly on the floors in the interior of the boat, so that they would not slide during underway operations. Our already cramped living quarters now became foxholes. Although the crew complained, war was war, and Germany urgently needed these materials. The raw rubber was squeezed into racks, and either placed under the deck planking or stowed in the free upper-deck torpedo tubes and the free flooding/diving tanks. For defense purposes we kept two tor-

The villa assigned to us at Penang is the former house of a British doctor. It provides comforts for tropical living—large rooms with high ceilings and a multitude of fans. We sleep on the airy veranda of the upper floor in wide beds covered with mosquito nets. Along with the house comes the doctor's former servant, Osman, who mixes excellent cocktails.

pedoes on board. With this large amount of additional weight, the fuel for our return trip had to be measured carefully, keeping some in reserve for emergencies.

Only a small number of our men could be sent on leave up to the beautiful resort, Penang Hill, where experienced Chinese cooks cared for their welfare. With nearly unlimited freedom, they felt as if they were in paradise. Penang Hill enjoyed a moderate climate and overlooked charming tropical scenery with views of colorful gardens in Georgetown below, azure blue seas around and towards Kedah, and countless hills and mountains on the distant mainland.

Those men who stayed behind could go into town after their hard day's work. There they had a chance to shop, drink Japanese beer, and meet girls. Additionally, the base had a club for them where they could order every imaginable drink and mix with more women. It was housed in a magnificent bungalow called the Shanghai Hotel.

During our loading, the *U-196* arrived in a tropical downpour. The docking maneuver in the powerful current took a long time, but we faithfully waited, soaked to the bone and shivering. The Japanese admiral and his staff seemed unmoved by all this. Finally, the boat got a line ashore, which one of our men picked up and put around a bollard about a hundred yards ahead of where we stood. Fine, we thought, it won't take long now, and soon we'll be enjoying a welcoming drink with our comrades in a dry place. But to our surprise we saw a Japanese army soldier go calmly to the bollard and unhook the line. The Japanese admiral didn't react. We were disturbed, since it took another hour for Captain Kentrat to get his boat docked at the place reserved for him.

Later we were to learn something instructive about the Japanese mentality. The other pier had belonged to the army, and it did not in the least way interest the soldier that high-ranking naval officers of his own country were waiting and that the arriving boat was a friendly ally and honored guest. This example was typical of the difficulties our base personnel had to overcome to gain the cooperation of the Japanese in supporting our front-line boats.

The U-boats operated pretty much on their own in the Far East. Neither the German Naval High Command with its operational staff nor the Japanese naval authorities were able to provide U-boat commandants with exact, extensive intelligence about such things as enemy bases, naval and air force strength, convoy systems, and routes of single fast-running vessels. Neither country appeared to have sufficient spies in the operational areas of the Indian Ocean. The only information the commandants had were reports and war journals from individual U-boats or their concise messages sent by wireless. Such reports in all probability were out of date because of the constant change in enemy tactics. Although the U-boats were directed by the tactical staff of the German Naval High Command, the BdU, and provided with the latest intelligence, it was usually left up to the individual commandant to conduct his own operation within his area. At the same time it was surprising and depressing to realize that the enemy was extremely well informed about the arrivals and departures, tactics, and in-theater movements of our boats.

The Japanese attitude towards us was cautiously friendly. It was tolerant, occasionally arrogant, and loosened by liquor it could become aggressive. It was so completely different from what I had previously experienced in Japan, but then I had dealt with civilians. Now we were working with soldiers.

A week after our arrival in Penang, many crewmembers of our boat were decorated. Captain Freiwald was among those honored. He also received a special greeting from Dönitz for being commandant of the most successful boat in the previous few months. I was awarded the Iron Cross First Class medal and shortly afterwards U-boat wings. I had already received the U-boat front medal, the Iron Cross Second Class, the blockade-runner medal, and the German sport medal in silver.

Some days later, our entire crew was invited to a garden party given in honor of a newly arrived U-boat. The affair was sponsored by the Japanese admiral and Captain Ariizumi, a quick-witted, slightly imperious officer with harsh manners. We could not help but admire him and his record as a successful submarine commandant operating in the Indian Ocean. However, we learned after the war through British intelligence officers in Singapore that Ariizumi had been cruel toward Allied seamen. He committed suicide when his last command, the *I-400*, was taken over by the U.S. Navy in August 1945.

We enjoyed the Japanese and Malayan entertainments at the garden party. The delicate Chinese and Malayan women wore tight-fitting long dresses, slit up the side, exposing their shapely legs. These women had husbands or fathers in good business standing with the Japanese authorities or German base personnel. Women of wealth, education, and grace, they were too reserved for our taste.

We enjoyed the drinks and especially the food, the wonderfully flavored frog legs. Soon the men, German and Japanese alike, were in high spirits and songs rang out over the green lawns. The Japanese admiral and Captain Ariizumi asked us to sing the Christmas tune *"Sah ein Knab ein Röslein Stehn"* ("Saw a boy standing a small rose"). The song came out a bit thin; we sounded much better belting out U-boat songs. Best of all, the Japanese started marching in place and singing our famous U-boat song with the refrain *"Wir sind die U-Bootleute . . . , die Grauen Wölfe auf dem Meer . . . "* ("We are the U-boatmen, the gray wolves of the sea"). They kept singing this until they were hoarse. How strange these people were, we thought— intelligent, traditional, ceremonial, but cruel and dangerous at the same time.

Preparing for a tiger hunt in the jungle. *Third from left,* Captain Junior Dommes; *fourth,* our doctor Lieutenant Senior Buchholz; *fifth,* Commander Kentrat; and *sixth,* Commander Ariizumi.

At times in the early morning on base we would hear the shrill signals of sirens and the dull *bum-bum-bum* of native drums. This was the Japanese exercise alarm for airplanes and raids. We often wondered how long it would take for the enemy to overrun these base points.

When not on board, we would watch the Tonga Ballet with its beautiful dancers, drive around Pulo Penang and visit with Professor Kudo at the turtle and snake temple, or have a snack at the Springtide Hotel.

Towards the end of August I joined a tiger-hunting party in Thailand with Captain Ariizumi, his staff, and the Japanese district officer. "You need a gun?" I was asked. "No, I'll take my own rifle with me," I responded. It was a heavy, modern German army rifle that I had managed to barter in the U-boat bunkers in Bordeaux. I had had the barrel shortened and the stock adjusted for hunting. Crouched in a couple of jeeps and trucks, we raced over narrow tracks through immense rubber forests and dense jungles. At our destination there

During our stay in Penang, I am fortunate to join a hunting party for some of the officers of our boat and Kentrat's. The party has been organized by Captain Ariizumi (*second from right*). The Japanese cooks will prepare a delicious suki yaki with our bagged animals, and we will flush it down with great quantities of saki.

were many natives with ferocious dogs assembled. Everything had been well organized; they even knew where our tiger was waiting.

After all the hunters had been positioned at small outlets, tunnels, and tracks, escape routes the cat might use in evading us, the battle was on. The noise the beaters made with their tin cans, drums, and sticks was such that I felt certain the tiger would succumb to heart failure before we could get a glimpse of him. My Japanese neighbor to the left had decided that instead of waiting for the tiger to come to us he would go looking for him.

I was afraid I might shoot the man by mistake if the tiger charged our way and he got in the line of fire. So I called loudly and whistled to him to get out of my range. This caused an uproar, and in the ensuing confusion what should break out of the jungle but several boars, which were immediately cut down by Japanese machine-gun fire. This proved too much for the tiger—he tore through the line of beaters and disappeared into the jungle. I was able to add a few monkeys to the cache, taking them from high in the trees with my powerful rifle. The Japanese were delighted, being partial to monkey meat. That evening we ate the delicious, juicy boar meat prepared in the form of suki yaki. The saki wine flowed freely, and soon some of our hosts were rolling under the tables. A big hunting day, indeed.

Our boat was ready to leave in early September. On the ninth, after a couple of farewell parties, we departed Penang and moved slowly off into the yellow waters of the Malacca straits. Although it was a soft, beautiful night, we maintained full alert while most of the crew not on duty stayed on deck. With Freiwald having been called to Tokyo, Lieutenant Commander Herwartz, captain of the *U-843,* had taken over command of the *U-181* to bring her to Singapore.

The boat ran at full speed, zigzagging. Herwartz remained on the bridge, not intending to leave his position until he had brought the boat safely into Singapore. All the men had put on their lifejackets. The situation became more tense the farther we got from Penang; if enemy submarines were waiting for us, it would be between Penang and the narrows of the inner straits. We made it through the inner straits safely, only to run aground on mud and sand south of the one-fathom bank. Navigation in these waters was a tricky business because of the lack of objects that could be used for accurate bearings. It was unmercifully hot, and in spite of the shark-infested waters around us, several of the seamen jumped overboard and enjoyed a brief swim while others watched with guns and pistols. One of our Arado planes passed over us with Captain Dommes, chief officer of the Southeast, on board, probably raising all kinds of hell. What a fine opportunity for the enemy to attack us! However, we waited stoically, trying to no avail to get the boat to move. Fortunately the next tide lifted the boat off the bar.

The *U-181* en route from Penang to Singapore. The boat has run aground in the Strait of Malacca, and on orders from First Watch Officer Düring, two men are in the water to check the extent of the sand bar.

The pier in Singapore was crowded with waiting officials, including Commander Wolfgang Ehrhardt (chief officer in Malaya, commandant of the naval base at Penang, and former executive officer of the auxiliary cruiser *Michel*) and his staff. We moved into quarters outside the town in the district of Pasir Panjang, nice, clean villas on the beach where we rested to make up for the sleep lost during the previous days.

The work on our boat at the Empire dock continued, with all hands participating and valuable assistance from the arsenal in Seletar, where the Japanese had taken over a large, closely guarded naval docking yard.

While Captain Freiwald was still in Tokyo, we kept in close touch with our base personnel in the Union building. We worked until we were covered with grease and dirt, then returned to our camps in the afternoons to get dressed and enjoy some leisure time. We often took strolls through beautiful tree-lined gardens that led to the *Tiger*, a large pavilion that once belonged to a Chinese multimillionaire who owned the world-famous Tiger Balm company. The ingredients in

Tiger Balm ointments were natural and of great value in treating a wide variety of illnesses.

Everything in the Tiger was round, including many small, intimate rooms running from the center hall. The hall was frequented by beautiful Eurasian girls who waited to be invited by the German officers for a drink or dance. The Tiger Club was run by a former Japanese dance star of the Takarazuka ballet, Mrs. Kadowaki, who, it was said, worked for the Japanese *Kempetai* (secret police). Our men were not forgotten; we turned a bungalow into a most comfortable haven for them with all the amenities afforded the officers. It was called the Jungle Club.

Freiwald had in the meantime returned from Tokyo. We were extremely happy to have him back with us. Most every day, I drove with my Japanese escort to Seletar to check on the status of our anti-aircraft gun and new radar-detection equipment, FUMB26 TUNIS, which received on the lowest frequencies and attained ranges up to thirty-eight nautical miles. Finally on 25 September, with all our equipment and supplies on board, we sailed for Batavia (it reverted to

The "Tiger," an officers' club in Singapore owned by the Chinese manufacturer of cure-all Tiger Balm.

Mrs. Kadowaki, Japanese manager of the Tiger.

A Eurasian dance girl who performed at the Tiger.

its Indonesian name, Djakarta, after the war). Our parting with the other U-boats, their officers and men, and the base personnel was cordial. Would we ever see each other again?

The military situation in Europe looked bleaker than ever. The enemy had closed in on Aachen, and paratroopers had landed near Eidhofen. A long line of Allied forces now moved steadily toward the German border.

After a rainy passage through the Banka Strait we docked at Tandjoeng Priok, about eight miles from the port of Batavia. We were warmly welcomed and housed in quarters managed by two Dutch ladies.

Captain Kandler, the base commander, had arranged a gala dinner for the *U-862* and our crew. Some twenty *djongos* (the Malay name for servants), dressed in colorful native costume, served us various dishes on silver trays. We learned how to cover our plates with fine, loose rice, build a crater in the center, fill it to the brim with spicy gravies, meats, chicken, and nuts, then mix it all with a spoon. What a delight!

The greater part of the crew of the *U-181* poses in front of living quarters at Pasir Panjang, Singapore. In the center is Captain Freiwald.

Since everything was cheap in town, and there was an abundance of merchandise in both the local and the black market, we made a lot of purchases that might bring a fortune back home. All these items were wrapped in thin rubber sheets for preservation. We figured the rubber could later serve as soles for shoes. Ah yes, we had some great ideas!

Suddenly, Freiwald was called to Batavia. The day before, 5 October, the *U-168* had sailed from there to Soerabaja to be rigged for an operation with the *U-537* and *U-862* around Australia. The *U-168* had been in Batavia for extended repair and the crew had made many intimate friends with natives and Eurasians. Shortly before their departure, kept as secret as possible, one of the men had led an Indonesian couple sightseeing through the U-boat without telling the commandant or the officers. About a hundred miles from Soerabaja, and nearly off Samarang on the morning of the sixth, the U-boat was torpedoed by the Dutch submarine *Zwaardvisch*. Twenty-eight men escaped the boat, which settled on the bottom, about 150 feet below. The men were taken aboard the submarine and supplied with seawater soap to wash off the oil that had covered them during their swim to the *Zwaardvisch*. They were given fresh clothes, coffee, and cigarettes.

Lieutenant Commander van Goosens, captain of the *Zwaardvisch*, called in two coastal sailing boats to carry twenty-three of the men ashore at Java. Commandant Pich, his chief engineer, the second watch officer, the U-boat's doctor, and a seaman remained on board the Dutch sub and were taken to Fremantle near Perth, Australia. The Dutchmen were surprisingly well informed about the movements of the German U-boat. They even knew the names of some of the girls who had entertained the crewmen of the boat. There was no doubt that the *U-168* was the victim of spying.[38]

Every day we watched Japanese soldiers attack straw dummies with bayonets while they yelled with hoarse, high-pitched voices.

Soon we were back in the work, sweat, and dust of Batavia, preparing our boat in Tandjoeng Priok for her big trip home. A

Captain Freiwald with his officers at the base in Singapore. *From left to right:* Second Watch Officer Giese; Engineer Lieutenant Hille; Captain Freiwald; Dr. Klaus Buchholz; Third Watch Officer Lieutenant Limbach; First Watch Officer Lieutenant Düring.

thousand small things still had to be done. I was glad that I had my artillery and the radar-detecting gear, completely updated according to the latest reports from the Atlantic front. We had hardly thought it possible that the enemy would work on such short frequencies. We had to find out which devices could detect these frequencies if we wanted to survive the hazardous voyage home, especially in a U-boat that had not been rigged with a *Schnorchel* (breathing pipe that made it possible for U-boats to run their diesel engines while submerged).

Although we had pleaded with the Japanese military officers not to have farewell festivities, which might tip the enemy off about our forthcoming departure, there were parties and dinners and even a champagne breakfast. On board, all was ready to go by 19 October. We left the crew in their quarters ashore and only a watch of a few men on board. In the afternoon, a truck drove around town advertising some of our crew's best boxers and inviting the people of Batavia to attend a big boxing match the next night. Around town there were additional displays announcing the event. The newspaper picked up on the boxing match and ran some quickly placed ads.

No sooner had darkness fallen on the town than a closed truck and some cars rushed from the crew's quarters to the pier in Tandjoeng Priok. A half an hour later the *U-181* slipped secretly out of the harbor basin. A hard wind met us from the sea. We did not look back at Batavia. We were moving forward at full speed with our watch on full alert, pressing to cover the distance to the Sunda straits before light.

Twenty-Two

Homeward Bound

. . . .

When the first morning rays appeared in the sky towards Bali, we submerged. During my watch at the depth rudders, I had time to look around and get adjusted to life on board again. Wherever my eye passed it rested on cargo, ship's equipment, provisions, and men. Gone were the days of romance and carefree parties, the land with its soft and sweet fragrance. We were back at war. Everything was primitive, filthy, and rough. What a contrast!

I felt forlorn and worn out. That might have been from overexerting myself during those last days ashore. Whatever the cause, I grew quiet and slept during much of my spare time.

During the day we ran submerged and at night surfaced. The sea was as rough and temperamental as we. Apparently the enemy did not detect us in the Sundra straits, because we reached the open sea unscathed. Gradually, very gradually, we regained our good humor. We were homeward bound!

We calculated that our trip would take about 120 days or so if we could pass the Denmark straits without incident. We only hoped that our troops would hold out in Norway. It would be difficult: The Russians were trying to break through our northern frontier at Kirkenes, the British were deep in Holland at s'-Hertogenbosch, the Americans were near the Rhine at Aachen and at the River Po in Italy. Prospects looked pretty gloomy.

In the afternoon of 1 November we sighted a smoke cloud on the horizon and closed in on a large tanker of about 10,000 tons. After zigzagging a few times with the ship, we found that she was doing about eighteen knots. "It'll be a hard job, but let's give it a try, Hille [the chief engineer]. Give us all best possible speed," said Freiwald. The commandant left the bridge only to go down to the control room

Third Watch Officer Lieutenant Johannes Limbach, who served under Lüth as navigator, has received the Knight's Cross in Singapore.

and check the enemy's movements, plotted by Watch Officer Limbach. All men remained on battle stations.

The pursuit was tedious and incredibly long. After some thirty hours, with just one hour left between sunset and moonrise, we had managed to get into the necessary forward position. The loudspeakers called out, "Boat attacks!" The tanker had just made a new change of course, exactly as we had calculated, when we approached her out of the dark sector showing only our narrow silhouette.

Our first torpedo was launched. We had come very close to our prey, so close that our glasses could no longer cover the entire tanker. We thought that we could see the watch officer walking up and down on her bridge. There was a muffled explosion and the tanker stopped dead in the water. Apparently we had scored a hit in the ship's engine room.

We stopped for a while, watching the tanker to see if her crew would man their guns. Then we circled her a few times to determine whether our single torpedo strike had done the job. If so, the ship would soon start to settle in the water. But she wasn't.

"Why not puncture her with our antiaircraft guns?" I suggested to Freiwald, because I knew that we had to save our last torpedo for other eventual incidents. "No," he responded. "That would certainly bring her crew to her guns, endanger us, and delay our mission. We have no chance with our artillery against theirs."

Thirty minutes after the first torpedo, we fired our second and last one and scored a hit amidships. Now there was action on board. To our surprise, however, there was no chaos. The lifeboats had not been damaged by the first torpedo aft, and now they all went into the water in orderly fashion. Through the darkness we saw many boats drifting, their lights moving up and down in the moderate sea.

Slowly we approached them. On orders from the commandant, I descended to the deck and called out: "If you have transmitters, do not use them immediately. Do you have enough provisions and water in the boats?" The men were extremely disciplined. They answered that everything was okay and that the name of their ship was the *Fort Lee*.[39] We thought she was a British naval supply vessel, but found out much later that she was a U.S. tanker of 10,000 gross tons. Tragically, only one lifeboat from the *Fort Lee* was to find its way to the coast of Timor, carrying two desperately ill men. One of the two survived. We learned later that search parties had been sent out, but because

The *U-181* in the southern Indian Ocean en route to Germany. I have the gunnery men on my watch check the 3.7-millimeter antiaircraft gun on the lower "Wintergarten." The man on the left is the gunnery mechanic.

the crew had given erroneous positions the other boats could not be found.

Before resuming our course down to the Cape of Good Hope, we departed on a deceptive northerly course, passing the dying ship exactly thirty-five minutes after the second torpedo had found its mark. On my evening watch on 3 November we detected another large freighter of about 7,000 gross tons heading on a course for Australia. We closed in, but with only antiaircraft guns as offensive weapons we decided an attack was not worth the risk and resumed course.

On the eighth, at 0000 Greenwich time, my watch congratulated me on my thirtieth birthday. At noon Captain Freiwald and the others joined in shaking my hand. Before lunch we each had a glass of champagne. The tablecloth, a gray-white bedsheet, was laid with flowers that our "sparks" had made of paper and scented with perfume. On my noon watch we had an exercise alarm dive, and while the boat ran submerged I made my tour of congratulations through all quarters with a bottle of Genever and sherry. The commandant

Dreaming of home in the Indian Ocean as the *U-181* attempts to return to Germany with much-needed cargo. We will soon be turning back when the babbitt of the main bearings gives way.

On watch with Chief Petty Officer Hannes Fröhlich (*right*), an extremely reliable seaman who served under Lüth.

made a speech over the loudspeaker: "Captain Freiwald, commandant of the famous U-boat *U-181*, requests that all crewmen congrat-
ulate Lieutenant Giese on his birthday. . . ." The boat rang with
cheers. I was given presents of fruits and cake. After dinner, we had
another sip of Genever and some card games, after which Freiwald
remarked, "Bad luck with cards, good luck with women in the new
year of your life, Ottokar!" Ottokar was my nautical academy nick-
name.

The quiet weather gave way to a storm from the west that brought
nothing but rain and low temperatures. The radio reports from the
front sounded optimistic, idiotically so. In reality, the situation
seemed desperate. We asked ourselves if we would reach home in
time for our valuable cargo to be useful.

There was a cockroach plague on board. No matter how many
years at sea, I could not get used to these creatures. We found them in
most of our provisions, which upon close inspection appeared to be
the oldest goods, from Batavia. The lube oil in the motors was getting
dirtier; we began to wonder if the diesels would hold out on the long
trip home. The engineer reported that the metal of the main bearings

was completely worn out. If the same level of wear continued for the next fourteen days, we would have to return to Batavia.

A day's run was now only about ninety miles because the boat was constantly being overrun by heavy seas. As she was thrown about in the swirling water, her interior was full of moving debris. Every forty to fifty hours, a new low-pressure center passed over the boat and we had to dive until a high-pressure center was reestablished. This further slowed our progress to about thirty miles a day. We also began to fight a strong countercurrent. There was still thirteen thousand miles to go. . .

On 20 November, we ran surfaced for three hours to charge the batteries in gale force winds of eleven, a sea force of ten, and a house-high swell from the port side nearly as bad as the swells around Cape Horn. On the lower balcony, my antiaircraft gun tore loose and was swinging in the gusting winds. Reluctantly, I sent the gunnery mechanic aft while I held the line around his chest. We had only a few seconds between the breakers to lash the gun tight. It was backbreaking work.

That day there was cherry brandy for the brave sea watch, because the Doc had his birthday and appeared on the bridge in spite of the roar of the elements. The temperature hovered around 4°C. Clouds chased by, shredded. There was not a second that the bridge was not whipped by biting, salty foam.

On 26 November, the boat at 43.5°S, 35.5°E, our chief engineer reported that the slackness in the main bearings was increasing rapidly. He could not guarantee further safe operation of the engines. The bearings appeared completely worn out, and the shafts were running on almost-bare metal. Oil pressure was at its lowest level. There was still 10,000 miles to go. How could we manage to withstand the hazards of the Atlantic and the Polar Sea?

There was only one bitter solution if we wished to save the boat and crew from falling into the hands of the enemy. We had to return to Batavia. We informed the BdU by short signal of our state and intention. We calculated that we would be back in Batavia around 25 December, a Christmas boat. We could return to the base provisions officer all of his rotten fruit preserves, many jars of which we had already thrown overboard.

The weather was still rough, heavy seas rolling over the boat from the rear. The safety belt of one of my seamen broke and he hung over the bulwark of the bridge, half drowned, before we could pull him back to safety at the last minute. Our eyes burned, our skin was raw and cracked, infections and carbuncles developed where our beards and the woolen necks of our heavy pullovers rubbed our throats. The port coupling began to give us serious trouble and we had to take it down. There being no repair parts on board, the port diesel was put out of action. The starboard diesel was fairly rattling away, and we had to save it for the dangerous night marches through the Sundra straits. We were forced to run now on diesel-electric power.

On the night of 17 December we were ordered to supply the *U-843* with our surplus fuel. She was about three hundred miles east of our position, near the Cocos islands. We tried in vain to give our position via short signal to the BdU. At nightfall we were in the rendezvous area. The *U-843* was nowhere to be seen. We spent the entire night running up and down on the surface, a risky matter, especially as we had been warned to be on the alert for enemy carrier planes.

At the beginning of my midnight watch, the other U-boat suddenly appeared alongside us. She had actually dived and located us by hydrophone. We tried to make contact with our hoses but failed because of the darkness and a high swell. After endless maneuvers, we made the transfer with the boats running a parallel course in high swells. Our men did their utmost to supply the *U-843* with as much fuel as possible, as otherwise she would be compelled to fuel from a front-line U-boat in the North Atlantic. On Christmas Eve we had completed our job, and with three "Hip-hip-hurrahs!" we sent the *U-843* off on her long journey home.

I should mention that *U-843* and her commandant, "Bully" Herwartz, reached Norway after a 16,000 mile trip on 2 April 1945, one of the few returning transport U-boats to make it back to home waters. However, while he was en route to Kiel and passing through the Kattegat, his boat was attacked by a British *Mosquito* bomber. Seriously damaged, she sunk, taking most of her crew down with her.

On course again after leaving the *U-843*, we began to think of Christmas at home with our loved ones. Soft carols came out of the loudspeakers in the boat and we drank our half bottle of beer. We switched on the fourth light of the advent wreath, made of toilet paper painted green, and silently pressed hands, then wished each other a merry Christmas.

For the next few days we ran on the surface to put some distance between ourselves and the refueling area. At dusk on the twenty-seventh we sighted a distant group of carrier planes and sounded the alarm. Although we continued on undetected, we were nervous, being uncertain about the enemy situation around us. Our commandant, down with diptheria for a week and a half, was suffering badly. He did manage to crawl out of his bunk and wish everyone a happy New Year over the loudspeakers.

On 3 January 1945, we received orders to proceed through the Sunda straits as far as Babi Island, where an Arado aircraft would pick us up and accompany us to Batavia. Message after message arrived warning us about enemy submarines in the straits. We felt certain that the enemy had intercepted our message reporting our arrival time at Babi.

As we proceeded toward our destination all men not needed on duty stayed on deck in their lifejackets. Aware of the various U-boats that had been attacked and sunk in the area, we remained on full alert. Later, we submerged and found ourselves fighting a terrific countercurrent. When we surfaced at 2200 on the fifth, we had great difficulty starting our diesel engine. Mountains and the shadows of many islands surrounded us, while flashes and thunder filled the sky. Where was the enemy hiding? We had not slept or eaten for three days.

Shortly after midnight we reached Babi Island and submerged, remaining under water until morning. Then we surfaced and exchanged recognition signals with the Arados. The boat proceeded submerged to Batavia. Around noon on the sixth we arrived at the pier in Tandjoeng Priok, which had been nearly destroyed by an ammunition transport that had exploded. Four other U-boats were tied up along the pier. The quarters were crowded but our comrades and friends were glad that *U-181* had returned safely.

Six days later orders came to proceed to Penang. It was extremely hot in the Banka Strait. Everyone remained on deck because of the ever-present danger of enemy submarine attack. Japanese guard vessels constantly signaled us. We didn't understand a single word of their messages so we just responded with affirmative signals. Off Lingga Island we received a message that the Japanese were expecting a large enemy air attack on Singapore. We submerged and rested on the bottom for the rest of the day, until the attack was over. Later we tied up at the pier in Singapore during a driving rain storm.

As it turned out, we couldn't proceed to Penang because the port had been fiercely attacked by British bombers and mines had been laid in the areas of approach. The senior German naval officer in Sin-

The *Bogota* arriving in Singapore from Central America, where she was stationed before the war as a tender for North German Lloyd.

gapore suggested that we get our boat ready and quickly back to sea, since the local situation might soon deteriorate.

Towards the end of January we finally celebrated our crossing of the equator. In this time-honored international ritual of initiation, anyone aboard ship who is "passing the line" for the first time has to be cleansed of the dirt from the other hemisphere. The ceremony is often wild, and always funny. We had about twenty victims for baptism, men who had crossed the line dirty and greasy, and with souls as dark as night. Never again could they appear on the high seas in this condition, not before the eyes of the omnipotent god Neptune and his fair lady Thetis.

The previous day, Admiral Triton and his colorful suite had heralded the arrival of Neptune and Thetis in eloquent and bombastic words, announcing the names of the black sheep soon to be washed clean. He had already hinted in a few careful remarks what those delinquents would have to expect from the ceremony. I'm sure none of these poor devils closed an eye that night.

At noon, Neptune and his wife and an endless camarilla of traditional court attendants and staff marched into the base camp, a procession many would never forget. The satellites, of which I was one,

Captain Kurt Freiwald in tropical rig waiting to inspect the crew at the base in Singapore.

Captain Freiwald decorates Radio Petty Officer Michalski with the EK I (Iron Cross First Class). Michalski served under Lüth.

were all greasy, dirty hard cases and oldtimers who had attended many baptisms. We took great pleasure in jumping out of column to give all those dressed in snow-white uniforms great big bear hugs.

The victims were then herded to the wooden pier on the beach of the camp, where, shivering, they listened to the barbarous speeches of the admiral, the priest, the astronomer, and finally Neptune. These were followed by a few high-pitched words from Thetis, who threw hand kisses all around, much to the disgust of her jealous husband.

The medical attendant, a nurse with blond hair made from rope strands and with "handsome" breasts, checked each victim and found something wrong with his health. As medicine she prescribed a concoction of castor oil, quinine powder, vomiting powder, oil, and flour, all baked together and forced down the throats of the victims with soap water.

With popping eyes, the victims had to crawl to Neptune and kiss his soot- and grease-covered leather boots before passing through a windbag into which powerful water jetted from both sides. The windbag led directly into the sea, where other satellites were waiting

A baptism is conducted at our base in Singapore for those crossing the line for the first time. Here, Neptune's Admiral Triton greets Captain Freiwald, who pleads for the life of those about to endure the ritual.

waist-deep in water. I was told later that cries for help could be heard miles away, especially from Doc.

That evening the Jungle Club saw all the red-eyed but exuberant men and officers celebrating the events of the day. Badges were distributed to the cheers of the men, and this wireless transmission from Neptune was addressed to the commandant of the *U-181*:

"My son, when my honorable wife Thetis could not detect your salty second watch officer among the assembled soldiers, she was very sad. Since he passed the line for the first time many, many years ago, I could hardly stop my wife Thetis from eloping with the then-coquettish young sailor. But then we received your cable about the names of the staff members of my suite. My wife Thetis nearly fell from her throne when she read the name Otto Giese. As a departure present I want to dedicate a special badge for him, because the crew has told me that he has been the sweetest-smelling man on board [I used an abundance of eau de cologne to keep my bearded face and body from itching]. Although he has tried several times and in many ports to break the hearts of fair ladies, and although he has tried to weave into his otherwise black hair distinguishing white strands, we will render him the badge of the 'Order of Man's Beauty' for his experiments with U-boat colognes."

Whereupon I had to step on a table raised high by strong sailors, notably those who had been among the victims of the baptism ceremony. I had to cling to the table like a monkey not to fall. U-boatmen, rough in manners, rough in battle, but comrades through and through.

We worked diligently to put everything in order aboard our boat and thereby hasten her return to sea. Our chief engineer and his staff built a primitive snorkel device from vague plans received from our naval attaché staff in Tokyo. Meanwhile waves of attacking planes would often interrupt us. We watched with awe as eighty to a hundred B-29 bombers droned overhead and attacked Keppel Harbor, Seletar, and Singapore. We also heard that Penang and Palembang had suffered attacks almost daily, and that heavy enemy naval forces had left Australia. This raised a state of alarm around Java and Sumatra. The Allies were gradually closing in.

News bulletins from the European front were crushing. In the east, the Russians had taken the towns of Gotenhafen and Danzig. To the west, Allied forces had crossed the Rhine and pushed from their bridgehead at Remagen to Giessen. German naval headquar-

The *U-181* in dry dock at Singapore for hull cleaning and engine repair. A snorkel will be built for our mid-May attempt to return home with cargo.

Without a snorkel, a transit through the Atlantic and the northern approaches to Norway would be impossible. Based on plans sent from Germany, and with the help of the Japanese shipyard and our able engineer Lieutenant Dieter Hille, we have constructed one.

ters reported that shipbuilding had to be curtailed and that in autumn 1944, 100,000 naval soldiers had been assigned ground-fighting duties.

We were still going strong, working closely with our Italian allies, former U-boat crewmembers who were helping us repair our boat. On 20 April, our entire crew celebrated Hitler's birthday with a special dinner at the base camp. That same week we completed construction of our makeshift snorkel. The engineers were proud of their work. We all wondered if the fast-closing war would allow us to make the long journey home safely. The reports and messages from inside Germany were anything but encouraging. The Russians were attacking Berlin, and British and American forces were crashing down on the German armies from the west. When would they meet and what would the outcome be? The ensuing and dramatic days ahead would answer our questions.

Four days later, the Russians had overrun Berlin's defenses and pushed from the northeast into the smoldering city. Koinew's and Chukow's armies had closed the ring around the outskirts of Berlin, and Hitler had taken over the command of German troops. We learned a few days later that the British had intensified the siege of my home town, Bremen, and that only a small group of defenders were holding out northeast of the town. Hamburg was completely surrounded. We could not get war news by short-wave radio and had to rely on what was reported in the Japanese newspaper *Shonan Shimbun*.

On board, we were working day and night. We heard that American troops had landed at Morobay and made attacks on the east coast of Borneo. All Japanese vessels had evacuated Balikpapan. On 29 April, again able to receive news via short wave, we learned that our troops at the River Elbe had been withdrawn from their positions and thrown into the battle for Berlin.

Then an officers meeting was called in "Chis" (chief officer, southeast) headquarters. We heard rumors that Hitler was surrounded in Berlin and that Himmler had made an offer of surrender to the Allies. It was decided that we would remain allies with the Japanese even if we had to go on fighting in the southeast area. There was some disagreement among the officers on this point.

The following day, 30 April, all leaves from the base camp were stopped and security was intensified around it. That evening we heard that rumors of peace offers had been denied by Prime Minister

Churchill and President Truman. We had planned for a trial trip on 10 May, a departure from Singapore for Batavia on the twentieth, and a cruise homeward starting on 1 June. This was confirmed by the BdU. All other U-boats in the southeast area were ordered to remain in their operational areas.

In the early morning hours of 3 May, Captain Freiwald called the crew together and spoke kind words about them. He then informed us that the Führer was dead. We were deeply shaken. In the afternoon all U-boat crews and base personnel assembled in camp no. 2. The Führer's picture was displayed, framed with green leaf and black silk garlands. Soldiers stood at attention when the Japanese commander, Lieutenant General Tomoyuki Yamashita, who had taken Singapore and was known as the Tiger of Malaya, and many other high-ranking Japanese officers arrived. They bowed deeply before the Führer's picture, as many of them had once met him personally in Berlin. Wreaths were placed in front of the picture and our chief in the southeast, Captain Dommes, made a solemn speech. In final tribute, our soldiers fired salutes over the blue waters of the beach at Pasir Panjang.

The following day we received an open message on U-boat frequency from Admiral of the Fleet Dönitz, now commanding officer of the German forces:

> The Führer is dead. True to his great idea to save the people of Europe from communism, he sacrificed his life. In proud reverence we lower the flags before him. The Führer has ordered me to be his successor and head of the state and highest commanding officer of the forces. I will follow this order with ambition, to continue the fight against communism until the hundreds of thousands of families of the German eastern area have been saved from slavery or annihilation. I have to continue fighting the British and Americans so long as they hinder me in carrying on the fight against Bolshevism. The situation asks from you, who are longing now for the termination of the war, further unconditional sacrifices. I demand discipline and obedience. Only by executing my orders without reservation will chaos be avoided. He, who at this moment withdraws from his duty and by this brings death and slavery to German women and children, is a coward and traitor. Your oath to the Führer passes over to me. The life of our people is at stake![40]

I was not politically inclined, and neither were the men with whom I served in U-boats and aboard the *Anneliese Essberger*. For those of us fighting the sea war in the far corners of the world, the Führer and the politics of the party were remote. Captain Freiwald and Admiral Dönitz had much more immediate bearing on our lives. But Hitler had still been Germany's Führer, and our supreme commander. Under oath, we had pledged our loyalty to him, to our country, and to our flag.

Twenty-Three

Surrender and Survival

． ． ． ． ． ． ． ． ． ． ． ． ． ． ． ． ． ． ． ．

The code word *Lübeck* meant that, according to an early agreement between Germany and Japan, if one nation lost and the other continued fighting, the former would render its war material to the latter. The *U-181* would be turned over to the Japanese should Germany surrender to the Allies. The air was loaded with electricity. The question foremost in our minds was, would we be able to sail for Germany before the code word was executed? Our anxiety was answered on 8 May when Admiral von Friedeburg, successor to Dönitz, surrendered all naval ports and their troops in northwest Germany, our country's last stronghold. *Lübeck* was to be followed by the code word *Regenbogen*. All U-boats at sea were to set a black flag and radio their position in the open, awaiting contact by Allied naval forces.

On 9 May 1945 the last report came from the German High Command:

> From midnight, on all fronts, a ceasefire has been in force. By command of Admiral Dönitz, the armed forces have given up the hopeless struggle. A heroic fight that has lasted nearly six years thus comes to an end. It has brought us resounding victories but also heavy defeats. Ultimately the German armed forces have succumbed to overwhelming superior strength.

> True to his oath, the German soldier has served his country in a manner that will never be forgotten. The people have endured the heavy sacrifices and have supported the armed forces to the utmost of their ability and to the very end. On the unique achievements of our fighting men at the front and our people at home, history will later pass its just verdict. The enemy, too, cannot but pay tribute to the feats of our armed forces on land, at sea, and in the air. Every German soldier, sailor, and airman can therefore lay aside his arms with justifiable pride and turn to the task of ensuring the everlasting life of our nation.

At this moment the thoughts of the armed forces will turn to their comrades who lost their lives fighting our enemies. To show obedience, discipline, and absolute loyalty to our Fatherland, bleeding from innumerable wounds, is the sacred duty our dead impose on us.

Over the following days I spent many hours under the palms, looking out to sea, trying to analyze why Germans had made so many enemies over the decades, especially people of our own racial heritage. The differences probably started at the time of Otto the Great's Holy Roman Empire, the background for Hitler's ideology of the Third Reich and a united Europe, in which he envisioned Germany would play an important role. A German nation that could draw on its powerful resources to lead Europe in a direction beneficial to all . . .

But why, if Hitler and the National Socialist party had wanted that goal, did the last sentence of his will, signed in Berlin on 29 April 1945, include these words: "Above all, I oblige the leaders of the government and nation and the followers to the strict observation of the racial laws and to unmerciful resistance towards the world poisoner of all people, international Jewry"? What about the equal rights of all races and creeds to live in freedom and justice before God?

How had it been possible that the majority of our people, the "nation of thinkers and planners," could have followed Hitler and his doctrines so closely? Many believed that Hitler was the only politician next to Hindenburg who, after the Versailles Treaty and the depression of the 1930s, promised Germans something to hold onto, something to be proud of again, perhaps not Germans of all classes but the majority, the workers and the middle classes.

But what about the atrocities of the concentration camps? In fairness to our people, it must be said that only a small portion knew about the institution of the camps and the horrible crimes committed in them, committed against human beings with feelings, hearts, and souls. Not many Germans had heard of gas chambers before or during the war. The revelation of such atrocities stunned those of us in the U-boat arm.

To prevent sabotage and accidents, I boarded the boat in the early morning hours of 6 May while the crew stayed in base camp. Our few guards, unaware of the situation at home, reported to me that all was well and in order. They were probably surprised that the rest of the crew didn't arrive with me, but they remained silent. The German war flag was still flying briskly in the morning breeze, a mere piece of cloth now but to us still a symbol of pride and honor. These were the colors to which we had once sworn a holy oath—an oath, I thought, even the enemy would have to respect, regardless of what he might think of National Socialism or Hitler.

I squeezed myself through the conning tower hatch into the central room and called the watch around me. "Well, men, the situation is very grave at home. Within a few hours we will have to expect final orders from our commandant. I want you all to stand your guard as usual. As always, strict orders remain in effect that nobody may enter the boat. Whatever happens, you are not to lose your nerve, commit sabotage or rash acts." That said, I stepped into our small radio room, took our two code-key machines, and went and dropped them into the yellow waters of Singapore Harbor, followed by most of the code books. Later I destroyed the rest of the cipher material in the camp.

I now had time to look around the boat and the pier, where the last parts of the diesels were waiting to be picked up and put together. I sat down on the rail of the *Wintergarten* and reminisced about happier and more active days, days long gone that would never, never return, days of glory, pride, and beauty, days of freedom and adventure. How good those days had been, so full of danger!

Towards noon the commander of the Japanese fleet, Admiral Fukudome, and three other admirals and their staffs called on Captain Dommes and other German officers and informed them of the imminent internment of all German soldiers in the southeast area.[41] He spoke without denunciation or rancor. He praised in precise military words the deeds of our men, especially the U-boat force, and earnestly promised the reconquest of Germany by Japanese imperial forces. To this day I'm sure that he believed what he said, though at the time we only smiled at his words. It did, however, prove to us that he and his officers were true friends and felt deeply for their German allies.

Later, Captain Freiwald appeared on the boat. He came alone. His expression was serious. When we saluted he smiled faintly. I knew then that it would be only minutes before we lost our boat. I looked automatically at my wristwatch: 1600. At that moment two trucks filled with Japanese soldiers carrying rifles and fixed bayonets sped round the shed and stopped at our pier with squeaking brakes. Within seconds, they had formed a line with their guns at the ready.

Freiwald and I stood on our bridge as the Japanese captain, Maru-jama, boarded and climbed up beside us. He saluted and explained that the *U-181* was "taken." I called to our men to come up instantly, for one of them already had his hands on the levers of the air-exhaust traps. We saluted stiffly as the German flag was lowered. Without further words, we stepped into the waiting trucks, the stonefaced Japanese soldiers boarded the *U-181*, and off we went to our base camp.

We had to stay in our camps until further notice. However, the area was spacious and we had our clubs. Two days later, Captain Dommes called all officers into his house and read a message to us from Admiral Wenneker, the German naval attaché in Tokyo:[42]

> Comrades, fate has decided against us. After a heroic fight, Germany has surrendered to the superior forces of the enemy. The decision *Lübeck* means an uncertain fate for the crews of the East Asia U-boats. This decision, however, was made out of respect for our former ally. History will recognize *Lübeck* as an honorable act between allies. I am certain that the Japanese navy will appreciate our great sacrifices by her future attitude towards us. We must bear our lot as upright men and remain disciplined and dignified soldiers to prove to our homeland, our hosts, and the world that Germany can master a desperate situation. Germany cannot and will not die in spite of all. I thank you for your faith and salute you in the hope of meeting you again in our home country.[43]

We took up work again on our boats, the *U-181* and *U-862*, to make them ready for the Japanese crewmen being shipped in from Japan. One day I was asked by the new Japanese officers to instruct them in the use of our 3.7-cm antiaircraft gun. While they stood watching in meticulous white uniforms, I had my gunner's mechanic go through the actions required to operate the gun. He also explained the procedure for taking the weapon apart and reassembling it. There were many *zsaaa* and *no-ne* responses, and everyone seemed to understand.

"Okay, Röhling," I said, "slam in a magazine and show them how the shells enter the chamber." I went on to explain that this was performed automatically. Suddenly there was a short, metallic click and then a *boooooommmm!* I yelled, "Who in God's name turned the trigger?"

Japanese soldiers were lying flat on their bellies on the deck and the pier. Those who had stayed close to the gun, observing the instructions, were spotted and striped with grease and oil. One of them must have turned the handle of the trigger by mistake. It was a wonder that we had not exploded the barrel, since it had been firmly stuffed with seawater-resistant grease.

I looked in the direction the gun was pointed, where the shell had hit its mark: the garden of a villa owned by a rich Chinese. Thank God it had not landed in the center of town! I felt certain that thereafter the Japanese would treat my beloved gun with awe and care.

In late June 1945 the Germans and Japanese agreed that all former German U-boat crews and base personnel at Singapore and Penang be transferred to the small Malayan jungle village of Batu Pahat, located on a river flowing into the Malacca straits. The village had some three thousand inhabitants, Malayans, Chinese, and Indians, and some bungalows and a school in the European section, where the former managers of a vast rubber plantation lived. Otherwise the village was an impoverished settlement that stretched along the southeast side of the riverbank. The natives lived in houses made of corrugated iron, wood, and bamboo, built on stilts about three feet above firm clay soil.

Captain Freiwald was put in command of the camp while I was charged with managing the stores and provisions, a tiresome job. While our men lived in the spacious school, we officers were housed all over the area in single-standing bungalows. Not wanting to leave us unwatched, the Japanese assigned an officer and several men to the camp. We knew then that the breakdown of the Japanese imperial forces was only a matter of time. We heard rumors that Chinese guerrilla fighters under the command of British "jungle rats" were advancing southward from the mountains of Thailand. The Japanese had wisely left us our arms, some rifles, machine guns, and pistols. We felt safe in Batu Pahat, as if it was sort of a sanctuary, amidst all the uproar. We did not yet hear the thunder of guns far beyond the horizon.

Then, one day, early in the morning when vapor still hung over the jungle, we saw in the far distance a dark smoke cloud rising in the pink sky. Bandits or guerrillas must have raided a Malayan village. I called to my provisions corporal, "Come on, Friedemann, take your machete and let's get over there and see what's happened!" I threw my pistol on the seat of our Austin sportscar and off we roared over bumpy jungle roads and small, narrow lanes in the direction of the smoke.

The thick jungle opened onto cultivated fields on both sides of us. There, ahead, were the charred and smoldering remnants of a village. We approached the site cautiously, only to find that all the natives had disappeared. Perhaps they had escaped before the bandits arrived or had been taken prisoner. The situation didn't look good. I ordered Friedemann to turn around immediately and head back at full speed. When the jungle had closed in on us again, we saw a man beckoning to us. We stopped, and out of nowhere a crowd of grim-looking Malayans gathered around us.

Friedemann, who spoke fluent Malay, asked them what they wanted. Our machete, they answered. We asked why, and calmly they pointed out that they needed the weapon to cut the heads off of some Chinese prisoners. The Germans always kept their tools in excellent condition. I had Friedemann tell them that we were pleased with the compliment but would be much happier if they would let us pass, which with a broad grin, they finally did. The only weapons they carried were some pointed bamboo poles as spears and bows and arrows, the heads of which were probably poisoned. I remembered hearing that these guerrillas fought the Japanese with any weapon available. There were no holds barred in jungle warfare.

On 6 August 1945 we heard that the Allies had dropped an atomic bomb on Hiroshima and that a few days later the Russians had declared war on the Japanese. The pressure on our former allies was tremendous. Finally, on 10 August, the Japanese made an offer of capitulation.

The jungle around us had come to life. Silent columns were marching. Now and then we could hear sticks breaking and branches brushing against unseen forces. We would often hear muffled Chinese curse words. The so-called *Chunking* guerrillas advanced quickly through the northern Malacca province, forcing the Japanese to withdraw to Johore. Only a few police stations held out. Heavily armed guerrilla fighters appeared sporadically in Ayer Itam and our village. They usually came at night, thundering along the road in their trucks, their fixed bayonets glittering now and then in the bright moonlight. They paid little attention to us. All the same, we posted an armed guard nightly around our provisions shed.

At night the Japanese and Malayan police in the village barricaded themselves in defensive positions. During the day, they took over the

. . . .

village. While the Japanese remained relatively calm, the Malayan police played havoc in the streets. Reprisals were the order of the day. Hundreds of suspicious Chinese were rounded up and thrown in trucks, taken to the slippery banks of the river, and shot in the neck. Their bodies would topple into the brown clay waters and drift silently down to the sea.

The killing continued day after day until the situation reached a point where we felt something explosive would happen. The Chinese sent feelers out to Captain Freiwald asking what he would do if the guerrilla fighters attacked Batu Pahat to liquidate the police stations. Freiwald answered that if the guerrillas left German soldiers unharmed and our provisions untouched, the Germans would stay where they were and not use their arms. Otherwise, we would take all necessary action in self-defense.

The attack on Batu Pahat was set for 20 August at 2000. That night we set up officer's watches in the schoolhouse and kept in close touch with the other houses by having an officer ride around in one of our Austin cars. The guerrillas started their hit-and-run raids later that night. In the midst of this uproar, our last men arrived from Singapore in trucks during a tropical downpour. The guerrillas did not succeed in their mission, at least not while we were in Batu Pahat.

We got news about the last stores and provisions being transported from our base at Penang. They were on board a Japanese train that had traveled through fierce fighting as it made its way along the jungle-canopied railway that ran between Penang and Singapore. The cargo had been guarded by our last ten men to leave Penang. They were all unarmed. Only the first platform car and the last car had machine guns manned by Japanese soldiers. Our men had built up sacks and cases in the cars as a bulwark against bullets fired by partisans from the dense jungle. The train passed burning villages and train stations, derailed cars, and the bodies of many who had fallen in battle. Debris was scattered as far as the eye could see. The guerrillas heavily engaged the Japanese soldiers, who fought on, refusing to surrender.

The train had made it beyond Ipoh when the engine suddenly derailed on a sharp turn, causing the following cars to ram into each other with a shrieking crash. Our men managed to jump out of the train in time, but one died upon hitting the ground and four others were seriously wounded. The men took shelter behind some debris and waited until the chatter of machine gun and rifle fire calmed down. Carefully scanning the area, they noted that all of the Japanese soldiers had been killed.

They tended to their wounded from a first-aid kit and cremated the dead man, whose ashes were put into a tin box for transport back to Germany.

The next day a Japanese auxiliary hospital train passed through from the Burma front. It stopped, and some Japanese rendered medical help to our men, then cleared the track ahead and took our men with them as far as Labis, where another guerrilla attack thundered around them. Fortunately, the guerrillas were more interested in a nearby train station that harbored Japanese and Malayan auxiliary troops. Our men barricaded themselves in a small Malayan hut, where they were deliberately left unharmed.

Since the Japanese guards in our camps at Batu Pahat and in the village had more than enough to do fending off the partisans, we formed a heavily armed expedition force under Commander Timm (former commandant of the *U-862*) and tried to reach Labis. The group returned the following day empty-handed. They had stopped at a broad jungle river where a wooden bridge had been destroyed.

The following day another expedition was formed under the leadership of Lieutenant Commander Grütznacher and Doc Buchholz. By some miracle they were able to reach Labis some forty miles away, pick up our men, and return them to our camp after suffering countless hardships. Fortunately, they were not once attacked by guerrillas.

Towards the end of the month, we learned that we were to be returned to our former camps in Singapore. We held an officer's meeting, and the younger officers recommended that we ignore these Japanese orders, remain in Batu Pahat, and make contact with the irregular Chinese troops, as we were capable of protecting ourselves. Even the mayor of Batu Pahat had come and asked us to take over police powers in his village until British troops arrived. Captain Freiwald, accompanied by Mr. Ahrens, a German businessman residing in Malaya, and a soldier drove to Singapore to check out the situation for himself. Treated coldly by the Japanese, he soon returned. It appeared that the Japanese wanted to have all Axis forces under their control assembled in Singapore before the day of surrender.

Our trip back to Singapore was not without incident. While our men sat on top of the bulky cargo in trucks, generally having a good time, our Japanese escorts were quite jittery. At night they fired wildly into the jungle with their rifles and machine guns. It happened that they wounded some of their own men as the trucks drove around sharp bends. In the villages and towns that we passed we noticed large bands of irregular troops, picturesquely dressed and sometimes armed with no more than bamboo poles and sticks to which they had tied knives. For the first time we saw many flags in the streets, the Union Jack, the Stars and Stripes, the Soviet banner, and the Chungking flag, a very strange sight. Suddenly the world had become international again.

We found our former camps in bad shape. To transport more provisions, we had left our beds in Batu Pahat. Now we found only torn-up beds in camp no. 1, where the Japanese crews of our U-boats had lived. With the help of former Chinese and Malayan friends and some money, we were soon well established again. Thank goodness for money—we had quite a bit of it as a result of the care Commander Ehrhardt had taken when he stayed in Singapore.

The opium and other valuable goods that had been stocked up in the sheds of the Empire dock and originally intended for transport in our U-boats were sold, not for paper money, the infamous Japanese "banana" dollars, but for pure, shiny gold. Gold bars were hidden in dark, moist vaults underground. With our return they were retrieved and turned over to some trustworthy Chinese friends who opened a secret account for us. The money permitted us to give our men a sort of clandestine war pay and allowed them to buy provisions and clothing up to the very day we shipped to England. Freiwald, now leader and spokesman for the Germans from our former bases at Penang and Singapore, signed responsibility for this special account.

Shortly before our departure, a protocol was set up, which the Chinese signed and which I copied. It stated that this account would belong entirely to a future German government, and that our Chinese friends would get a specified indemnity for their faithful services. I folded my copy in aluminum paper from a pack of cigarettes and squeezed it into a tube of toothpaste, which I kept with me through the ensuing years in POW camps in England and then at home. One day in 1948 I was visited by Captain Freiwald in Bremen–St. Magnus. I handed the protocol to him. He in turn passed it on to the German government after the country's financial situation stabilized.

On Sunday, 2 September 1945, we read of the Japanese surrender on board the U.S. battleship *Missouri* in the last issue of the Japanese newspaper *Shonan Shimbun*. It was suddenly very calm in our camps. We realized that what would be a great celebration for the Allies

Our honor guard at ease, awaiting the command to fire salvos during a funeral for one of the civilians at our base in Singapore.

would be our darkest and saddest hour. Little hope remained, at least for the near future.

On 4 September we watched from the beaches as the first British warships appeared off Singapore. Among them was the heavy cruiser *Sussex*. They departed within a short while, probably to have minesweepers clear the entrance before the main British force with the battleship *Nelson* arrived. It was on this vessel that Japanese Admiral Uosumi signed the formal surrender of our former base at Penang.

The Japanese had tried hard to be conscientious allies, up to a certain point. I personally felt that they had been friendly to us as long as we were successful on the battlefield, at sea, and in the air. When the situation went from bad to worse at the fronts, we seemed to lose face with them. To sound out their mentality and their thinking was difficult. They were either smiling or stonefaced—no middle ground. The upper class, especially those who had some samurai blood, displayed their superiority through arrogance. I was acquainted with a lady of this class. One day when we had used the cable car to go to the

Rokko, a hill in Kobe, she refused to stay in line with the people at the ticket counter, just walked on ahead. Seeing that I was ill at ease, she turned to me and said, "This is my right!"

In general, I felt, the Japanese were not burdened with as many emotional feelings and problems as Westerners. I never saw anyone crying out of fear, sadness, happiness, anger, patriotism, pain. Perhaps they repressed these feelings. Life, their own and that of others, apparently was not valued as much as in the West, Hitler and his henchmen aside. I had had long discussions with a Japanese officer about these topics while sharing a bungalow at Batu Pahat. When Chinese guerrillas had advanced close to our small village, I did not detect any fear in the man. His heavy sword was always leaning against his bed ready for immediate use to defend himself, and his small *hara-kiri* knife was always available to kill himself in case he was taken prisoner. The Japanese were truly tough people.

Waves of Hurricane fighter planes frequently roared over Singapore. The Japanese did everything possible to maintain control of the general situation, not an easy task. British doctors parachuted into the city to start medical care for the thousands of Allied prisoners of war. Driving through the overcrowded streets, I saw prisoners dressed in the strangest uniforms. In the New World Amusement Park, I saw the first Australian soldiers to arrive in Singapore. They caused a great sensation and were received like heroes by the local population.

One evening there was heavy fighting among Indians, Malays, and Chinese. Hundreds were slaughtered. After this the Japanese seemed to lose control of the situation. The next day they ordered Germans to remain in their camps. Freiwald was conducted to Seletar to provide a list of our names to Japanese military authorities. The town was put under martial law, and despite the order to remain in camp we were left to our own devices, almost as if we didn't exist.

On 15 August Japan surrendered, and to prevent a bloodbath the emperor released his soldiers from any obligation to perform *hara-kiri*. However, about three hundred Japanese officers committed suicide in Singapore when General Itagaki told them he was surrendering by order of the emperor. They had a *saki* party, then blew themselves up with hand grenades. A whole platoon of Japanese soldiers followed suit.

In the meantime, British forces were landing without much fanfare. I took the car and frequently went into town with Friedemann. We passed colorfully uniformed Indian soldiers who cordially saluted us. They had not the slightest idea that we were German naval personnel. We passed "Aussies" and "Tommies" in splendid uniforms, and there were flags everywhere. Suddenly the streets were jammed with cars again, cars that had been scarce for so many years. Friedemann told me about how clever the Chinese had been: They took their vehicles apart when the Japanese conquered Singapore and distributed the parts among their kinfolks, waiting for this very moment to resurrect them.

Twenty-Four

Prisoner of War and Repatriation

· · · · · · · · · · · · · · · · · · · ·

Finally, on 7 September, our contingent was discovered by the commanding officer of the British military administration, who came to our camp along with several members of his staff. I interpreted their questions, asked in a formal, polite way. Were our higher-ranking officers flag officers? Were there any intelligence officers on our naval staff? Where did we get our provisions? How did we operate our base and organize our personnel? What was our connection with the Japanese navy? What documents, plans, reports did we possess? We answered all queries truthfully, without mentioning the gold. Then the following day, much to our disbelief, a British officer accompanied by a heavily armed military guard escorted Commander Ehrhardt to the city prison, claiming that he was a war criminal. Our own Ehrhardt, once executive officer on the grand raider *Michel* under the command of Captain von Ruckteschell, and afterwards chief officer of Malaya! We were at a loss concerning this sudden turn of events.

On 12 September 1945 Admiral Lord Louis Mountbatten, as supreme commander, Allied powers Southeast Asia, received nine high-ranking officers representing the Japanese forces in Singapore's municipal building to sign the instrument of surrender. It was a day of celebration for the town, which waited to see the best-known Japanese soldier in Southeast Asia, Lieutenant General Yamashita. However, at the time General Yamashita was a prisoner of war in the Philippines.[44]

German civilians were initially imprisoned at Adams Road and dealt with harshly. There seemed to have been an error in the interpretation of their activities and status. Quite haggard, they appeared one day and took lodging in one of our former clubs. Just as unexpectedly Ehrhardt, looking depressed, returned in the company of the director of the jail, a British army captain. He told us about the sufferings of the former inhabitants of the jail, victims of the Japanese, whose one-time director was himself behind bars there. The director left us with some cheery words. Ehrhardt, however, followed his departure with wary eyes. Months later, Ehrhardt was returned to jail on the orders of the prison director. He suffered terribly at the hands of this officer, and all because of an erroneous report by British intelligence mistakenly identifying Captain Ehrhardt as someone else. To the honor of the British, it must be said that a military inquiry regarding the actions of the officer was subsequently conducted with Ehrhardt as a witness. The matter was rectified and justice prevailed.

On 17 October orders arrived that all German soldiers were to be moved from Pasir Panjang to the Changi jail some twenty-two miles away, not in trucks but on foot. Freiwald protested strenuously to the officer in charge of our district. The officer replied that he had his orders and they would be complied with. He added, tapping his baton on our war medals, "I would appreciate it very much if these Nazi distinctions would disappear. Good morning, gentlemen!"

The sun was shining brightly, the air was sultry and humid as we waited to begin our long march. We had packed our few belongings and stood inside the camps, leisurely waiting for things to develop. Several jeeps and trucks suddenly appeared on the road to our camps. Stopping in a swirl of dust, the vehicles discharged Gurkha soldiers with rifles and fixed bayonets led by a young Scottish officer. "Damn, where are the Germans?" he yelled, running around, baton swinging like the wings of a windmill. Calmly, Captain Freiwald ordered the men to line up, and when both companies were formed he reported to the young officer that all men were present.

With Freiwald at the head of the column, 260 German seamen of former U-boats and raiders moved forward, slowly at first to save their strength for the last part of the march. We sang "Lili Marlene" and many other marching songs. The Pasir Panjang road was long, but soon we entered town. The formation closed up and the marching steps grew faster and echoed loudly from the walls of the houses. Natives surfaced from the sidestreets. They ran alongside the Gurkhas lined up along our flanks. At first the natives didn't know who the silently marching troops were, but soon a face here and there was recognized and friends called out in jubilation. Soon a crowd had gathered around the column. The guards shoved them back with their gun butts. We were viewed with mixed reactions by passing Allied military personnel. Several British officers averted their eyes, others, Indian guards, saluted us until the column had passed. "Fine men," we thought. "Thank you!"

Soon we had passed the town and moved towards Changi Road. The Gurkhas who could not keep up our fast pace were relieved by Indian troops. Cameramen ordered to film our march for the news media came much too late, and what they did film was never presented to the public, for what reason I do not know. The sun had now reached its highest point and mercilessly burned down on us. Not an inch of our clothing was dry. Sweat dripped down our backs and legs and into our shoes. Blisters formed and broke on the soles of our feet. We attempted to sing, but by now our throats were dry and our voices cracked. Some of the younger men fainted and collapsed; they were afterwards picked up by trucks. Our Scottish officer had become quiet by now; he was looking tired. We didn't bear him any grudge. He had only followed orders.

Finally, Changi jail came into sight. It appeared to us like a huge old castle. We didn't know it then, but it was one of the most modern and best guarded jails in Southeast Asia. A young captain drove up to Captain Freiwald and informed him that a lieutenant colonel would meet our group at a cross-section of the road up ahead. However, when we arrived at the intersection there was no officer in sight, so we branched off to the right, hoping that we had made the proper turn. The Indian soldiers followed us to the rear. Suddenly we heard a jeep approaching from that direction. It was the Scottish officer, loudly cursing the Indian troops: "Stop, all of you, you've chosen the wrong way!" Weary beyond belief, we turned around and made our way along the gray jail walls to the huge dark iron doors. We straightened up, grim faced.

Freiwald ordered us to enter with pride in ourselves as courageous seamen. We mustered up a marching song and quickened our step. The walls were manned by British and Australian soldiers, and what we heard to our surprise and satisfaction was applause in rhythm to our marching. We could not have expected a warmer reception by soldiers who were once our bitter enemies. The huge doors closed behind us. Looking ahead, we detected a long row of stone bungalows. The Scottish officer halted us and said to Captain Freiwald, "That's where you and your men will stay from now on. Good night, gentlemen, have a good rest." With that, he smiled and left us.

Changi jail, on the island of Singapore, the notorious prison built like a fortress with high walls and numerous watch towers. The huts where we live can be seen next to the palm trees. A Chinese man protects himself from the blazing sun with an umbrella. For us, Changi is just one more way station en route home. Accordingly, we bear whatever happens to us rather stoically.

It was late in the afternoon and we had hoped to find some place to rest after our long march, but all the tiny rooms were bare and dirty. The stone blocks had formerly served as quarters for Malayan camp and jail guards and their families. Next to us were housed Australian soldiers who, knowing of our filthy lodgings and lack of running water, offered us tea and their week's ration of beer. We collapsed on the dirty cement floors and spent the night in fitful sleep, fighting off swarms of mosquitoes.

The next day we were visited by a British lieutenant colonel and some officers of the Eighth Indian Division. Since we hadn't eaten for the past twenty-four hours we were anxious about getting provisions to feed the men. The British officer wasn't particularly concerned about our plight. He let us know that we were prisoners and would be treated as such. He took us into the vaults of the main prison building and pointed to a heap of dirty rice in a far corner. That would last us for some time, he said. There was a small garden within the jail where some Japanese were digging. I asked the officer if we could forage in the garden for vegetables to eat with our rice. He gave his permission but went on to say that our request for tea would not be allowed. Water would be good enough for us.

It was perplexing to us, the variety of characters we met among the Allied soldiers. The British lieutenant colonel was hard and insensitive. Some would prove to be among the finest men I ever met. Most were tough as nails. Grudgingly, I came to admire them.

It became clear to me then and there that if we wanted to survive, we would have to cooperate with pride, be innovative, and keep our men busy and disciplined. We had a truck mobilized to pick up corned beef from our former camp. This was distributed to our men instead of the dirty rice. They worked on the jail's plumbing system and soon water ran out of each tap and shower. Using brushes and brooms made out of branches and shrubs, we cleaned debris out of the rooms and salvaged what could be used, including some light-bulbs.

Soon we received permission to retrieve our belongings and provisions from the camp in Pasir Panjang. The small gardens between the rows of barracks were cleaned and planted with shrubs and flowers from the fields around. And we built, much to the pride of our camp, a kitchen with a range and stoves made from old bricks and clay and whatever else we could find abandoned—a large rice bowl, iron rods, tin pipes, iron doors. Next to the kitchen we rammed logs into the clay ground and built tables and benches, and over the whole area we built a huge roof covered with palm leaves.

Unknown to the British, I made contact with our Chinese friends, who supplied us with fresh provisions and other necessary items. Often I drove secretly into town with them to buy pigs and poultry, which we raised within sight of the jail guards positioned along the high walls. There was no barbed wire around our camp, although there were times when the subject was brought up after one of our men, dressed in his best civilian clothes, would be caught in one of the local dance halls. We would usually offset any reprisals by holding a nightly roll call with a British officer present. What he didn't notice was that some of his paratroopers were in line substituting for some of our men, who were off in town.

The Germans at Changi build a kitchen and a mess room using old iron bars, clay, mud, wood from palm trees, and fronds for the roof. Here are the former cook of the *U-181* and his able and innovative helpers.

Our neighbors, the British Thirteenth Paratroop Brigade, left us and were sent to Indonesia to bolster British troops fighting indigenous forces following the surrender of the Japanese. A unique situation occurred when the British command in Java requested that 350 German seamen from our former bases in Batavia and Soerabaja be armed again and assist the British in their struggle with the Indonesians, especially in the area around Buitenzorg. It was reported to us that our soldiers fought under the command of their own officers, did extremely well, and distinguished themselves through bravery in the field, battling shoulder to shoulder with their British comrades. Many of us who remained behind tried our best to join our comrades but without success, since transportation was extremely limited. The German force was not withdrawn until reinforcements arrived from Malaya. They were later encamped under Dutch guards on the small island of Onrost off Batavia, which had the dubious distinction of being named Jail Island.[45]

The cooks, having prepared chow in our primitive open-air kitchen, are serving up rice-based food from large containers. The "mess boys" will bring the food in all sorts of containers to the tables in the mess hall. On this particular day, Commander Heinrich Timm (*second from right*), former commandant of the *U-862*, is performing the job of mess boy.

After we were comfortably installed in our camp at Changi, the British began to request working details, which we were happy to provide since it was the only real and honest way to preserve relative freedom. We soon became the "masters" of the jail electrical system and were readily called upon to remedy outages. If we found our men in some sort of trouble we might cause an outage on our own to negotiate a cancellation of the punishment. Negotiations, conducted in pitch dark, usually lasted but a few minutes.

The British were very rough with the Japanese war criminals in Changi jail, probably as rough as the Allies were with ours at Spandau. Daily truckloads of them arrived, former staff officers, *Kampetai* (secret police), police, and guards from concentration camps. The men were hollow-eyed, emaciated, and shrunken. Still they tried to walk and bear themselves upright. They were put in small cells with concrete beds and toilet bowls in the ground. It was a pitiful sight, and whenever we needed assistance in the garden we would ask for these men, thus helping them in a small way to bear their plight.

On my daily reports to the director's office, I passed a window that looked directly down on the inner yard. A large rectangular platform with three traps painted with white circles had been erected, and on it was a beam structure with three ropes and nooses hanging down. Usually I avoided the jail when hangings were taking place, but one day I was called to the office and had to wait. It was in the morning, and there were many people gathered around the gallows, men and women, something that surprised me. From the passages of the opposite building I heard hoarse calls of *Banzai! Banzai!* again and again as the doomed were led into the courtyard, now steaming in the hot sun.

I watched the guards on the turrets, and all were looking down at the terrible scene. The three Japanese had their hands tied behind their backs. Large numbers had been painted on their oversized clothing. Without hesitation the victims were led up the steps to the platform and lined up. Hoods were slipped over their heads and the nooses followed. The hangman stepped back and muffled cries of *Banzai!* could still be heard from behind the hoods. I wanted to cover my ears, but there were other men standing around me, Gurkhas and British soldiers. A single harsh command rang out, instantly followed by the dull thuds of the trapdoors banging against the inner walls of the platform. The calls stopped and the ropes started to swing and suddenly all was deadly calm. I had to sit down, for my legs had become weak. It had taken no more than two and a half minutes for the Japanese to step out of their cell and die.

When the jail director came back, I mentioned my surprise at seeing women attending this macabre drama. He explained that they had been nurses on the Adaman islands and, after falling into the hands of the Japanese, suffered unmentionable atrocities.

Finally we received the news that all Germans, soldiers and civilians, would be shipped back to England on 26 June 1946 on a passenger liner. Before leaving I passed one last time through the plantations, gardens, and native huts to our tropical beach. I slowly scanned the sand, the azure water, the gray-green palms, and the blue sky with its sailing clouds as my thoughts slipped back to all those times in Malaya and Java. Another chapter of my life had come to an end, a chapter dictated by the necessities of war. A new life would have to be started now under entirely different conditions. Slowly I walked back into camp. England, and eventual repatriation to Germany, were deep in my thoughts.

We soon checked on board the old liner *Empress of Australia*, where we were quartered in the forward sections of the ship. En route to England, we spent the days sitting on deck talking about our past adventures and what might lay ahead. While passing through the Suez Canal we watched some deeply tanned Germans, former members of General Rommel's Afrika Corps, laboring on the banks. We called down and threw them some cigarette packages. When they heard that we were en route from Singapore they were surprised that there had been German soldiers farther east than they. Finally, the Brits told us to step back from the railings.

Upon our arrival at Liverpool in July 1946, we were taken to camp no. 23 in Sudbury, Rugby. We marched through the wide gates in close formation with officers in the vanguard. Our marching song brought cheers from the inmates; they clapped their hands in time with our steps. A month or so later we were transferred to Camp Crew Hall, in Cheshire, where we were quartered in Nissen huts. The food was scarce and we suffered from boredom. However, I found a way out by working on a farm, the Fox Farm. I enjoyed working in the fields resetting bundles of stacked corn to prevent mildew, driving the tractor or horse-drawn wagons, repairing farm tools, and attending to the cows, horses, pigs, and poultry. I drank gallons of good coffee and milk and, above all, enjoyed being with the lovable Fox family, who wanted me to stay with them permanently.

Then we were suddenly moved to Camp Abergavenny in Wales. Winter had gradually replaced the colorful fall days and we shivered around a small stove in our drafty hut. The daily food was held at a minimum of about 800 calories per man. We were always hungry. To supplement our meager rations, we secretly picked up acorns on our daily walks and roasted them on our stove. Unfortunately, our stomachs took exception to this menu and we spent many nights suffering from severe cramps. The guards in the high wooden towers around the camp were Polish soldiers who continually displayed their dislike for Germans.

In February 1947 we were shifted again, this time to camp no. 18 in Featherstone Park, Newcastle upon Tyne. This camp was well run. It even had a university, a theater, concerts, colloquiums, speeches about interesting topics, and trips to Durham University. I took courses in history and philosophy at the camp university. In the course of my studies I came across a book written by the British historian Trevor Roper relating a story about a letter written by Albert Speer. In it he pleaded with Hitler to mitigate the suffering of the German people. I cannot recall the exact words of Hitler's answer. In essence, he wrote that the German people had not followed his reforms, understood his doctrine, or fulfilled his expectations and therefore did not deserve a better fate. If I had any feelings left for this man, they were killed at that moment. Since that time many years ago I have refused to read any books or articles or watch any movies or television documentaries about this villain.

I admired Churchill as a leader and statesman. I studied his writings in depth and gave some lectures. During my spare time I worked in the kitchen as a dishwasher, mainly to improve the quality of my meals.

It so happened that my status was upgraded, and I was cleared for repatriation. After saying a hearty good-bye to Freiwald, the officers of our boat, and many old and new friends, I went to "through camp" no. 4 at Leicester. I was processed in a few days and then put aboard a Pullman car that rolled to Harwich, where I took the channel ferry to the mainland.

I passed the German border at Bentheim and there was transferred to a cattle car, which brought me to the general collecting camp at Munsterlager. Here the situation was depressing in every respect. The food was scarce and hardly eatable. While we awaited processing we had to clear mines outside the camp. I still have in my possession a small English Bible that was given to me by a friend at Featherstone Park. He was repatriated a short time after I left the park. I received a letter from his wife later informing me that he had lost his life at Munsterlager clearing mines. He had survived the bitter war in Russia and was killed just a few days before he was to arrive home.

On 24 August 1947, after a slow and difficult journey, our train finally rolled into the terminal at Bremen. German soldiers were running all over the place. Some were dressed in English battle dress, others in shabby German uniforms, gray, green, and khaki. Locomotive smoke hung in the air and escaped through the shattered glass of the high terminal ceiling. I carried my heavy bag down the dirty steps and through the crowded hall onto the wide square, where I waited for streetcar no. 3. A conductor helped me lift my bag through the narrow door of the car. A passenger remarked rather jokingly, "Hey, soldier, you must have come through the war pretty well."

We drove through the streets I remembered so well. There was nothing but ruins. I wondered how people had survived such devastation. My heart pounded as we came closer to where I was to disembark. I stepped down from the car and started to walk, presently arriving at the gate of the house my parents and sister had found as a temporary home. The house was partly damaged, most of its windows boarded up. My family was unaware that I had been repatriated.

I had to take a deep breath to control my emotions before ringing the bell. The next moments were the most intense and rewarding of my life. The "lost son" had finally come home.

Home at last!

Epilogue

· · · · · · · · · · · · · · · · · · · ·

The war had been over for almost two and a half years when I arrived in Bremen from the British POW camps. Our family lived in narrow quarters in the partially damaged home of a relative who had moved to his summer house on the Baltic Sea.

As soon as I was settled in, I enrolled in a course towards a master's license (unlimited seas) at the nautical academy. My British battle dress had to be discarded for a suit, which I bought with some scarce ration cards when reporting to the German authorities. A while later I happened to walk through some rain. The next morning my suit had shrunk by at least an inch.

Bremen lay in ruins, and life for its citizens was very hard. During the war some four thousand tons of bombs had been dropped on the city, destroying sixty-five thousand houses. Now and then my father went by train to farms outside of the city to trade our few carpets, which had escaped the war, for meat and sausage. I tried to make some money on the black market like so many of my friends. I soon found out that I was not the right man for this kind of business.

As soon as I had received my master's license from the city, I tried to find a job at the port. The stevedoring company Friedrich Tiemann was able to hire me as an inspector. I supervised the loading of ships with logs from German forests and material from demolished German factories. Laborers were always happy to unload vessels bringing flour, cornmeal, and other staples. Everybody had a so-called sample bag, which held about one pound of such food. As we finished work each day, the bag was pushed under our belts. The custom's officer at the gate usually just touched the bag, smiled, and waved us through.

In 1948, during the tension surrounding the Berlin blockade, my boss, his manager, and their families felt that it would be safer to relocate to South America. They asked me to find a seagoing fishing boat, supply it, and prepare it for sea under my command. However, when the tension eased I was asked instead to learn the fishing trade and fish with the boat in the waters of the outer Weser River. We had no problem filling our bins daily and selling our catch at the large fishing basins of Geestemünde. Occasionally I took my boat plowing up the Weser and supplied the entire company with fresh fish.

Soon my father asked me to help him with his bunker business. Standard Oil Company (ESSO) had offered him a tanker with which to supply tugs and motorized Weser barges with bunkers, oil, fresh water, and a large variety of supplies. The business went exceedingly well, but after about two years I felt a strong urge to return to sea.

In port at Bremen and on the Weser River, I often saw small, modern seagoing vessels of about 420 gross tons making about ten knots. They were known as *Volkswagen zur See* (Volkswagons of the Sea). They traded between the waters of the North Sea and the Baltic, carrying deals and battens (lumber) westbound and coke and coal eastbound. The banks financed the vessels using funds from the Marshall Plan. In 1952, I obtained financing and a contract with Pape Shipyard at Rönnebeck to build just such a ship, the *Ann-Christin*.

In the winter the Baltic was solidly frozen. The bow of my vessel was fortified for ice breaking; still, it was rough going and much time was lost. This and a generally weak market made me decide to go into the charter trading business in the Caribbean. It was not easy for a little German vessel to compete with Dutch and local companies so soon after the war in a competitive market. In 1957, I realized that the vessel was too small to bring sufficient profit. Therefore I contracted with Jade Shipyard in Wilhelmshaven to have the vessel enlarged by about 230 tons.

In general, the years in the Caribbean were rather successful. I survived hurricanes, northers, revolutions, and some treacherous reefs. My crewmembers were mostly handpicked locals, tested and reliable. I had gradually made friends in most of the ports of call, and there was no lack of offers for cargo shipments. For the Atlantic crossing, I loaded a cargo of timbers in the holds and on the hatches on deck. These were well lashed with heavy manila ropes and chains.

In spring 1957, after clearing the vessel with the customs people at Man of War Keys on the Nicaraguan coast, I sailed for Bermuda to take bunkers, oil, water, and provisions and to send my last telegrams. The weather reports did not give any reason for concern.

I set course for the Azores, radioing my positions to some of the weatherships without receiving any response. Gradually a swell started to roll in and dark heavy clouds appeared in the sky. The wind increased to force 11. Soon a full storm was howling and the small vessel was laboring badly in the monstrous breakers. I had the crew remain on the bridge. The cargo hold made water. The bilge pumps were clogged by the chafing of heavy timber. Our prayers were heard: After two days the storm abated. But the stanchions of the hatch coamings had cracked the deck. We hammered lead into the cracks and saved the vessel. In Rotterdam we discharged the cargo, which had to dry out before being delivered to the consignee.

In 1958, forced back into the old trade in European waters, I saw that little profit could be made because of a dismally low market rate for timber. Without losing time, I chartered the *Ann-Christin* out, sending her to East India (Colombo) under another captain. Half a year earlier I had bought a second, 650-gross-ton vessel in Denmark, the *Ann-Charlott*. Again I entered the Caribbean market and was soon busy trading between Newfoundland and Trinidad.

I later expanded my business in the mahogany trade between Mexico and the United States. This venture brought me into close contact with importers in Gulf Coast ports and during numerous port calls I made many close American friends. I liked the small, easygoing coastal towns, the snow-white beaches, and being close to the sea.

In 1963, while a cargo of mahogany was being unloaded in a U.S. port, I had to undergo an operation at the local hospital that ended my life at sea. It was during my recovery that I began to think of settling down in that city.

Living in America had always been a distant dream of mine. I have mentioned boyhood days spent reading about the Wild West and listening to my father talk of the experiences his family had had in Wisconsin, the beautiful land of lakes. Visits to New York while I was a crewmember of the *Columbus* and my New Jersey sweetheart deepened my appreciation of Americans and their magnificent country. My trip across America as a distressed seaman opened my eyes to the vast beauty of the land. After the war while I was conducting trade in the Carribean and the Gulf of Mexico, my love affair with America resumed.

The opportunity had now arrived for me to make a long lost dream a reality. I took that opportunity and became a citizen of the United States. Subsequently I became a port superintendent for a shipping agency and in 1973, its manager. I married a lovely American woman in 1967 and we raised two sons from a previous marriage of mine, one of whom graduated from the U.S. Air Force Academy and fought in Operation Desert Storm.

Looking back on my life, I consider myself fortunate to have survived the ordeals of a world war and the ventures that followed. The sea continues to hold a special place in my heart. Whenever I look out on quiet waters, I feel an urge to sail towards some distant horizon. But I know those days are gone, and so I spend my time close to the sea marveling at its ever-changing, breathtaking beauty. There is a freedom of spirit at sea known to only those who experience it. How blessed we are.

U-Boat Characteristics

· · · · · · · · · · · · · · · · · · · ·

The *U-405*

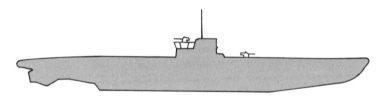

Type	VIIC
Displacement (tons)	
Surfaced	761
Submerged	865
Length (meters)	67.1
Beam (meters)	6.2
Draft (meters)	4.8
Propulsion (no. ×hp/type)	
Diesel	2 × 1,400
Electric	2 × 375
Fuel capacity (tons)	113
Speed (knots)	
Surfaced	17.0
Submerged	7.6
Range (nautical miles/knot)	
Surfaced	6,500/12
Submerged	80/4
Armament	
Bow torpedo tubes	4
Stern torpedo tubes	1
Torpedoes carried	14
Guns (centimeters)	1 × 8.8
	1 × 2
Crew	44

The *U-181*

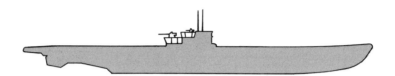

Type	IXD2
Displacement (tons)	
Surfaced	1,616
Submerged	1,804
Length (meters)	87.6
Beam (meters)	7.5
Draft (meters)	5.4
Propulsion (no. ×hp/type)	
Diesel	2 × 2,200 MAN
Electric	2 × 580 MWM gen.
	2 × 500
Fuel capacity (tons)	442
Speed (knots)	
Surfaced	19.2
Submerged	6.9
Range (nautical miles/knot)	
Surfaced	23,700/12
Submerged	57/4
Armament	
Bow torpedo tubes	4
Stern torpedo tubes	2
Torpedoes carried	24
Guns (centimeters)	1 × 3.7
	2 × twin 2
Crew	57

Source: Rossler, *The U-Boat*, 335 and 337, and Giese.

U-Boat Far East Operations

. . . .

On 6 February 1945, the *U-862* sent the American troop ship SS *Peter Sylvester* to the bottom some seven hundred miles west of Perth, Australia. The sinking signaled the end of U-boat war patrols in the Far East. When Germany surrendered three months later six U-boats lay in Far East ports. According to terms of an Axis accord signed early in the war, the boats were promptly taken over by the Japanese.

German U-boats had first rounded the Cape of Good Hope in late June 1942. Italy, Germany, and Japan agreed in December 1941 to a line of demarcation in assigning Far East submarine operations, for example, the 70th meridian of East longitude (west of Bombay, the Laccadive islands, the Maldives, and southward through Kerguelen). Germany and Italy would confine their activity west of this line, while the Japanese would run submarine patrols east into the Pacific.

Some fifty-seven U-boats ranged in the Indian Ocean and Pacific waters during the war. The initial group of four 740-ton boats, called *Eisbär* (polar bear), departed French bases for Cape Town in August 1942. One of the group, the *U-156*, was lost en route; the remaining force, joined by the first of the new long-range Type IXD boats, achieved remarkable success. During October 1942 *Eisbär* boats sank twenty-four Allied ships totaling 163,000 gross tons.

The next group, called *Kap U-Boote* (cape U-boats), was dispatched southward by Admiral Dönitz in September 1942 while the *Eisbär* group was still en route to Cape Town. This group subsequently operated off the cape and northward into Mozambique channel. Operating practically unopposed, cape U-boats sank thirty-six merchant ships sailing independently during the last three months of the year. All U-boats of this group returned safely to their home bases.

The *Seehund* (seal) force, led by *U-182* commander Nicolai Clausen, sailed into Far East waters in early 1943. Clausen's group included five U-boats and five Italian submarines. Another twenty-four ships were destroyed by this mixed force. Clausen and Italian commander Grazzana were credited with the majority of the kills. While homeward bound, the *U-182* was depth-charged and sunk by U.S. escort destroyers *Mackenzie* (DD 614) and *Laub* (DD 613) some two hundred miles west-northwest of Funchal in the Madeira islands. Clausen and his entire crew were lost in the action.

In March 1943, a new group of U-boats arrived in the western Indian Ocean. Although the boats sank thirty-four merchantmen in a three-month period, Allied convoys were sighted only for the first time. This latest tactic, along with strengthened antisubmarine forces, began to take its toll on patrolling U-boats.

Among this group of U-boat commanders was Captain Junior Wolfgang Lüth, one of Germany's most accomplished submariners. Lüth completed the longest continuous war patrol in submarine history (211 days) during this sortie, adding ten ships to his record. Following the patrol, he received the Swords and Diamonds of the Oak Leaves Award, worn with the Knight's Cross. He was the seventh German to receive this decoration and the first navy man. As Lüth's group of U-boats departed from the area, one, the *U-178*, proceeded to Penang, an island off the Malay Peninsula, to establish a German submarine base.

By June 1943 the happy days of western and mid-Atlantic U-boat operations were over. U-boat losses mounted as Allied convoy systems and techniques improved. New hunter-killer antisubmarine groups roamed the ocean freely in search of their underseas enemy. Between January and July of 1943, 130 U-boats went to the bottom, more than half of the total U-boat operating force.

Dönitz began to look for new areas of operation where Allied shipping remained relatively undefended. Early Indian Ocean operations had reaped an impressive harvest. Between September 1942 and July 1943 U-boats claimed 116 ships for 600,000 gross tons, with only three U-boats lost.

Dönitz, commander in chief of the German navy in 1943, and his new U-boat chief, Admiral Hans-Georg von Friedeburg, faced other problems that further directed their attention toward increased U-boat activity in that area. German blockade-runners that moved war materials between Japan and Germany were being lost to British air and naval forces at an alarming rate. The U-boat headquarters staff was convinced that U-boats could readily assume the transporting of vital goods. Type X-B and Type XIV cargo-carrying U-boats were available, along with a number of Type IX-D boats that were rapidly joining the operational fleet in 1943. These 1,600-ton boats had a surface operational radius of 23,700 miles. Additionally, the Japanese had opened their bases at Penang, Singapore, and Batavia (later renamed Djakarta) to German U-boats.

A plan was developed by the U-boat operational staff that would send large U-boat patrollers (IX-C and IX-D) and transports (VII-F, X-B, and XIV) to the Far East for extensive operations. Groups of boats would proceed to the Indian Ocean independently. Roundtrip missions would include refueling from U-tankers in the Atlantic and surface ships in the Indian Ocean, war patrols in assigned areas, then in-port periods at Far East bases for repair, overhaul, and rest. The boats would then either sortie out on other patrols or take on vital cargoes of tungsten, rubber, tin, quinine, opium, and molybdenum and head for home waters. The operational schedule called for a continuous stream of boats moving to and from the Far East.

The Monsoon campaign commenced in June 1943 with the departure of eleven U-boats from Norwegian, French, and German bases. The group met almost immediately with fierce enemy opposition. On 24 June the *U-200* was sunk by VP-84 PBY-5A aircraft south of Iceland. The U-tankers *U-462* and *U-514* were sent to the bottom the following month by British air patrols in the Bay of Biscay. U.S. Army Corps Liberators destroyed the *U-506* west of Vigo, Spain, on 12 July. And finally, American hunter-killer antisubmarine groups, which included the carriers *Card*, *Core*, and *Santee*, claimed the *U-487*, *U-509*, and *U-847* as they were transiting the Atlantic. The *U-509* and *U-847* were lost with all hands.

Of the original eleven Monsoon boats, five made it into the Indian Ocean. Operating mostly in the Madagascar straits, the Gulf of Aden, and off the west coast of India, the group, joined by the *U-178* out of Penang, achieved notable success, sinking twenty-one ships for a total of 121,625 gross tons.

Dönitz sent out the second Monsoon fleet in the fall of 1943. Three of the four boats in the group were lost in the Atlantic as they made their way south towards Cape Town. The *U-848* and *U-849* were sunk by American land-based patrol and carrier aircraft near Ascension Island in November, while the *U-850* was dispatched by aircraft from the USS *Bogue* (CVE 9) southwest of the Azores. Only the *U-510* made it through to Penang, after sinking five ships in her assigned patrol area.

U-boats and UIT (ex-Italian) submarines now operated out of Far East bases. The Italian boats were taken over by the Japanese when Italy surrendered in September 1943. They were subsequently refitted and manned by German officers and mixed crews. They were used primarily for cargo carrying between Japan and the southeast bases. In addition to losing Monsoon U-tankers, the German navy experienced mounting refueling problems as its two surface tankers *Charlotte Schiemann* and *Brake* were lost to British naval forces in early 1944.

By the spring of 1944, Dönitz had committed forty-two German and Italian submarines to Indian Ocean operations. Twelve boats had been lost; twenty-three had made it through to patrol and to attack Allied shipping and returned safely to their home ports. One, the *U-511*, had been turned over to Japan as a gift, and six boats remained in Far East bases. Monsoon boats had sunk thirty-three ships. Despite rising losses, the Far East still offered the best hunting ground for U-boat offensive operations. Plans were made to sortie additional groups, strengthen Far East operating bases, and improve the efficiency of command and control in the area.

Five bases supported Far East U-boat operations by the end of the year. Penang was the principal operating base, Kobe, Japan, and Singapore were used as repair facilities, Batavia became the main cargo-loading port, and Soerabaja was used as both a repair base and a loading facility.

The third Monsoon group of seven boats suffered much the same fate as its predecessors. Only three of the seven boats escaped to operate in their assigned areas. Allied antisubmarine units all but stopped the group during its Atlantic transit.

Eleven more boats went out in the spring of 1944. Aboard one, the *U-181*, was Second Watch Officer Otto Giese. Of this group, the *U-181* and *U-862* enjoyed the most successful patrols. Between June and October of 1944, only eighteen Allied ships were sunk. Patrolling U-boats now found that most merchantmen traveled in convoy. The *U-860*, *U-198*, and *U-859* were lost to massive attacks by British air, surface, and submarine forces.

One more group of seven patrollers and cargo boats left European bases for the Far East in late 1944. Only two boats, the *U-195* and

U-219, made it through Allied antisubmarine barriers. The U-boat arm lost nineteen of twenty-four Monsoon boats sent out that year. Allied shipping losses for the year totaled twenty-eight vessels, or 150,000 gross tons. This was less than half the previous year's count.

Only two boats, the *U-861* and *U-862*, were operational in late 1944 and early 1945. Eight more boats lay in various southeast ports undergoing repair or loading cargo. The *U-861*, *U-510*, and *U-532*, ordered to return home, were transiting Atlantic waters at the time of Germany's capitulation in May 1945. The *U-861* made port in Trondheim, Norway, and was delivered to the British. The *U-510* surrendered at St. Nazaire in August, while the *U-532* sailed into Liverpool and captivity a few months later.

The *U-862* made the last successful Monsoon U-boat patrol in the Far East. She sank the liberty ship *Robert J. Walker* off Sidney, Australia, the day before Christmas 1944 and the SS *Peter Sylvester* off Perth the following February before returning to Batavia. The *U-183* left Penang in April to operate off the Philippines, the first U-boat endeavor to disrupt U.S. naval operations in the Pacific. The boat was torpedoed and sunk by the American submarine SS *Besugo* (SS 321) in the Java Sea late that month. Warrant Officer Karl Wisniewski, the boat's navigator and sole survivor of the sinking, was picked up by the *Besugo*. The *U-183* was the last U-boat loss in the Far East.

When Germany surrendered, six patrollers and two cargo carriers lay in Far East ports. In compliance with Axis treaties, the boats were promptly taken over by the Japanese. The veteran crews immediately set to work training the Japanese submariners who were to man the commandeered U-boats.

The German U-boat endeavor in the Indian Ocean was a notable success when one considers the loss in Allied gross tonnage and the fact that Far East U-boat operations did not begin until the war was into its third year. Between October 1942 and February 1945, 151 Allied ships were sent to the bottom for a loss of 935,000 gross tons. Fifty-seven U-boats were committed to Far East operations (some boats made multiple deployments). Thirty-nine boats were lost to Allied naval and air units while they were in transit or on patrol in the Indian Ocean and Pacific waters. Of the eighteen remaining U-boats, fourteen survived the war.

Notes

. . . .

1. Giese's war diaries.
2. Ship's log entries, Giese's files.
3. At the outbreak of the war, the *Bremen* was in New York. President Roosevelt directed the State Department to make a thorough search of the ship for concealed ordnance, hoping to delay the ship until HMAS *Perth* and HMS *Berwick* could be in position to intercept her. Though the search took three days the *Bremen*, aided by fog off Newfoundland and an unsuspected route, reached Germany safely (Abbazia, *Roosevelt's Navy*, 70).
4. Giese's war diaries.
5. A 5,083-ton freighter owned by Hamburg-Amerikanische Paket Aktien Gesellschaft (HAPAG). The *Spreewald* had an unfortunate demise. While operating in the North Atlantic in early January 1942, she was identified by Lieutenant Commander Peter Cremer in the *U-333* as a British passenger-carrying freighter and sunk following a torpedo attack. The ship carried some three hundred British civilian prisoners. After a massive search for survivors, the *U-105* found three lifeboats and three rafts with twenty-four German merchant seamen and fifty-eight British prisoners, the only survivors (Brice, *Axis Blockade Runners*, 101, 105; and Cremer, *U-Boat Commander,* 43–47).
6. The *Elbe* was a 9,179-ton North German Lloyd (NDL) freighter. The blockade-runner was sighted and sunk by Swordfish aircraft from the British carrier *Eagle* near the Azores on 6 June 1941 (Brice, *Axis Blockade Runners,* 97).

   The *Regensburg* was an 8,068-ton NDL freighter. While inbound from the Far East on 30 March 1943, she was intercepted by British warships in the Denmark straits. To escape capture, the crew scuttled the ship and took to their lifeboats in a thick snow shower. Fearful of a U-boat attack, the British cruiser *Glasgow* finished off the slow-settling derelict with her 4- and 6-inch guns (Brice, *Axis Blockade Runners*, 102, 121, 122).

   The *Odenwald* was a 5,098-ton HAPAG freighter. She was captured by the U.S. cruiser *Omaha* and destroyer *Somers* on 6 Novem-

269

ber 1941. It was assumed that a German raider had attacked the British oiler *Olwen*. The Royal Navy dispatched several warships to hunt down the raider. Since the attack had taken place in the Pan-American neutrality zone, which extended to 70°W, the U.S. Navy was informed of the action. The *Odenwald* was sighted by U.S. Task Group 3.6 during the early morning of 6 November 1941. The ship was ordered to stop and the *Omaha* sent away a boarding party. The *Odenwald* immediately signaled "Am sinking, send boats," and began abandoning ship. As they boarded, the American boarding party heard explosions below decks. They quickly secured the ship from further damage, closing the seacocks, replacing manhole covers, and dispersing the dense fumes caused by scuttling charges. Captain Löhrs, the *Odenwald*'s commander, had not been instructed to scuttle his ship in case of an American interception. When he realized his ship was about to be seized, he ordered his crew to hurry the process, which resulted in an ineffective operation. The *Odenwald* was subsequently escorted to Port of Spain, Trinidad. The ship and her cargo of 3,800 tons of raw rubber remained in American custody. American justification for seizing the *Odenwald* was based on an 1819 law that gave the U.S. Navy the right to stop and seize any ship suspected of carrying slaves or being engaged in the slave trade. The German government protested but to no avail (Brice, *Axis Blockade Runners*, 104, 105).

The *Havelland* was a 6,334-ton HAPAG cargo ship. Later transferred to the Japanese and renamed the *Tatsumiya Maru*, she was sunk by U.S. Navy carrier aircraft on 30 July 1945 off Kyoga-saki, Japan (Joint Army-Navy Assessment Committee, *Japanese Naval and Merchant Shipping Losses during World War II by All Causes,* 198; and Prager, *Blohm und Voss,* 247).

7. The *Anneliese Essberger* was a 5,173-ton freighter owned by John T. Essberger. On 21 November 1942, while bound for Japan disguised as a Norwegian merchantman, she was scuttled by her crew in the Atlantic narrows between Brazil and West Africa. She had been stopped by the U.S. cruisers *Cincinnati* and *Milwaukee* and the destroyer *Somers*. The entire crew of sixty-two was rescued and interned (Brice, *Axis Blockade Runners,* 112, 113; and Roscoe, *United States Destroyer Operations in World War II,* 136).

8. She was a 6,104-ton freighter owned by John T. Essberger. The *Elsa Essberger* departed Sasebo, Japan, on her maiden blockade run in November 1941. She was attacked and damaged by British Coastal Command aircraft, forcing her to seek refuge in the Spanish port of El Ferrol, where she arrived on 12 January 1942. While in port, she transferred her cargo to smaller vessels for further transport. She eventually made her way safely to Bordeaux. However, while outbound in early November of that year she was again attacked by British Coastal Command and Bomber Command aircraft off the entrance to the Gironde River that put her out of action as a

blockade-runner for the remainder of the war (Brice, *Axis Blockade Runners*, 101, 106, 112; and Roskill, *The War at Sea, 1939–45*, 2: 183, 274).

9. The *Ermland* was a 6,528-ton HAPAG freighter. She was the oldest blockade-runner, built by Blohm and Voss in 1922. She was renamed the *Weserland* in 1942 to avoid any confusion with the naval auxiliary *Ermland*. At 0826 on 3 January 1944, the *Weserland* was sunk by point-blank 5-inch gunfire from the U.S. destroyer *Somers* about halfway between Ascension and Caravellas. One hundred and thirty-four uniformed survivors were picked up. Before being intercepted by the *Somers*, antiaircraft fire from the *Weserland* had damaged two U.S. Navy PB4Y-1 patrol craft of Bomb Squadron 107. One of the damaged bombers crashed seventy miles short of Ascension with the loss of all hands (Roscoe, *United States Destroyer Operations in World War II*, 296, 297; Morison, *History of United States Naval Operations in World War II*, 10: 227; and Brice, *Axis Blockade Runners*, 18, 139–41).

10. The *Münsterland* was a 6,408-ton HAPAG freighter. She was assigned to supply the raiders *Komet, Orion,* and *Atlantis*. She made one blockade run, departing the Far East in February 1942 and arriving in Europe the following May. The *Münsterland* was retired from blockade running and relocated to German waters for employment in the Baltic trade. However, before she could make her run up the channel, she was damaged by British Fighter Command aircraft during an air raid on Cherbourg in October 1943. She eventually ran aground off Cap Gris Nez and was destroyed by the Dover batteries on 20 January 1944 (Roskill, *The War at Sea, 1939–45*, 1: 607, 2: 482, 3: part 1, 93, 291; and Brice, *Axis Blockade Runners*, 136, 137).

The *Winnetou* was a 15,105-ton tanker. At the start of the war the old tanker, enjoying an extended stay at Las Palmas, was ordered to sea as the supply oiler for the raider *Orion*. Slowed by marine growth on her hull and belching funnel smoke, she often arrived late at secret rendezvous points. She was eventually transferred to the Japanese and renamed the *Teiko Maru*. The ship was sunk by the U.S. submarine *Puffer* on 22 February 1944 in the Koti Passage off Borneo (Brice, *Axis Blockade Runners*, 80, 81; Roskill, *The War at Sea, 1939–45*, 1: 607; and Roscoe, *United States Submarine Operations in World War II*, 546).

11. The *Scharnhorst* was an NDL freighter/passenger ship. She was transferred to the Japanese navy and rebuilt as the escort carrier *Jinyo*. In November 1944, while in company with six destroyers, an oiler, and seven transports carrying the Twenty-third Infantry Division from Manchuria to Luzon, the *Jinyo* and her group encountered an American submarine wolf pack. One transport was sunk by the USS *Queenfish* in the East China Sea on the fifteenth. Another transport fell victim to the USS *Picuda* on the seventeenth in the Yellow Sea. That same night the USS *Spadefish*, flag of the wolf pack under

Commander G. W. Underwood, sent the *Jinyo* to the bottom with a six-torpedo attack. Planes could be seen sliding off the flight deck as the carrier became engulfed in fire and settled by the stern (Morison, *History of United States Naval Operations in World War II*, 12: 409).

The *Kulmerland* was a 7,363-ton HAPAG freighter. She acted as supply ship for the *Komet, Orion*, and *Kormoran*. The *Kulmerland* also delivered full loads of oil, stores, provisions, drinking water, and iced beer to lonely Pacific anchorages. Along with the *Regensburg*, she served as an unarmed scouting ship, rescued survivors, and collected intelligence. She made a single blockade run from Dairen to Bordeaux in late 1942. The ship was destroyed during an air raid on Nantes, France, in September 1943 (Brice, *Axis Blockade Runners*, 84, 110; and Roskill, *The War at Sea, 1939–45*, 1: 607, 2: 483).

The *R. C. Rickmers*, a 5,198-ton freighter, was transferred to the Japanese in 1942 and renamed the *Teifuku Maru*. She was sunk by the U.S. submarine *Trigger* off Nojima-Zaki, Japan, on 22 December 1942 (Roscoe, *United States Submarine Operations in World War II*, 561).

The *Burgenland* was a 7,320-ton HAPAG freighter. She made a successful run from Kobe to Bordeaux in the fall of 1941 and returned to the Far East in January 1943. Disguised as the merchant ship *Floridian*, the *Burgenland* was challenged on 5 January 1944 by a U.S. Navy PBM patrol bomber some five hundred miles northeast of Brazil. The U.S. warships *Omaha* and *Jouett* arrived on the scene and fired shots across the freighter's bow. Scuttling charges were detonated by the crew, and the ship settled stern-first into the sea. One hundred and fifty crewmen were rescued, along with two thousand bales of rubber, enough for the manufacture of five thousand aircraft tires. The *Burgenland* was one of the last German blockade-runners to attempt to bring home cargoes from the Far East (Brice, *Axis Blockade Runners*, 101, 116, 117, 142; and Roskill, *The War at Sea, 1939–45*, 2: 482, 484).

The *Ramses* was a 7,983-ton HAPAG freighter. She served as a prisoner ship for German raiders visiting Japan. While attempting to transport a cargo of raw rubber, quinine, and tea from Batavia to Bordeaux via the Indian Ocean, she was sighted and intercepted on 28 November 1942 by an Allied naval force six hundred miles west of Australia. Cruisers HMAS *Adelaide* and RNN *Jacob van Heemskerck* opened fire on the blockade-runner after she had lowered her lifeboats and set off scuttling charges. Seventy-eight Germans, ten Norwegians, a pig, and a dog were picked up (Brice, *Axis Blockade Runners*, 110–13).

12. The *Pinguin* was a 7,766-ton freighter owned by the Hansa Line. Within a forty-eight-hour period in January 1941, she captured the Norwegian factory ships *Ole Wegger, Solglimt*, and *Pelagos* with their whale catchers *Star XIV, Star XIX, Star XX, Star XXI, Star XXII, Star XXIII, Star XXV, Pol VIII, Pol IX, Pol X*, and *Torlyn*. Cargoes totaled

10,300 tons of fuel oil and 20,500 tons of whale oil. The first of the raiders to be sunk, the *Pinguin* was intercepted by the British heavy cruiser *Cornwall* on 8 May 1941 and destroyed when a cruiser shell exploded among mines on her deck. Twenty-two British and Indian prisoners and sixty German survivors were picked up. During ten months of operation, the *Pinguin* had accounted for twenty-eight ships of 136,551 tons (Brice, *Axis Blockade Runners*, 83; Woodward, *The Secret Raiders*, 154; and Roskill, *The War at Sea, 1939–45*, 1: 385).

13. The *Elbe* was sunk by Swordfish aircraft from the British carrier *Eagle* near the Azores on 6 June 1941. The *Regensburg* arrived safely in Bordeaux on 27 June 1941 (Roskill, *The War at Sea, 1939–45*, 2: 183, 482).

14. The *Alstertor*, owned by Hamburg-Südamerika, was assigned to provision the raiders *Pinguin, Komet, Orion*, and *Kormoran*. She was scuttled on 13 June 1941 west of Gibraltar after an attack by British aircraft, Force H destroyers (Eighth Destroyer Flotilla), and the OBV *Marsdale* (Roskill, *The War at Sea, 1939–45*, 1: 606; and Brice, *Axis Blockade Runners*, 97).

15. The *Emden, Möwe*, and *Wolf* were the most successful raiders during World War I. Between them they accounted for the destruction of over 320,000 tons of Allied shipping (Woodward, *The Secret Raiders*, 283).

16. Nine German armed merchant raiders operated between 1940 and 1943. They included the *Atlantis, Komet, Kormoran, Michel, Orion, Pinguin, Stier, Thor*, and *Widder*. Three additional vessels, the *Coronel, Hansa*, and *Togo*, were converted to auxiliary cruisers but were damaged by British air and sea forces before they could break into the Atlantic. The *Coronel* was forced to return to Germany after being attacked by British forces on the night of 8 February 1943. She was subsequently refitted as an auxiliary minesweeper and served as such in the Baltic. The *Hansa*, damaged in an air raid, was used for target practice and training in the Baltic. The *Togo* was attacked and damaged by British aircraft while passing down the English Channel on 13 February 1943. She returned to Germany and was not active as a raider thereafter (Roskill, *The War at Sea, 1939–45*, 1: 604, 605, 2: 387, 388, 481; and Showell, *The German Navy in World War Two*, 119–22).

17. The raider force held 675 prisoners, but regular soldiers and RAF volunteers taken from the passenger ship *Rangitane* and officers and men of the merchant navy were not released. Fifty-two women and eight children were among those landed on Emirau Island. The captain of the *Komet*, Robert Eyssen, provided the prisoners with radios, kerosene, foodstuffs, cigarettes, and four rifles. He joined the prisoners on his ship before they departed and pointed to the nearby palmy island: "Well, tomorrow you'll be drinking whiskey and soda over there." The prisoners went ashore the following morning and were picked up a short time later by the British (Woodward, *The Se-*

cret *Raiders*, 109–11; Muggenthaler, *German Raiders of World War II*, 68, 69; and Roskill, *The War at Sea, 1939–45*, 1: 283).

18. Admiral Eyssen was later appointed naval liaison officer with Luft-flotte IV. From August 1942 to July 1944 he commanded the navy office in Oslo, Norway. Following this tour of duty he was sent to Vienna to the Inspectorate of Reserves for the Armed Forces, and in April 1945, a month before the war ended, he retired from the navy (Woodward, *The Secret Raiders*, 199).

19. On 28 July 1940, the *Thor* encountered the 22,000-ton British auxil-iary cruiser *Alcantara* near the island of Trinidad. The *Thor* easily outranged and outfought her opponent, causing the merchant cruiser to move to quiet South Atlantic waters for repair and replen-ishment. The *Thor*'s first cruise lasted 329 days. During that time she either sank or captured twelve ships. Her second cruise, which lasted 321 days, found her operating in Indian Ocean and Pacific waters, where she accounted for ten more ships. In late fall of 1942, while she was moored in Yokohama alongside the supply ship *Uckermark*, an explosion and subsequent fire destroyed both ships (Showell, *The German Navy in World War Two*, 122; and Roskill, *The War at Sea, 1939–45*, 1: 285).

20. Unbeknownst to the crew of the *Anneliese Essberger*, the *Orion* had arrived in Bordeaux on 23 August 1941 via the Indian Ocean. The raider had been at sea for 510 days and had accounted for twelve and a half ships of 80,279 tons (she shared the sinking of seven ships while operating with the *Komet*). Built in 1930 for passenger service, "Ship 36" was a single-screw vessel of 22,000 tons. Plagued by engine prob-lems during her days as a raider, she was not sent to sea again after her long initial cruise. The ship was stripped of her armament and special equipment for use aboard other raiders. She was converted to a repair and workshop ship, then commissioned as the artillery train-ing ship *Hektor* in 1944. The ship was sunk by Allied aircraft off Swinemunde on 14 May 1945 (Woodward, *The Secret Raiders*, 97, 116; and Showell, *The German Navy in World War Two*, 120–22).

21. Prior to her rendezvous with the *Anneliese Essberger*, the *U-106* had a successful year of operations in the Atlantic. Between January and May 1941, the Type IXB U-boat sank eight Allied merchant ships of 36,000 tons. On 20 March she made a torpedo attack on the shadow of a merchant ship during poor visibility and, without realizing it, damaged the British battleship *Malaya*. Later that year, tragedy struck the U-boat on a calm October day just outside of the Bay of Biscay when an unexpected wave from the stern carried the entire unstrapped bridge watch overboard. The four men vanished into the sea. The boat was depth-charged and sunk by Sunderland aircraft of RAF and RAAF Squadrons 228 and 461 northwest of Cape Ortegal on 8 February 1943. The final war record for the *U-106* was twenty-one ships sunk, totaling 131,703 tons. *U-106* captain Lieutenant Com-mander Jürgen v. Oesten survived the war, surrendering his last com-

mand, the *U-861*, to Allied forces at Trondheim, Norway, in May 1945 (MacDonald, *German Submarines*, 1: 91; Gannon, *Operation Drumbeat*, 192; *United States Submarine Losses in World War II*, 236; and Rohwer, *Axis Submarine Successes, 1939–45*, 41, 45–47, 54, 55).

22. Hans-Rudolf Rösing commanded U-Flotilla Emsmann at the start of the war. During the summer of 1940 he commanded the *U-48* and sunk fifteen ships of 75,589 tons. After leaving the *U-48*, he became liaison officer with the flag officer of U-boats in Bordeaux. He later took control of the Third Flotilla. From July 1942 until the end of the war he served as flag officer for U-Boats West, which was initially headquartered in France, then Norway, and finally Germany (Rohwer, *Axis Submarine Successes, 1939–45*, 18, 19, 20, 25, 26; and Showell, *The German Navy in World War Two*, 179).

23. Prange, *Hitler's Words*, 367–77.

24. The *St. Louis* was a former Hamburg Amerika liner. Many HAL vessels had American names.

25. Homeward-bound convoy QP-11 consisted of thirteen merchantmen and a covering force of cruiser HMS *Edinburgh*, six destroyers, four corvettes, and a trawler. The *U-456* (Teichert) torpedoed the *Edinburgh* and blew off her stern, forcing her to turn about and head back to Murmansk. She was later attacked by German destroyers and disabled. Following the evacuation of the ship, she was sunk by the British destroyer *Foresight*. The *U-251* (Timm) sunk the 6,000-ton merchant ship *Jutland* and the *U-589* (Horrer) and *U-88* (Bohmann) heard detonations following torpedo attacks on ships in the convoy (Rohwer, *Axis Submarine Successes, 1939–45*, 198; and Roskill, *The War at Sea, 1939–45*, 2: 128, 129.

26. Germany invaded Norway on 9 April 1940 at points from Oslo to Narvik. Though British naval units attempted to deter the invading forces, all German objectives were quickly attained. The only serious threat to the invasion was at Narvik where British destroyers sunk two German destroyers, two freighters, and an ammunition ship while suffering the loss of the *Hunter* and *Hardy*. On 13 April a large British naval force, which included the battleship *Warspite* and the carrier *Furious*, attacked the German-held Ofot Fjord and sunk the eight German destroyers that had survived the earlier battle. On 28 May a British expeditionary force landed at Narvik and destroyed the town's ore quays, its electric power supply, and the railway before being evacuated on 8 June (Potter, *Sea Power*, 246; and Roskill, *The War at Sea, 1939–45*, 1: 193).

27. Roskill, *The War at Sea, 1939–45*, 2: 143.

28. Ibid., 2: 280–85.

29. The *U-405*'s *Kriegstagebuch* (war diary) entry for 14 September 1942 reads as follows: "1615 AC.1438. The wounded men cannot get to our U-boat, so Mr. Otto Giese ties a rope to himself and dives in to pull the capsized raft with the men to us. We take aboard the two men who are still alive. They both are unconscious. We try for al-

most three hours to revive them. Sargeant Haase has a severe head injury. Petty Officer Gudzent regains consciousness but both die."

30. Captain Kurt Freiwald was aide (adjutant) to Admiral of the Fleet Räder until the latter was relieved of his post as supreme commander about 1 February 1943. After that he served as Admiral of the Fleet Dönitz's aide for about six months, then was assigned to command the *U-181* (Freiwald, *Office of Naval Intelligence Review*, August 1953, 362).

31. Captain Wolfgang Lüth was credited with sinking forty-seven Allied ships and a submarine during World War II. At the end of the war he was in command of the naval school at Flensburg, situated adjacent to the Dönitz government complex, a former PT school. Tragically, a week after the armistice, he was shot and killed by one of his own sentries as he walked through the grounds one cold and rainy night. In his eulogy at the memorial service, Dönitz said, "Wolfgang Lüth, we now take leave of you. . . . It is not mine to describe your family's loss; we, your comrades, have lost a great warrior, a true and noble friend, and I, a beloved member of the old guard of my *U-Bootwaffe*, to which my entire heart once belonged and belongs still. . . ." (Vause, *U-Boat Ace*, 202, 203, 209).

32. The *Janeta* was a 5,312-ton freighter owned by Glasgow United Shipping. Built in 1929, the *Janeta* was sunk on 1 May 1944 at 18.14°S, 20.00°W (Rohwer, *Axis Submarine Successes, 1939–45*, 180).

33. A 7,118-ton freighter owned by Rotterdamsche Lloyd of Rotterdam. Built in 1917, the *Garoet* was sunk on 19 June 1944 at 12.30°S, 64.00°E. The fate of the crewmembers of the ship would never have been learned if several were not saved by accident. The ship was on a voyage from Portuguese Goa to South Africa when she was hit by two torpedoes. Within a few minutes she had disappeared beneath the waves, taking with her the manned boats alongside. Three Dutchmen, an Australian, and six Laskars were able to get into the boats. They jumped from their boats to escape the fast-sinking ship and were lucky enough to board two rafts that popped up to the surface after the vessel was gone. Five Laskars reached the island of Mauritius, the remaining five survivors were picked up by a passing ship after eleven days at sea and landed at Durban, South Africa. Of almost one hundred crewmembers, only ten survived the sinking (Rohwer, *Axis Submarine Successes, 1939–45*, 275).

34. The *Tanda* was a 7,174-ton freighter owned by Eastern and Australian Steamship. Built in 1914, she was sunk on 15 July 1944 at 13.22°N, 74.09°E (Rohwer, *Axis Submarine Successes, 1939–45*, 276).

35. Rohwer and Hummelchen, *Chronik des Seekrieges, 1939–45*, 417.

36. This 5,265-ton freighter was owned by King Line. Built in 1920, the *King Frederick* was sunk on 19 July 1944 at 09.29°N, 71.45°E (Rohwer, *Axis Submarine Successes, 1939–45*, 276).

37. The other boat was HMS *Stratagem*, which dived to make an attack on the *U-181* but lost the U-boat after an extensive search. The fol-

lowing November, the *Stratagem* was caught in the dangerously shallow waters of the Malacca straits and sunk by a Japanese destroyer (Rohwer and Hummelchen, *Chronik des Seekrieges, 1939–45,* 417; and Roskill, *The War at Sea, 1939–45,* 3: part 2, 203, 204).

38. The *Zwaardvisch* was on her first mission when she sank the *U-168.* Eleven days later she sank the Japanese minelayer *Itsukshima.* The Dutch boat was attached to the British Eighth Flotilla under the operational control of U.S. Rear Admiral Ralph Christie, whose submarine forces operated out of Fremantle and patrolled the South China and Java seas (Gray, *Operation Pacific,* 168).

39. The *Fort Lee* was a 10,198-ton tanker owned by the U.S. Maritime Commission. Built in 1943, she was sunk on 2 November 1944 at 27.35°S, 83.11°E (Rohwer, *Axis Submarine Successes, 1939–45,* 277).

40. Dönitz's message to all U-boats, dated 3 May 1945 (Giese's files).

41. Admiral Shigeru Fukodome was a senior naval aviator and chief of staff to Admiral Isoroku Yamamoto, commander in chief, Combined Fleet, prior to the war. He was one of the primary planners of carrier strike operations against warships anchored in harbors. His study, completed in January 1941, was subsequently utilized in the attack on Pearl Harbor on 7 December 1941. Later in the war he commanded the Sixth Base Air Force, which covered southern Kyushu, the Ryukyus, and Formosa (Dull, *The Imperial Japanese Navy, 1941–45,* 8, 315, 316).

42. Admiral Paul Wenneker was commander of the pocket battleship *Deutschland* until November 1939, then he became German naval attaché to Japan. He remained in that position until the end of the war (Showell, *The German Navy in World War Two,* 180).

43. Giese's files.

44. General Tomoyuki Yamashita was in command of the Twenty-fifth Army when the Japanese attacked Pearl Harbor on 7 December 1941. He invaded Malaya and captured Singapore on 15 February 1942. Following his victory he became known as the Tiger of Malaya. He was posted to command the First Army Group in Manchuria and later designated supreme commander in the Philippines to oppose invading American forces. Because of atrocities committed by Japanese units during the battle for Manila, Yamashita was put on trial after the war and hanged at the Luzon prisoner-of-war camp on 27 February 1946 (Tunney, *Biographical Dictionary of World War II,* 213).

45. Brennecke, *Haie im Paradies,* 316, 317.

Bibliography

· · · · · · · · · · · · · · · · · · · ·

Abbazia, Patrick. *Mr. Roosevelt's Navy: The Private War of the U.S. Atlantic Fleet, 1939–42*. Annapolis: Naval Institute Press, 1975.

Beaver, Paul. *U-Boats in the Atlantic*. Cambridge, England: Patrick Stephens, 1979.

Brennecke, Jochen. *Haie im Paradies*. Preetz/Holstein, Germany: Ernst Gerdes Verlag, 1961.

Brice, Martin. *Axis Blockade Runners*. Annapolis: Naval Institute Press, 1981.

Cocker, Maurice. *Destroyers of the Royal Navy, 1893–1981*. London: Ian Allan, 1981.

Cremer, Peter. *U-Boat Commander: A Periscope View of the Battle of the Atlantic*. Annapolis: Naval Institute Press, 1985.

Dictionary of American Naval Fighting Ships. Vol. 7. Washington, D.C.: Naval History Division, Department of the Navy, 1981.

Dull, Paul S. *A Battle History of the Imperial Japanese Navy, 1941–45*. Annapolis: Naval Institute Press, 1978.

Freiwald, Kurt. "German U-Boats in the Indian Ocean." *The ONI Review* (August 1953): 362–70.

Gannon, Michael. *Operation Drumbeat*. New York: Harper and Row, 1990.

Giese, Otto, and James Wise. "Hitler's 'Monsoon' U-Boats." *Sea Classics* (June 1991): 12–17, 64–66.

Gleichauf, Justin F. *Unsung Sailors*. Annapolis: Naval Institute Press, 1990.

Goralski, Robert C. *World War II Almanac: 1931–45*. New York: Putnam's, 1981.

Gray, Edwyn. *Operation Pacific*. Annapolis: Naval Institute Press, 1989.

Hickam, H. H., Jr. *Torpedo Junction*. Annapolis: Naval Institute Press, 1989.

Jane's Fighting Aircraft of World War II. London: Studio Editions, 1990.

The Joint Army-Navy Assessment Committee. *Japanese Naval and Merchant Shipping Losses during World War II by All Causes*. Washington, D.C.: U.S. Government Printing Office, 1947.

Kriegstagebüch (KTB) War Diary of U-405. National Archives. Microfilm publication T1022, roll 2939, ONI roll T-202-D. 1 March–23 December 1942.

Lenton, H. T. *Navies of the Second World War: German Submarines 1 and 2.* London: Macdonald, 1965.

Morison, S. E. *History of United States Naval Operations in World War II.* Boston: Little, Brown, 1975.

Muggenthaler, August Karl. *German Raiders of World War II.* Englewood Cliffs: Prentice-Hall, 1977.

Pawlak, Manfred. *Lexikon des Zweiten Weltkrieges.* Herrsching: Verlagsgesellschaft mbH, 1977.

Potter, F.. B. *Sea Power: A Naval History.* Annapolis: Naval Institute Press, 1981.

Prager, Hans Georg. *Blohm und Voss.* Herford: Koehlers Verlagsgesellschaft mbH, 1977.

Prange, Gordon W. *Hitler's Words.* Washington, D.C.: American Council on Public Affairs, 1944.

Robertson, Terence. *Escort Commander.* New York: Nelson Doubleday, 1956.

Rohwer, Jürgen. *Axis Submarine Successes, 1939–45.* Annapolis: Naval Institute Press, 1983.

Rohwer, Jürgen, and Gerhard Hummelchen. *Chronik des Seekrieges, 1939–45.* Oldenburg: G. Stalling, 1968.

Roscoe, Theodore. *United States Destroyer Operations in World War II.* Annapolis: Naval Institute Press, 1953.

———. *United States Submarine Operations in World War II.* Annapolis: Naval Institute Press, 1949.

Roskill, S. W. *The War at Sea, 1939–45.* Vols. 1–3. London: Her Majesty's Stationery Office, 1956.

Rossler, Eberhard. *The U-Boat: The Evolution and Technical History of German Submarines.* London: Arms and Armour Press, Lionel Leventhal, 1981.

Saville, Allison. "German Submarines in the Far East." U.S. Naval Institute *Proceedings* (August 1961): 80–92.

Schmalenbach, Paul. *German Raiders.* Annapolis: Naval Institute Press, 1980.

Showell, Jak P. Mallmann. *The German Navy in World War Two.* Annapolis: Naval Institute Press, 1979.

———. *U-Boats under the Swastika.* New York: Arco, 1977.

Stern, Robert C. *Type VII U-Boats.* Annapolis: Naval Institute Press, 1991.

Stokesbury, James L. *A Short History of World War II.* New York: William Morrow, 1980.

Tunney, Christopher. *Biographical Dictionary of World War II.* New York: St. Martin's Press, 1972.

United States Submarine Losses, World War II. Washington, D.C.: Naval History Division, Office of the Chief of Naval Operations, 1963.

Van Limburg Stirum, S. J. Graaf. *Varen in Oorlogstijd.* Amsterdam: Uitgeverij v. h. C. de Boer, 1948.

Vause, Jordan. *U-Boat Ace.* Annapolis: Naval Institute Press, 1990.

Woodward, David. *The Secret Raiders.* New York: W. W. Norton, 1955.

Index

About the Authors

. . . .

OTTO GIESE was born in 1914 in Bremen, Germany. Starting in 1933, he served aboard square-riggers and numerous oceangoing freighters, after which he attended the nautical academy for his mate's license.

After World War II he obtained a master's license and started his own shipping line, which operated in the North Sea, the Baltic, the Caribbean, and the Far East. In 1964 he moved to Florida, where he was pier superintendent and manager of a steamship agency until he retired in 1981. He and his wife presently reside in the panhandle of Florida. One of their two sons graduated from the U.S. Air Force Academy and served in the Gulf war.

JAMES E. WISE, JR., was born in 1930 in Chicago. He became a naval aviator in 1953 following graduation from Northwestern University. He attended naval intelligence school and served as ship's intelligence officer aboard the USS *America* (CVA 66) during that carrier's deployment to Vietnam in 1968. Later he served as commanding officer of various naval intelligence units. He retired in 1975 with the rank of captain.

Since his retirement he has held several senior executive posts in private-sector companies. He has also published many historical articles in naval and maritime journals. He and his wife presently reside in Alexandria, Virginia.